The IDEA MAGAZINE FOR TEACHERS.

MAILBOX.

2011–2012 YEARBOOK

The Education Center, Inc.
Greensboro, North Carolina

The Mailbox® 2011–2012 Kindergarten Yearbook

Managing Editor, *The Mailbox* Magazine: Lynn Drolet

Editorial Team: Becky S. Andrews, Diane Badden, Kimberley Bruck, Karen A. Brudnak, Kimberly Ann Brugger, Pam Crane, Chris Curry, David Drews, Amy Erickson Corkhill, Tazmen Hansen, Marsha Heim, Lori Z. Henry, Troy Lawrence, Kitty Lowrance, Tina Petersen, Gary Phillips (COVER ARTIST), Mark Rainey, Greg D. Rieves, Kelly Robertson, Hope Rodgers-Medina, Rebecca Saunders, Donna K. Teal, Zane Williard

ISBN 978-1-61276-243-2
ISSN 1088-5552

©2012 The Education Center, Inc., PO Box 9753, Greensboro, NC 27429-0753

Printed in the United States of America.

The Mailbox® Yearbook
PO Box 6189
Harlan, IA 51593-1689

Look for *The Mailbox*® 2012–2013 Kindergarten Yearbook in the summer of 2013. The Education Center, Inc., is the publisher of *The Mailbox*®, *Teacher's Helper*®, and *Learning*® magazines, as well as other fine products. Look for these wherever quality teacher materials are sold, call 1-866-477-4273, or visit www.themailbox.com.

Contents

Math Units

Seasonal Units

Teacher's Resource

www.themailbox.com

Arts & Crafts

Arts & Crafts

Here's Johnny!

Make these adorable projects during the month of September in honor of Johnny Appleseed's birthday (September 26).

Materials for one project:
9" x 12" sheet of red construction paper
4" x 9" gray construction paper rectangle
5" flesh-color construction paper circle
brown and green construction paper scraps
scissors
crayons
glue

Steps:
1. Cut a large apple shape from the red paper.
2. Cut a stem and a leaf from the paper scraps and glue them to the apple.
3. Cut hair from the brown construction paper scrap and glue the hair to the circle (head). Draw a face on the head.
4. Cut out a pot shape from the gray paper. Glue it atop the hair to make a hat.
5. Glue the head on the apple.

Sue Fleischmann, Sussex, WI

Oink!

These precious pigs are simple to make and are the perfect addition to a farm unit.

Materials for one pig:
9" pink construction paper square
3" x 9" pink construction paper rectangle
scissors
crayons
glue

Steps:
1. Fold in the four corners of the square.
2. Unfold the bottom two corners. Cut along the fold lines to make the body.
3. Draw a pig face on the body.
4. Cut the rectangle in half to make two legs. Draw hooves on the bottom of each leg.
5. Glue the legs to the bottom of the body.

Step 1

Arts & Crafts

Sock-Print Snowpals

These adorable snowpals make great holiday gifts! Attach a ribbon loop to the back of each completed craft to make an ornament or put a strip of magnetic tape on the back to make it a magnet.

Materials for one snowpal:

white craft foam   scissors
black craft foam   glue
felt scraps   markers

Steps:

1. Keeping your sock on, trace your foot on the white craft foam. Cut out the tracing (snowpal).
2. Cut a hat from the black craft foam and glue it on the heel of the snowpal.
3. Glue felt scraps to the snowpal to make a scarf.
4. Use markers to draw eyes, a nose, a mouth, and buttons.

Beth Staab, Scribes and Scribblers
Middleberg Heights, OH

Red-Nosed Rudy

Invite students to wave these puppets as you lead them in singing "Rudolph the Red-Nosed Reindeer."

Materials for one puppet:

9" x 12" sheet of brown construction paper   red pom-pom
3" brown paper circle   glue
two 1" x 4" brown paper strips   scissors
four 1" x 2" brown paper strips   crayons

Steps:

1. Fold the sheet of paper in half. Unfold it. Put glue on the top and the side, leaving the bottom open, and refold. Trim the bottom corners of the resulting pocket to make the reindeer's head.
2. Cut the paper circle in half (ears). Glue the ears to the head.
3. Glue the paper strips to the head to make antlers.
4. Glue on the red pom-pom to make a nose.
5. Draw eyes and a mouth.

Janet Boyce, Cokato, MN

Step 1

Arts & Crafts

Colorful Creations

After discussing the methods different artists use to create their artwork, invite your students to create this holiday masterpiece. Provide different-colored paint to feature holidays—blue and yellow for Hanukkah, red and green for Christmas, and red, black, and green for Kwanzaa.

Materials for one project:
9" x 12" color construction paper
8½" x 11" white paper
paint

variety of painting supplies (such as string, yarn, paintbrushes, plastic forks, and turkey basters)

Steps:
1. Use different-colored paint and desired painting supplies to create a unique design on the white paper.
2. Set the project aside to dry.
3. When the paint is dry, glue the project to a sheet of construction paper to make a frame.

Marianne Cerra
Riverside Elementary
Reading, PA

Shiny Ornaments

These glossy projects may take several days to dry, but the finished product is worth the wait!

Materials for one ornament:
tagboard circle
small construction paper rectangle
different colors of light corn syrup
   (Tint the syrup with food coloring.)

permanent marker
paintbrush
ribbon
tape

Steps:
1. Use the marker to draw designs on the circle (ornament). Write your name on the back.
2. Paint over the designs with a thin layer of syrup.
3. Tape a ribbon loop to the paper rectangle.
4. Put the rectangle on the sticky ornament to make an ornament topper.
5. Set the ornament aside to dry.

Phyllis Prestridge
West Amory Elementary
Amory, MS

Arts & Crafts

A Lovely Butterfly

This butterfly's heart-shaped wings and antennae make it a perfect Valentine's Day project.

Materials for one butterfly:

9" paper oval	two ½" x 4" paper strips
2 large heart cutouts	crayons
2 small heart cutouts	glue

Steps:

1. Draw a face on the oval.
2. Glue the large hearts (wings) to the oval.
3. Glue the paper strips (antennae) to the top of the oval.
4. Glue the small hearts to the antennae.
5. Draw details on the wings.

Sue Fleischmann
Sussex, WI

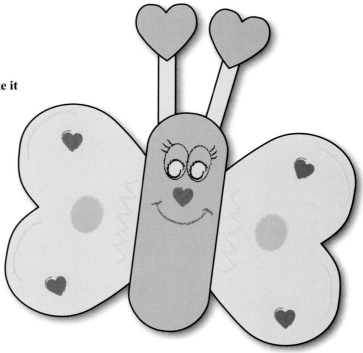

Lucky Leprechaun

As a follow-up to making this project, have students respond to the writing prompt "If I met a leprechaun,…"

Materials for one leprechaun:

7" manila oval	scissors
6" green half circle	glue
1½" x 8" green paper strip	crayons
orange construction paper scraps	

Steps:

1. Round the corners of the paper strip. Then glue it to the half circle so it looks like a hat.
2. Glue the hat to a short end of the oval.
3. Draw a face and hat details.
4. Tear orange paper scraps into small pieces and glue them to the face so they resemble a beard and eyebrows.

Janet Boyce, Cokato, MN

Arts & Crafts

April Showers

These simple-to-make scenes form an appealing rainy-day display!

Materials for one scene:

sheet of white construction paper
blue-tinted water or diluted blue paint
sheet of newspaper
paper towel
paintbrush
crayons

Steps:

1. Use crayons to draw a springtime scene on the paper.
2. Put the drawing on the newspaper.
3. Dip the paintbrush in the blue mixture. Tap the brush on a paper towel.
4. Run your fingers over the paintbrush bristles to flick the blue mixture (raindrops) onto the drawing.
5. Repeat Steps 2–4 to add more raindrops to the drawing.

Karen Guess
St. Richard's School
Indianapolis, IN

Bunny Bag

Put cellophane grass in these completed bags and youngsters will have a soft place to store springtime treats.

Materials for one bunny:

construction paper
   —5" white circle
   —two 5" white ovals
   —two 3" white ovals
   —two 3" pink ovals
   —2" white circle
white paper lunch bag
cotton ball
crayons
glue

Steps:

1. Draw a bunny face on the large white circle (head).
2. Glue the pink ovals atop the larger white ovals so they look like bunny ears. Glue the ears to the head.
3. Put the flat side of the bag faceup. Glue the head to the top of the bag.
4. Draw details on each of the smaller white ovals so they look like bunny feet. Glue the feet to the bottom of the bag.
5. Cut the small circle in half. Draw lines on the circle halves (paws). Glue the paws to the bag.
6. Open the bag. Glue the cotton ball (tail) to the back of the bag.

Walma Rios-Hutchinson
Tamarac Elementary
Tamarac, FL

 **One Shape**

6 Super Spring Crafts!

Follow the directions below to lead students in making these heart-shaped crafts. Then use the completed crafts to decorate the classroom, inspire creative writing, or explore other spring things that can be made with this shape.

ideas contributed by Mary Davis, Keokuk Christian Academy, Keokuk, IA

1 Daisy

Glue the points of white heart cutouts around the edge of a yellow paper plate. If desired, add a stem and leaves to the project.

2 Butterfly

Glue decorated heart cutouts to a jumbo craft stick (butterfly body) so they resemble wings. Then attach wiggle-eye stickers or eye cutouts above the wings.

3 Ladybug

Glue a black heart cutout (head) to a red heart cutout (body). Then add legs, antennae, and spots!

4 Bunny

Draw a bunny face on a heart cutout. Glue on ear cutouts to complete the bunny.

5 Frog

Attach four small green hearts (feet) to a large green heart (body). Then glue on circle cutouts (eyes) and a length of red string (mouth) to finish the frog.

6 Bee

Draw black stripes and an eye on a yellow heart cutout. Attach white heart cutouts to resemble wings.

Lots of Learning Fun!

Students are sure to enjoy using these crafts to complete skill-related activities! Have each child make a craft. Then follow up with one or more of the skill boosters.

Spotted Ladybug

Craft

For one ladybug, cut away two corners of a red sheet of paper to make the body. Use a white crayon to draw a face on a black circle (head) and glue the head to the body. Then cut construction paper scraps to make six legs, two antennae, and several spots.

Skill Boosters

- **Making a graph:** Write "more than 5," "5," and "less than 5" to label three rows of a floor grid. Have each child count the number of spots on his ladybug and put his ladybug in the corresponding row.
- **Problem solving:** Invite two or more students to stand with their ladybugs. Lead youngsters to determine the total number of heads, eyes, and legs there are in all.
- **Writing:** Have each child write to tell what her ladybug might see if it were to fly around her room at home.

craft by Sue Fleischmann, Sussex, WI

Caleb's Fireflies

Fingertip Fireflies

Craft

To make a jar of fireflies, use yellow paint to make ten fingerprints on a simple jar cutout. After the paint is dry, use a black marker to draw head, wing, and antenna details on each bug. Then write to label the jar with your name as shown.

Skill Boosters

- **Counting by tens:** Use the completed crafts to lead youngsters in counting by tens.
- **Number order:** Have youngsters write the total number of fireflies in a featured set of jars. Then lead each child to write each number that comes before and after that number. Continue with different jar sets as time permits.
- **Writing:** Have each child pretend the fireflies in his jar glow bright at night. Then have him write or draw to tell how his bug jar could be helpful in the dark!

craft by Laurie K. Gibbons, Huntsville, AL

THE BOOK CORNER

The Gingerbread Cowboy

Written by Janet Squires
Illustrated by Holly Berry

In this southwestern version of the traditional tale, the Gingerbread Cowboy outruns the rancher, a pack of javelinas, grazing cattle, and others before finally being eaten by a crafty coyote!

This story elements display is decorated with the Gingerbread Cowboy's runaway boots! Read the story aloud. Then give each child a brown construction paper copy of the cowboy boot on page 20. Encourage her to use a cotton swab to add white paint (icing) to the boot so it resembles a cookie. Next, help students name the title, author, illustrator, characters, and setting. Write the information on a sheet of poster board. Then have youngsters glue their cowboy boot cookies around the board. Mount the resulting display in your classroom.
Story elements

Phyllis Prestridge, West Amory Elementary, Amory, MS

The Gingerbread Cowboy
Written by Janet Squires
Illustrated by Holly Berry
Characters:
rancher
rancher's wife
Gingerbread Cowboy
horned lizard
roadrunner
javelinas
cattle
cowboys
coyote
Setting:
a desert in the southwest

Elmer

By David McKee

Elmer, a patchwork elephant, keeps the other elephants happy with his games and jokes. Unfortunately, Elmer is not happy and wishes he looked like the other elephants. When he manages to camouflage himself to look gray like the others, he discovers that he misses the attention and laughter.

Youngsters discover the meaning of the word *unique* when they make their own creative elephants! After the read-aloud, explain that Elmer is a unique elephant. Prompt youngsters to tell you what they think *unique* means, leading them to conclude that something unique stands out as being different. Next, give each youngster an enlarged copy of the elephant pattern on page 20. Encourage him to use crayons and collage items to make a truly unique elephant. Prompt each child to dictate a sentence explaining why his elephant is unique. Write the sentence on his paper. Then encourage him to share his unique elephant with the class. ***Dictating information***

Jennifer Reidy, Halifax Elementary, Halifax, MA

My elephant is unique because it is covered with purple cars!

Sam

The Book Corner

Literacy Ideas for Teachers®

Chicka Chicka Boom Boom

Written by Bill Martin Jr. and John Archambault
Illustrated by Lois Ehlert

Mischievous lowercase letters decide to congregate at the top of the coconut tree, which bends lower and lower until all the letters end up in a pile on the ground. The letters wiggle free, but this beloved story doesn't end there!

Write different letters on individual brown paper circles (coconuts) to make a class supply. Then invite each child to crumple a coconut to make it 3-D. Have youngsters hold their coconuts and stand in a circle. Then, on your signal, encourage the students to toss the coconuts in the center of the circle. Next, have each child pick up a new coconut and smooth out the paper. Then go around the circle and prompt each child to hold up his coconut, identify the letter, and say its sound. **For an added challenge**, have each child name a word that begins with his letter's sound. *Identifying letters and sounds*

Elouise Phipps
Hobbton Elementary
Newton Grove, NC

I Like Me!

by Nancy Carlson

The happy pig in this story has a best friend, and that best friend is herself! When she's sad, she cheers herself up; when she makes mistakes, she tries again; and when she falls down, she picks herself up. No wonder she can say, "I like me!"

After this activity, each youngster will be able to say, "I like me!" as well. Read the story aloud. Then give each student a paper programmed with the prompts shown. Help her write three things she likes about herself and then encourage her to write "I like me!" Showcase the finished papers with youngsters' photos or self-portraits. Then add the title "I Like Me!" to the display. *Writing*

Michelle Freed
Peru, NE

I like <u>my hair</u>.
I like <u>my eyes</u>.
I like <u>my clothes</u>.
I like me!   Sarah

Russell and the Lost Treasure
By Rob Scotton

When Russell the Sheep discovers a treasure map, he immediately makes a treasure finder. Then he and his frog friend, Frankie, go on a treasure hunt. Although the treasure is not what they expect, it turns out to be a great deal of fun!

Making predictions: Frankie the frog pops up repeatedly in the story. Why not add another frog to keep him company! Make copies of the frog cards on page 21 and use Sticky-Tac adhesive to attach the cards in the book where desired. Read the story aloud. Whenever you encounter a frog card, stop and have students predict what will happen next in the story.

Constructing simple maps: Encourage students to create a treasure map similar to Russell's! Make a copy of the map key on page 21 and attach it to a table. Provide sheets of newsprint and crayons. A child constructs his own treasure map, using the symbols from the key. For added fun, have each child draw a treasure on the back of his map.

The Emperor's Egg
Written by Martin Jenkins
Illustrated by Jane Chapman

An emperor penguin, the biggest penguin in the world, sits on his egg waiting for it to hatch. He doesn't eat breakfast, lunch, or dinner. It's rough being an emperor penguin, but the reward is a sweet little penguin chick!

Students pretend to be emperor penguins with this adorable display-worthy activity! Use play dough to form a large egg shape. For each child, place the egg on her feet and take a photo. Help her trim the photo and glue it to a simple iceberg cutout. Encourage her to write on the iceberg how she would feel if she were the penguin in the story. Then display the finished projects with a title such as "We Are Emperor Penguins!" ***Writing sentences***

I feel very cold and hungry.

tip → For a different egg prop, try using a plastic egg lawn ornament.

The Umbrella
by Jan Brett

When Carlos climbs a tree in the rain forest to look for animals, he leaves his green umbrella on the forest floor. The umbrella proves to be a perfect resting place for the animals that Carlos is looking for!

This story-inspired umbrella project is a handy tool for retelling the plot! Guide each child to glue eight large leaf cutouts to a disposable paper plate as shown. Then use a pushpin to poke a hole in the center of the plate. Have him push a pipe cleaner through the hole and bend the ends so they resemble the tip of an umbrella and its handle. Next, have him cut out a copy of the animal cards on page 22 and glue each card, in order, to the underside of a different leaf. Encourage him to point to each character at the appropriate time as he retells the story. **For a home-school connection,** have him carry the umbrella home so he can share a dramatic retelling of the story with his family! *Retelling a story*

adapted from an idea by Janice Burch
Tri-Valley Elementary
Downs, IL

Green Eggs and Ham
by Dr. Seuss

Do you like green eggs and ham? Sam poses this question and goes through a series of outlandish scenarios in order to tempt the main character to try this colorful cuisine.

Youngsters get a rhyming workout with this engaging group activity! Place green play dough on a tray so it resembles green eggs and ham. Give the tray to a child and say, "Would you like it with a frog?" and encourage the child to say, "Would you like it with a [rhyming word]?" Then have all youngsters chant, "Not with a frog! Not with a [rhyming word]!" Next, direct the child to give the tray to a classmate and begin a new rhyming sequence, replacing *frog* with a different word. *Rhyming*

Would you like it with a dog?

The Book Corner

Literacy Ideas for Teachers®

Rain

By Manya Stojic

The animals of the African grasslands use their senses to alert them to the upcoming rainstorm. After the rain, the earth blooms and the animals sensitively enjoy its gifts. Then, when the dry times return, the animals know that the rain will come again.

Choose one or both of the ideas below to integrate science and vocabulary in your literacy lessons.

- Invite students to make a variety of masks to match the animals in the story. Then encourage youngsters to take turns exaggerating their animals' roles in telling the tale. For example, have a child holding a lion mask speak with a deep voice and say, "Yes, the rain is here. I can taste it." Then have him stick his tongue way out as if to taste the rain. ***Five senses, dialogue***

- Put a layer of clay in a shallow pan and have youngsters compare it to the dry ground in the story. Then set the pan out in the sun for youngsters to observe over time. When cracks begin to form, revisit the matching pages in the book. Continue to read aloud to review how rain affects the ground. Then lead youngsters to make real-life connections as you add water, representing rain, to the dry clay in the pan. ***Effects of weather, text-to-world connections***

Stacey Helders-Pevan, Prince of Peace School, Milwaukee, WI

The Very Hungry Caterpillar

By Eric Carle

Each day for a week, a growing caterpillar eats increasingly larger amounts of food. He then retreats into a cocoon before he emerges as a beautiful butterfly!

Choose from the hands-on ideas below to pair this book with different math skills!

- Attach red and green linking cubes so they resemble the caterpillar from the story. Then have each child make his own caterpillar with linking cubes. Briefly hold up your caterpillar and prompt each child to predict whether his caterpillar is longer than, shorter than, or the same length as your caterpillar. Then encourage each child to hold his caterpillar next to yours and evaluate his prediction. ***Estimating and comparing length***

- Tell students that the caterpillar liked the food he ate, and he wants more! Using color paper squares to represent food—such as red squares for strawberries and brown squares for cake—tell story problems related to how much food the caterpillar eats. Guide youngsters to write and solve the corresponding number sentences. For each correct response, prompt youngsters to say, "Mmmm, good!" ***Counting, addition***

Mary Ann Craven, Fallbrook United Methodist School, Fallbrook, CA

The Mightiest
By Keiko Kasza

When a bear, a lion, and an elephant come upon a crown designated "For the Mightiest," they each feel they deserve to wear it. But after an encounter with a giant and his formidable little mother, they know the true meaning of the word mightiest!

Youngsters are sure to want to share their predictions throughout this engaging story with the assistance of a very mighty prop! Make a student-size paper crown so it resembles the one in the book. Ask youngsters to look at the front cover and predict what the story is about. Then, as you read the book aloud, stop periodically to ask questions such as "What do you think 'for the mightiest' means?" and "What do you think will happen next?" As a child responds, encourage him to wear the crown. After reading the story, lead youngsters to conclude that the mightiest is not necessarily the strongest or the biggest and that the mightiest does not need to wear a crown! ***Making predictions, drawing conclusions***

Andrea Patnaude, William Winsor Elementary, Greenville, RI

Chester's Way
By Kevin Henkes

Chester and Wilson are best friends and they do everything the same way. When Lilly moves into the neighborhood, she has her own way of doing things. Can Chester and Wilson and Lilly all be friends? They sure can!

To prepare for this comparison activity, cut blue and yellow construction paper to make strips. Label each of several yellow strips with different activities Chester and Wilson like to do together, such as riding bikes, cutting sandwiches diagonally, and raking leaves. Glue each prepared strip to form separate loops. To begin, encourage each child to determine how he feels about each of the activities. For each activity he enjoys, have him personalize a yellow strip and attach it to the original loop. If he does not enjoy the activity, have him attach a personalized blue strip. Then guide youngsters to conclude they have varying opinions—just like the characters in the story—but, regardless of their differences, they can be friends too. **For a math connection**, use the data to form graphs and have youngsters use the graphs to determine if they are more similar to or different from the characters in the story. ***Making connections, identifying the main idea of a story***

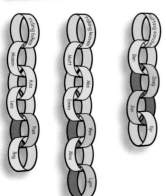

Colleen Dabney, Williamsburg, VA

Cowboy Boot Pattern
Use with "The Gingerbread Cowboy" on page 14.

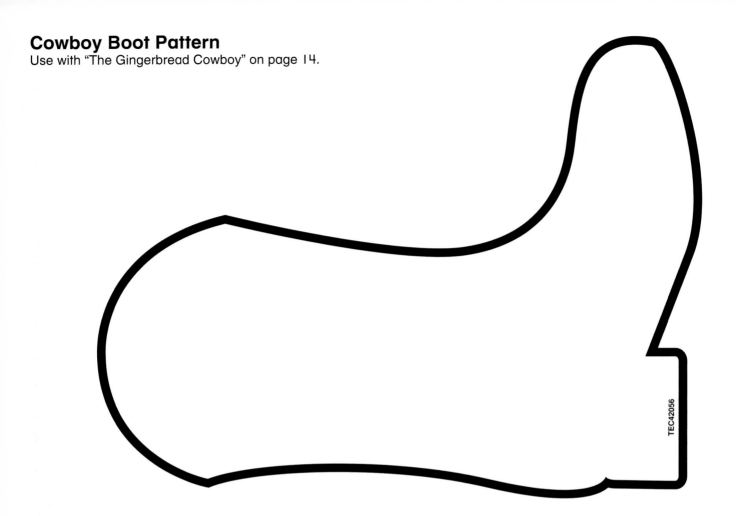

TEC42056

Elephant Pattern
Use with "Elmer" on page 14.

TEC42056

What happens next?   What happens next?

TEC42058   TEC42058

Key

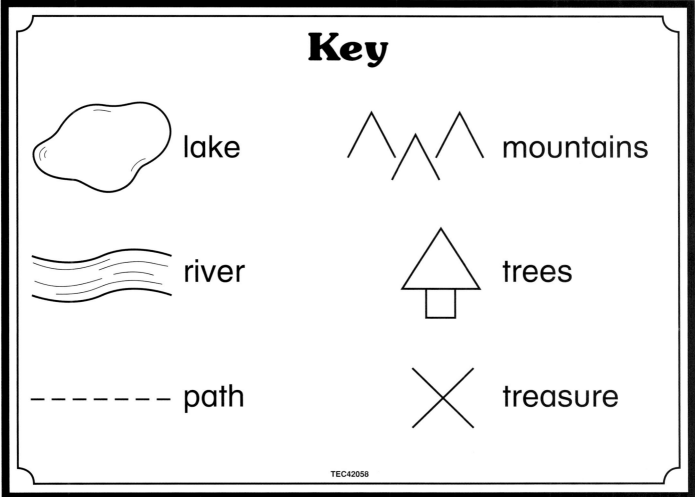

lake   mountains

river   trees

path   treasure

TEC42058

Animal Cards

Use with "*The Umbrella*" on page 17.

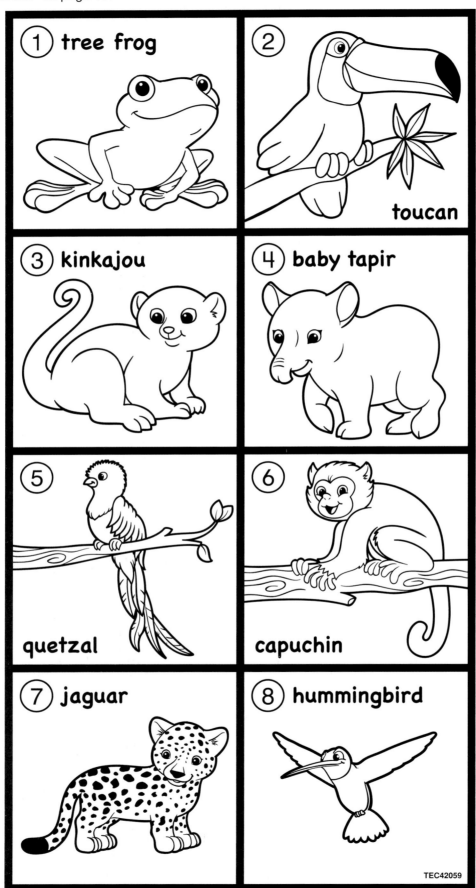

1. tree frog
2. toucan
3. kinkajou
4. baby tapir
5. quetzal
6. capuchin
7. jaguar
8. hummingbird

TEC42059

BUILDING MATH SKILLS

Piece by Piece

Number recognition, counting

Youngsters count their way to the 100th day of school with this calendar-time idea. Prior to the first day of school, put together a kindergarten-friendly 100 piece puzzle. On a sheet of tagboard, trace the outer edge of the puzzle to make a frame. Next, turn the puzzle over and write "1" on a corner piece. Number the remaining pieces from 2 to 100, making sure each consecutive number is interlocking. Then label a resealable plastic bag "up to 20"; label bags for 40, 60, 80, and 100 too. Put the corresponding puzzle pieces in the bags. On the first day of school, have a child find the puzzle piece that is labeled "1" and help her glue it to the appropriate corner of the frame. Explain that a new piece will be added each day as youngsters count to 100 and reveal the puzzle's picture.

Judy Rintel
Chesterbrook Academy
Manalapan, NJ

Snazzy Shape Books

Shapes in the environment

A hat is a triangle.

At the end of this five-day project, your kindergartners are sure to be eager to read these books with their families! Cut out a class supply of each of the following shapes: circles, squares, triangles, ovals, and rectangles. To make a page, show the group a shape and encourage students to name objects in the environment that have the same shape. Then have each child glue a corresponding shape cutout to a sheet of paper, leaving room at the bottom for writing. Instruct him to draw or add craft details to the shape so it resembles an object in the environment. Next, help him write a sentence about the shape. Each day, lead youngsters to make a different shape page. To complete the book, help each child staple her pages between construction paper covers.

Mary Ann Craven
Fallbrook United Methodist School
Fallbrook, CA

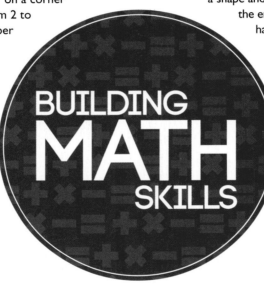

BUILDING
MATH
SKILLS

Math Mats

Comparing sets

These color-coded mats establish students' workspace and are perfect for quickly assessing progress at a glance. For each child, glue a half sheet of yellow paper atop one side of a full sheet of blue paper as shown. Laminate the mats for durability. Then give each child a mat and a desired number of counters. Lead students to compare sets by giving directions, such as "Put more counters on the blue side than on the yellow side" and "Put two counters on the blue side; show a set on the yellow side that has one more." From across the room, it is quick and easy to check for accuracy!

Vanessa Rivera, La Luz Elementary, La Luz, NM

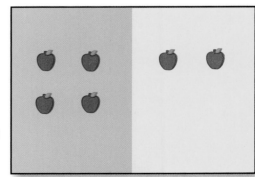

 See page 30 for a **practice page** on comparing sets.

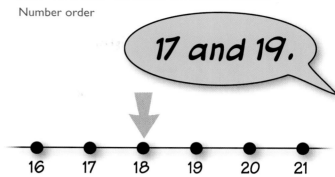

17 and 19.

Which one do you like best?		
9		
8		
7		
6		
5		
4		
3	Louisa	
2	Gorge	
1	Tara	Evan

Great Bar

Print Preferences
Data collection

This graphing idea showcases environmental print. Gather several pieces of environmental print, such as restaurant bags and food packages. Prepare a reusable graph similar to the one shown. Display the graph in a student-accessible location, leaving some space below the graph for the graph elements. Below each column of the graph, display a piece of environmental print. Have each child tape a personalized card in the column that shows his preference. Repeat this activity over the next several days using different environmental print each time.

Suzanne Kobb, Swanson Primary Center, South Bend, IN

In Tune With Numbers
Number order

16 17 18 19 20 21

Sing this toe-tapping ditty each day to reinforce youngsters' number line skills. Display a large number line in a student-accessible location. Sing the song shown, inserting a desired number where indicated. At the end of the song, invite a volunteer to point to the featured number on the line and name each neighboring number. Then ask the group number-related questions as time permits.

Jodi Darter, Cabool Elementary, Cabool, MO

(sung to the tune of "Pop! Goes the Weasel")

Up and down the big number line,
The numbers are in order.
Find [18] and look on each side.
What are the numbers?

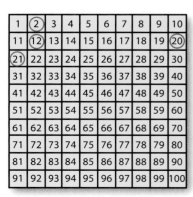

BUILDING MATH SKILLS

Two Cheers for "Two's day"
Review

1	②	3	4	5	6	7	8	9	10
11	⑫	13	14	15	16	17	18	19	⑳
㉑	22	23	24	25	26	27	28	29	30
31	32	33	34	35	36	37	38	39	40
41	42	43	44	45	46	47	48	49	50
51	52	53	54	55	56	57	58	59	60
61	62	63	64	65	66	67	68	69	70
71	72	73	74	75	76	77	78	79	80
81	82	83	84	85	86	87	88	89	90
91	92	93	94	95	96	97	98	99	100

Turn every Tuesday into "Two's-day" using the following activities all related to the number 2. As the year progresses, be sure to incorporate newly learned skills into your two-themed activities.

Jodi Darter

- Display a reusable hundred chart. Have kindergartners circle each number that contains a two.
- Enlist students' help in dividing a group of objects into two equal groups.
- Invite youngsters to make a pattern using two different shapes.

- Display a number line and say a number. Have a child name the number two places ahead (+ 2) and two places behind (– 2).
- Lead students in counting by twos.
- Ask youngsters to name things that come in pairs.

See page 31 for a **skill sheet** on measurement.

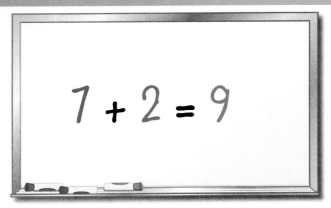

Bus Stops
Addition and subtraction

Students act out word problems by getting on and off this imaginary bus. Arrange student chairs so they resemble passenger seats on a bus. Tell youngsters they are going to take an imaginary bus trip across the country. Then invite several students to "board" the bus; write the number on the board. Then ask a few more children to get on the bus. Lead youngsters to complete the corresponding addition sentence. To continue, pretend the bus moves along to different cities. At each stop, invite passengers on and off the bus to create different math sentences as you go. For added fun, have riders pretend they are on a bumpy country road between destinations.

Catherine Mullins
Munford Elementary
Memphis, TN

Spill It!
Number skills, graphing

BUILDING
MATH
SKILLS

Tuck in a variety of skills with this small-group graphing activity. For each student, place several double-sided counters in a cup. Give each child a cup and a blank two-column graph. Have him spill the counters and sort them on the graph by color. Then encourage him to count the total number of counters; compare the color columns using words such as *more*, *fewer*, and *equal*; and construct number sentences related to the graph. For added fun, put the counters in seasonal containers, such as small red stockings in December or plastic eggs in April. **For early finishers**, encourage youngsters to trade cups for a different graphing experience.

Chantelle Schroeder
Meadow Lane Elementary
Lincoln, NE

Seconds, Minutes, and More!
Equivalent units of time

Discuss with youngsters how the hands on a clock show the passage of time. Then use this little ditty to help students make connections related to time.

(sung to the tune of "If You're Happy and You Know It")

Sixty seconds in a minute, round and round.
Sixty minutes in an hour, round and round.
Sixty seconds in a minute; sixty minutes in an hour,
Time passes as the hands go round and round.

Twenty-four hours in a day, round and round.
Seven days in a week, round and round.
Twenty-four hours in a day; seven days in a week,
Time passes as the hands go round and round.

Donna Williams
River Ridge Elementary
Moore, SC

See page 32 for a **practice sheet** on number order.

Have a Cupcake!
Addition

To prepare this partner game, label each hole on a jumbo-size cupcake pan with a different number from 1 to 6. Cut apart copies of the cupcake cards on page 34. To make the activity self-checking, write the answer on the back of each card. Set out the pan, cards, and a number cube along with birthday candles to use as counters. To begin, players put two cards faceup in each hole of the pan. To take a turn, a child rolls the number cube and takes a card from the matching section. She solves the problem and checks her answer. If she is correct, she keeps the card; if not, she returns the card to the pan. If a player rolls and there is no card in the matching section, her turn is over. Play continues until each problem is solved or as time permits. The player with more cards wins.

Janice Burch, Tri-Valley Elementary Downs, IL

Tip the Ship
Comparing weight

Which is heavier—a slice of watermelon or a car? Students make many comparisons with this small-group activity. To make a ship, color and cut out a copy of page 33. Use brads to attach the circles to the ship so the pictures show through the portholes. Tape a straw to the back of the ship's mast to make it sturdy. Next, invite a child to be a sailor. Have him move the ship's circles to show two pictures and then hold up the ship. Encourage group members to lean left or right in the direction of the heavier object. Then have the sailor tip the ship, lowering the side with the heavier load. Confirm students' accuracy before asking a different sailor to take a turn.

Jennifer Reidy
Halifax Elementary
Halifax, MA

Switcheroo
Number identification, number order

This pocket chart activity is sure to be a class favorite! Write the numbers from 1 to 20 on separate cards and shuffle the deck. Have students name the number as you place each card in your pocket chart. Then invite a volunteer to swap the number 1 card's position with the card in the top left corner. (If 1 is already in the top left corner, begin with the number 2 card.) Lead youngsters to continue switching pairs of cards until the numbers are in order.

Krista Sadlers, Liberty Magnet School, Vero Beach, FL

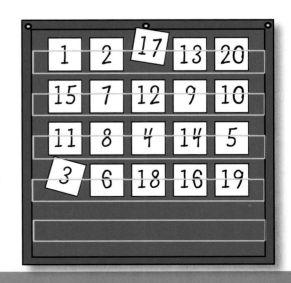

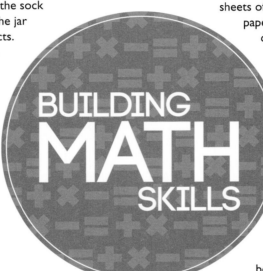

BUILDING MATH SKILLS

A Busy Book!
Concepts of calendar time, telling time

At nine o'clock, I go to music class.

Students keep track of a busy day with this hands-on booklet project. For each child, put four half sheets of paper behind a half sheet of construction paper. Staple the resulting booklet pages and cover to the bottom half of a 9" x 12" sheet of construction paper (booklet backing). Give each child a booklet and a copy of page 35. Direct her to cut out the clock patterns. Then help her secure the clock hands with a brad and glue the clock to the top of the booklet backing. Next, have her write "[student name]'s Schedule" on the front cover. For each booklet page, direct the student to refer to the sentence starter card to help her write a sentence about something she does at a particular time during the day. **(For extra support,** list activities on the board as a reference.) Then have her illustrate the activity on the page. When she reads her completed book, have her manipulate the clock hands to match the time on each page.

Layla Ciptak, Layla's Homeschool, Elizabethton, TN

Guess and Group
Estimation, exploring tens and ones

Pass the sock around? Youngsters are sure to enjoy this estimation activity. Put like objects in a small plastic jar and secure the lid. Slide the jar inside a sock to conceal its contents. Have students sit in a circle and pass the sock around. Encourage youngsters to shake the sock and guess what is inside. Then remove the jar from the sock to show the hidden objects. To continue, draw a number line on the board. Invite each student to estimate how many objects are in the jar and plot his guess on the number line. Next, have students count aloud as you put the objects in groups of ten. Then lead the group in counting the total number of objects. Using a different color marker, write the answer on the number line and have students compare their estimates to the answer.

Tammy Willey
Pine Street Elementary
Presque Isle, ME

 See page 36 for a skill sheet that reinforces tens and ones.

Got Seven?
Addition to 12

All that is needed for this partner game is a pair of dice, blank paper, and pencils. To play, a child rolls the dice. If the sum of the dots rolled equals seven, he says, "Got seven!" and writes the corresponding number sentence. If not, his turn is over. The first player to write seven number sentences wins.

adapted from an idea by Cathy Wroten
Bear Branch Elementary
Magnolia, TX

$3 + 4 = 7$
$1 + 6 = 7$

The Hands of Time
Time

Take your class outside to a large paved surface for this entertaining review activity. Use chalk to draw a jumbo-size clockface without hands. Then announce a time and invite a pair of youngsters to pretend to be the hands of the clock, guiding the shorter child to show the hour. (If desired, have each child position a folded towel in the correct location before lying on the pavement.) Have the remaining students confirm the positions for the announced time; then continue with more telling-time practice.

Darlene Parks
Effort Christian School
Palmyra, VA

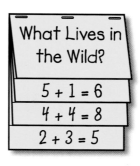

Wild Critters
Addition

This flap-book activity is sure to foster each student's ability to solve story problems. To make a flap book for each child, stack one sheet of paper one inch lower than another sheet of paper and then fold the two sheets to create four tabs as shown. Staple the pages near the fold and draw a line along the bottom edge of the top three tabs.

To begin, enlist students' help in creating a list of wild critters (or other animals) on the board. Then have each child write an appropriate title on the top flap of her booklet as shown. Have her lift the top flap and select an animal from the list. Then roll a die and have her draw her animal that number of times on the space above the staples. Roll the die again and have her draw her animal that number of times below the staples and above the line. Guide her to write a corresponding number sentence below the line. Continue with the two remaining flaps to complete the booklet.

Marie Christiansen
Bushkill Elementary
Dingman's Ferry, PA

Spot the Differences!
Subtraction

Ladybugs "land" to show matching differences with this center idea. Write "4," "5," and "6" on separate cards. Set out the number cards with a cutout copy of the ladybug cards on page 37. When a child visits the center, he puts the number cards faceup in a row. Then he solves the problem on each ladybug card and "flies" it under the number card with the matching difference.

Lauren Harms, Oakland, CA

Turn this subtraction center into a game!
Invite each of three players to take a number card. Stack the ladybug cards facedown. To take a turn, a player takes a card and solves the problem. If it matches her number, she keeps the card; if not, she returns the card to the bottom of the stack. The first player to get four ladybug cards is the winner.

See page 38 for a skill sheet on probability.

Name _____

Seed Munch

✂ Cut.
🔖 Glue to match.

more than 5 seeds

less than 5 seeds

Bonus: Draw a 🌻 with 8 ●. Draw another 🌻 with more than 8 ●.
sunflower   seeds   sunflower   seeds

©The Mailbox® • TEC42056 • Aug./Sept. 2011

Name

Toy Time

✏ Write 1, 2, and 3 to order each set of toys from **shortest** to **longest**.

©The Mailbox® • TEC42057 • Oct./Nov. 2011

Bones, Bones, Bones!

✏️ Write the numbers in order.

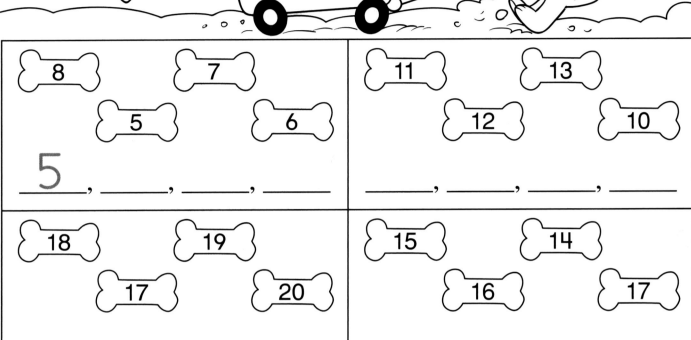

Box 1	Box 2
8 7	11 13
5 6	12 10
5 ___, ___, ___, ___	___, ___, ___, ___
18 19	15 14
17 20	16 17
___, ___, ___, ___	___, ___, ___, ___

✏️ Draw 🦴 to show the number that comes next.

✏️ Circle the number.

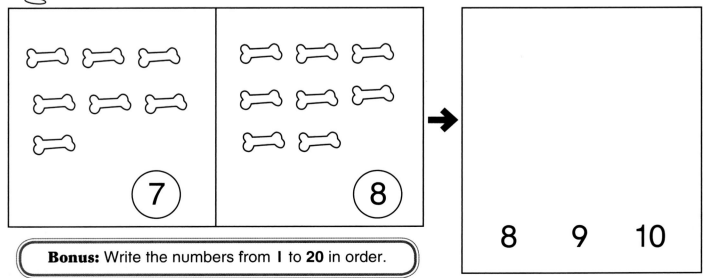

7   8   →   8   9   10

Bonus: Write the numbers from **1** to **20** in order.

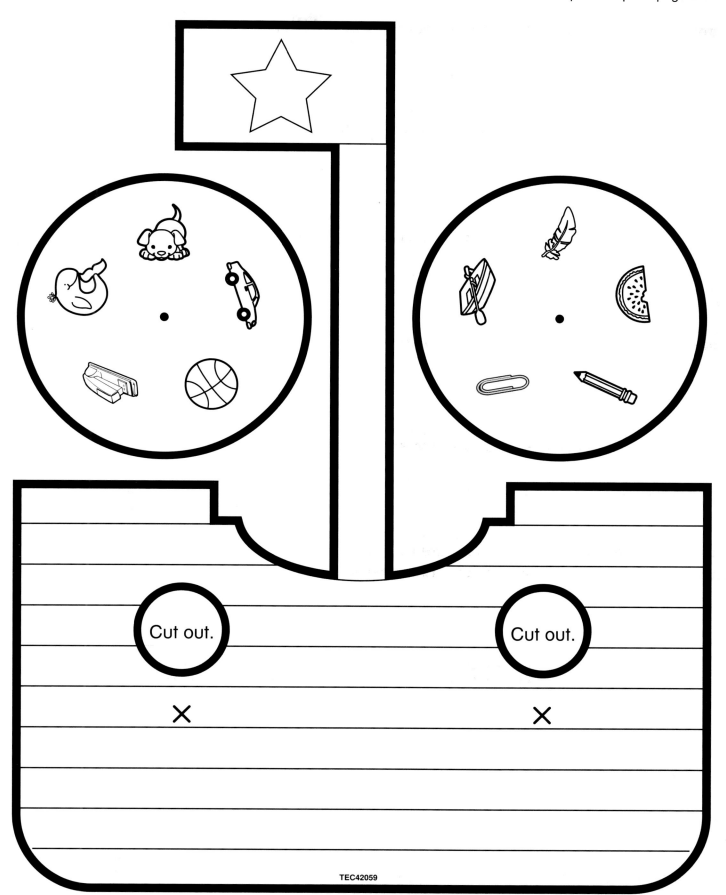

Cut out.

Cut out.

TEC42059

Cupcake Cards
Use with "Have a Cupcake!" on page 27.

2 + 3
TEC42059

8 + 1
TEC42059

5 + 2
TEC42059

1 + 6
TEC42059

3 + 3
TEC42059

9 + 0
TEC42059

4 + 4
TEC42059

2 + 8
TEC42059

6 + 4
TEC42059

3 + 5
TEC42059

7 + 3
TEC42059

5 + 4
TEC42059

TEC42060

At _____ o'clock, I _____ .

Number Words

1 one	4 four	7 seven	10 ten
2 two	5 five	8 eight	11 eleven
3 three	6 six	9 nine	12 twelve

TEC42060

Name _____

Squeaky Can Count!

 Count.

Write how many tens and ones.

Write the number.

Bonus: Draw a ten frame and gumballs to show 19.

_____ _____   _____

_____ ten _____ ones   _____

_____ _____   _____

_____ ten _____ ones   _____

_____ _____   _____

_____ ten _____ ones   _____

_____ _____   _____

_____ ten _____ ones   _____

_____ _____   _____

_____ ten _____ ones   _____

Draw circles to show each number.   Write the number.

| 1 ten   4 ones   _____ | 1 ten   7 ones   _____ |

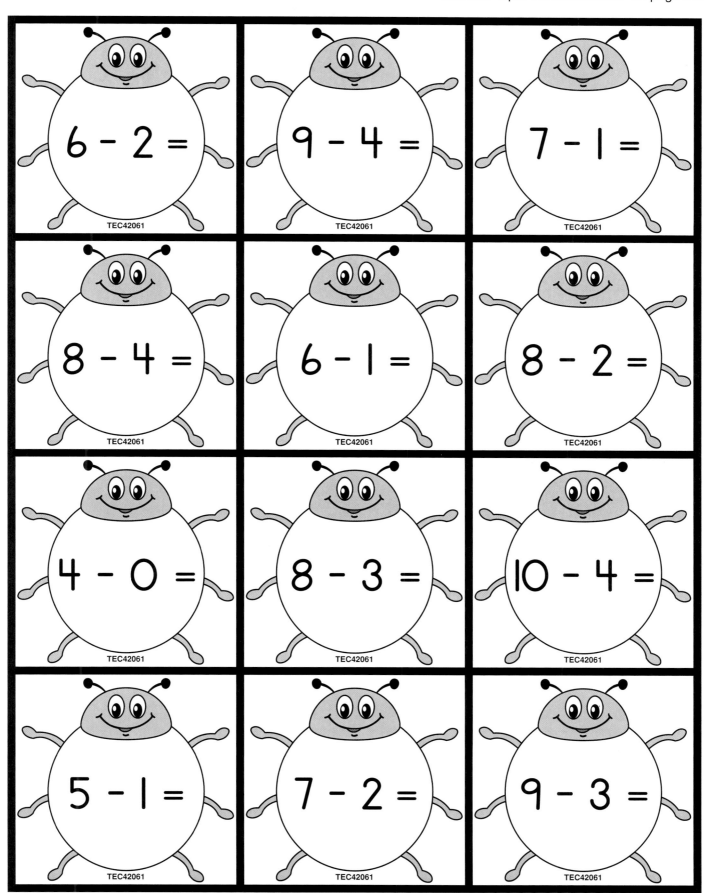

6 - 2 = TEC42061

9 - 4 = TEC42061

7 - 1 = TEC42061

8 - 4 = TEC42061

6 - 1 = TEC42061

8 - 2 = TEC42061

4 - 0 = TEC42061

8 - 3 = TEC42061

10 - 4 = TEC42061

5 - 1 = TEC42061

7 - 2 = TEC42061

9 - 3 = TEC42061

Name _____

Beach Treasures

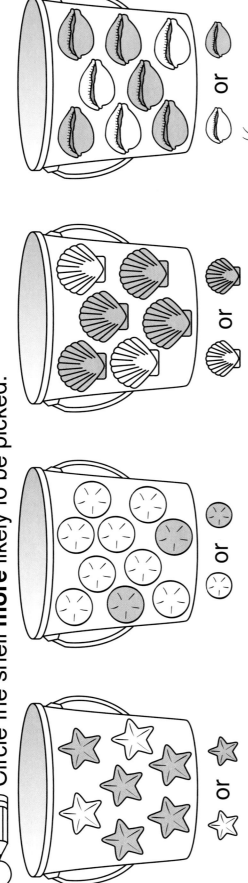

✏ Circle the shell **more** likely to be picked.

or

or

or

✏ Circle the shell **less** likely to be picked.

or

or

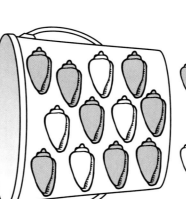

Bonus: Draw a picture with six yellow fish and one red fish. Write to tell which color fish you are **more** likely to catch if you were fishing.

Classroom Displays

Look Who's Popping Up In Our Class!

For this welcome display, color and cut out an enlarged copy of the toaster pattern on page 45. Display the toaster with the title shown. For each child, post a toast cutout and a personalized knife cutout (or plastic knife). Put a yellow square with the corners rounded (butter) on her desk. To complete the display, help each child find her name and glue the butter to her toast. **Antonio Kling, Haw Creek Elementary, Asheville, NC**

This sweet apple features a star, and these bright stars feature your sweet students! Post an enlarged cross-section of an apple as shown. Write each student's name or glue each child's photograph on an individual star cutout. Arrange the stars around the apple, along with the title and sentences shown. To promote communication skills, prompt a discussion about the stars on the display. **Patty Henderson, Early Childhood Learning Center, Titusville, PA**

A Sunny "Kinder-garden"

Students' smiles are featured in the center of these sunflowers. Guide youngsters to round the corners of yellow paper rectangles to form flower petals. Have each child glue his petals to a brown circle to make a flower head and then glue the flower head to a green rectangle strip (stem). Encourage him to cut green paper scraps to make leaves and glue the leaves to the stem. Then help each child glue a photograph of himself to the center of his flower. (For a 3-D effect, glue a muffin liner to the center of each flower before gluing the photo.) Arrange the completed flowers on a wall display with desired details and the title shown. **Elouise Miller, Lincoln School, Hays, KS**

Here's an eye-catching display that is ready to read! In advance, gather a supply of objects that feature environmental print, such as take-out bags, cereal boxes, and candy wrappers. Color and cut out an enlarged copy of the ant pattern on page 45. Feature the gathered materials, ant, speech bubble, and title, along with desired details, to create a picnic scene. Students are sure to show they *can* read right away in kindergarten! **Lacy Underwood, Janet Brockett Elementary, Arlington, TX**

DISPLAYS That Do More Than Decorate!

After reading your favorite version of *The Night Before Christmas* aloud, discuss with youngsters how the sleepy character had visions of sugarplums dancing in his head. Next, take a photograph of each child taking a turn wearing a Santa hat, pretending to sleep, and dreaming about a holiday surprise. Then help her write to complete the sentence on a cutout copy of the thought bubble on page 46. Post the trimmed photos, corresponding thought bubbles, desired details, and a title for a perfectly dreamy display.

Amy Fleener, Early Learning Center, Effingham, IL

This paper candy display serves as a reminder for your students to be nice, not naughty! Have each child cut out a copy of the candy pattern on page 46 and glue it to a small paper plate. Then have her paint three of the alternating sections red to resemble a peppermint candy. After the paint dries, help her slip the candy between a folded sheet of waxed paper and then twist the edges. Tape the completed candies to a display and add the title shown. When a child demonstrates kindness, record it on a card and post it by her candy to encourage her sweet attitude.

Patty Henderson
Early Childhood Learning Center
Titusville, PA

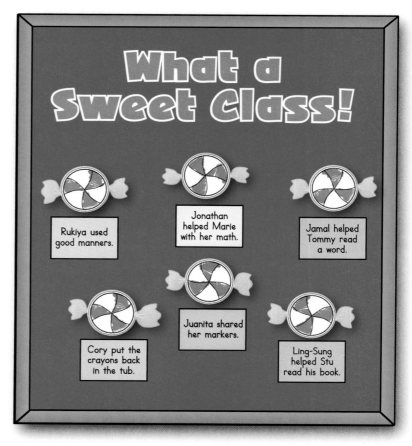

DISPLAYS That Do More Than Decorate!

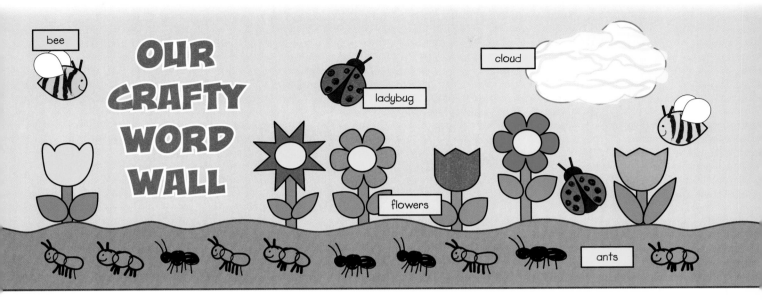

OUR CRAFTY WORD WALL

bee

ladybug

cloud

flowers

ants

Students' artwork makes this wall display a sensational spring scene! Have students draw ants on a long strip of brown bulletin board paper. Trim the top edge and post the paper along the bottom of a wall to represent the ground. Next, have youngsters make paper flowers to add to the wall. Continue to add other student-made crafts, such as painted yellow raindrop shapes with details (bees), cotton balls pulled apart and glued to a white paper shape (cloud), and paper ladybugs. Then label the completed scene and encourage youngsters to use the vocabulary to help them write spring-related stories.

Dawn Best
Dunkerton Elementary, Dunkerton, IA

Try this motivational display! Label mitt cutouts (pattern on page 47) with different springtime skills. Personalize a copy of the baseball pattern on page 47 for each student. Then arrange the mitts, baseballs, and an enlarged copy of the coach pattern on page 47 on a board. When a child masters a featured skill, invite him to put a sticker on his baseball. **For a positive behavior display**, label a mitt with a desired behavior, such as working quietly, and post personalized baseballs along the bottom of the board. When a child demonstrates the behavior, help him move his ball off the ground, symbolizing a home run!

Marilyn Barton
Ozark Early Learning Center
Ozark, MO

Spring Training

Write numbers to 30.

Fran

Lou

Name the shapes.

Nina

Bella

Read the color words.

Know addition facts to 10.

Pete

COACH K

Josh

Matching sun crafts to drawings is the final step of this summery display. Instruct each child to paint a paper plate yellow (sun). When the paint is dry, guide her to cut triangle shapes all around the outside of the plate (sunrays). Next, encourage her to cut paper scraps to add details to her sun. Post the completed crafts with the title shown. Then have each child draw a picture of her sun craft on story paper and write a sentence that tells what she likes to do on a sunny day. Invite each child to read her sentence and have classmates match her illustration to her craft.

Kate Wonders, Carlisle Elementary, Carlisle, Iowa

Kindergarten Graduates!

These graduation portraits make the perfect farewell display! Guide each child to draw a self-portrait. Instruct him to write his name on a card and glue it to his portrait. Next, have him color and cut out a tagboard copy of the graduation cap pattern on page 48. For added detail, encourage him to glue or tape a tassel to his cap. Help him glue the cap to his drawing. Post each resulting graduate portrait on a wall display. **For a writing connection,** have him write and draw about a kindergarten memory, roll the paper to form a scroll, and post it with his portrait.

Sandra Albrecht-Conrad, Grand Traverse Academy, Traverse City, Michigan

Toaster Pattern
Use with "Look Who's Popping Up In Our Class!" on page 40.

TEC42056

Ant Pattern
Use with "Reading Is a Picnic" on page 41.

TEC42056

Thought Bubble Pattern
Use with "Dreaming About the Holidays"
on page 42.

I have visions of

_____

dancing in my head.

TEC42058

Candy Pattern
Use with "What a Sweet Class!"
on page 42.

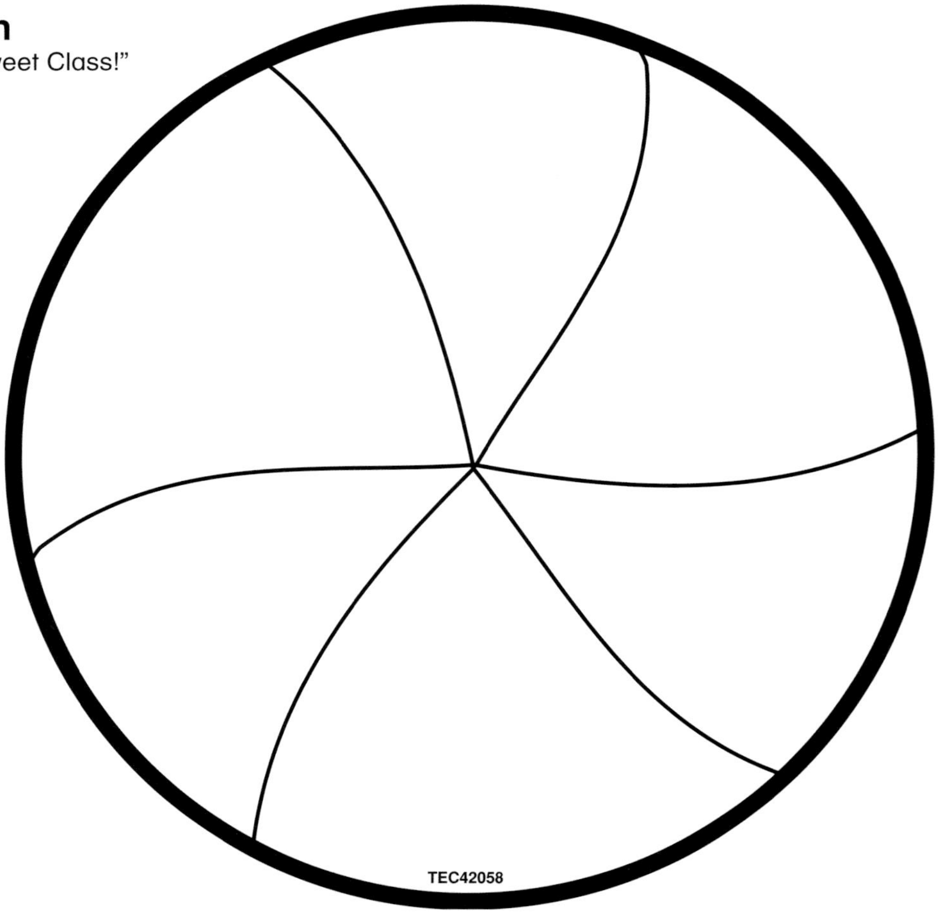

TEC42058

©The Mailbox® • TEC42058 • Dec./Jan. 2011–12

COACH K

TEC42060

TEC42060

TEC42060

Graduation Cap Pattern

Use with "Kindergarten Graduates!" on page 44.

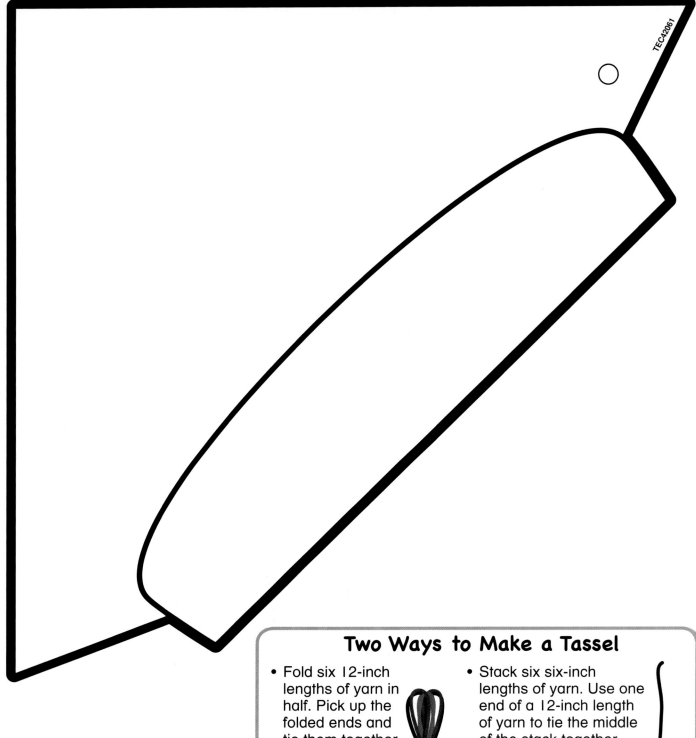

TEC42061

Two Ways to Make a Tassel

- Fold six 12-inch lengths of yarn in half. Pick up the folded ends and tie them together in a knot. Glue the knot to the cap where indicated.

- Stack six six-inch lengths of yarn. Use one end of a 12-inch length of yarn to tie the middle of the stack together. Poke a small hole in the cap where indicated and thread the other end of the 12-inch yarn length through the hole. Tape the end to the back of the cap.

LEARNING CENTERS

Learning Centers

Soup Sort
Math Center

Students are sure to enjoy this hands-on activity with noodles! To prepare, attach a copy of the label on page 58 to a container with a lid to make a soup can. Then partially fill the can with differing amounts of uncooked elbow, bow tie, rotini, and penne pasta. Set out the can, a small pot, four plastic bowls, and student copies of the recording sheet on page 58. A child pours the contents of the soup can into the pot and then sorts the pasta into the bowls. He counts the pasta pieces in each bowl and writes each amount on his paper. Then he answers the questions at the bottom of his recording sheet. *Sorting*

Jodi Darter
Cabool Elementary
Cabool, MO

Red, Yellow, and Green
Literacy and Math Center

Practice a variety of skills at this versatile center. Simply prepare apple cutouts (see suggestions) and display a pocket chart.

ABC order: Label each of 26 apple cutouts with a different letter. Place the apples and an alphabet chart near the pocket chart. A child arranges the apples in the chart in ABC order, using the alphabet chart as a reference.

Matching: For this partner center, program same-colored pairs of apple cutouts with matching letters, matching numbers, or matching uppercase and lowercase letters. Place the apples facedown in the pocket chart. In turn, each child turns over two apples. If the pair matches, he takes the apples. If they do not match, he turns the apples over and the other child takes a turn.

Matching numbers to sets: Program each of several apples with a different number. Then draw matching dot sets on several more apples. Place the apples with dot sets faceup in the pocket chart and the numbered apples nearby. A child matches each number to a dot set and stacks the matching pair.

Patterning: Glue different-color apples to sentence strips to create pattern starters. Place each strip in a separate row of the pocket chart and place the remaining apple cutouts nearby. A child extends each pattern using the cutouts.

Vanessa Rivera
La Luz Elementary
La Luz, NM

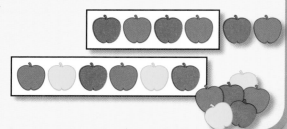

Cups to Count On!
Math Center

Reuse clean, plastic pudding or fruit cups with this counting center. Set out several cups, number cards, and a supply of small seasonal erasers. A child takes a card and sets it in front of a cup. Then she reads the number, counts a matching number of erasers, and places them in the cup. She repeats the process as time permits. *Making sets*

Amy Chevalier, Prickly Pear School, Tijersas, NM

Learning Centers

Fancy Formations
Literacy Center

To prepare for this hands-on activity, label each of several resealable plastic bags with a different letter pair. Put in each bag a supply of objects whose beginning sound matches the featured letter—such as cotton balls for *Cc*, foam flower cutouts for *Ff*, and noodles for *Nn*. A child empties a bag and uses the items to form the corresponding uppercase and lowercase letter. Then he points to each object and makes the corresponding beginning sound, tracing each letter as he goes. He returns the objects to the bag and continues with different bags as time permits. ***Letter formation, letter-sound association***

Jodi Darter
Cabool Elementary
Cabool, MO

Bony Backs
Math Center

Use the dinosaur pattern on page 59 to prepare one or both of the options below.

Counting: Glue a different number of paper triangles (bony plates) to each of several dinosaur cutouts. Prepare a set of number cards to match the number of plates on the dinosaurs. A child counts the plates on each dinosaur and places the matching number card on its body. If desired, color-code the back of matching pairs to make the activity self-checking.

Comparing sets: For this partner center, set out two dinosaur cutouts, 24 triangular pattern blocks (plates), and two pairs of dice. Simultaneously, each child rolls a pair of dice, counts the dots, and places a matching number of plates on his dinosaur's back. Then the partners compare their dinosaurs to determine which has more and which has fewer plates.

Karen Hoover
Asbury Preschool
Raleigh, NC

My dinosaur has more.

Make "Chunk-y" Soup!
Literacy Center

Serve a heaping helping of reading with this word chunk (rime) sort. Cut apart a copy of the noodle cards on page 60. Use the largest cards to label each of three small pots and put the remaining cards in an empty pasta box. Place the pots and the pasta box at a center. A student sorts the noodle cards into the matching pots to make three kinds of "chunk-y" soup. Then, for each pot, he matches each word to its picture. **To extend the activity,** have him choose one pot and write the words, draw matching pictures, and write two more word-family words of his choice. ***Word families***

Kimberli Carrier, Wise Owl Preschool, Nashua, NH

Learning Centers

How Many Scoops?
Math Center

This hands-on center can be adapted for any time of year. Set out four different containers and, for each one, a supply of corresponding items—such as a plastic candy dish and seasonal candies, a wintry mug and marshmallows, a pail and cotton balls (snowballs), and a gift box and holiday trinkets. Provide a measuring scoop or large spoon and copies of the recording sheet on page 61.

A child draws an object to be measured on his recording sheet. Next, he writes an estimate of how many level scoops it will take to fill the container. Then he scoops objects into the corresponding container and records a tally mark on his paper for each scoop. When the container is full, he counts the tallies, writes the actual number of scoops, and compares it to his estimate. He repeats the activity for each remaining object to complete his paper. *Estimation*

Tracy Shaner
Eastside Christian School
Marietta, GA

Colorful Tails
Math Center

Reinforce patterning skills with these cute mice. To make a mouse, fold a paper circle in half and glue the sides together; draw mouse details as shown. Label each mouse with a pattern unit, such as *AB*, *ABC*, and *AABB*. Then laminate the mice for durability, punch a hole where each tail should be attached, and secure one math link to each mouse. Place the mice and math links at a center. A child identifies the pattern unit and then connects links to create a long tail with the matching pattern. **To provide extra support**, display examples of each pattern unit featured. *Patterning*

Jodi Darter, Cabool Elementary, Cabool, MO

Dress That Snowpal!
Literacy Center

These labeled accessories lead to super sentence writing! To prepare, write color words on a large hat cutout, high-frequency words on a pair of large paper mittens, and seasonal words on a large paper scarf. Display the resulting posters at a center and set out a class supply of page 62 and 11" x 17" paper. A child chooses words from the posters and labels each of her corresponding clothes patterns. Next, she cuts out the patterns and glues the snowpal to a sheet of paper. To dress the snowpal, she glues on the accessories. Then she uses the words to write one or more sentences on her paper. *Writing sentences*

Doria Owen, William Paca/Old Post Road Elementary, Abingdon, MD

Learning Centers

That's a Real Word!
Literacy Center

Youngsters make a list and check it twice at this word family center. Label each of several envelopes with a rime. Slide into each envelope consonant cards, most of which make real words with the rime. Set out the envelopes with a seasonal notepad. A child empties an envelope, places a card in front of the rime, and reads the word. If it is a real word, he writes it on his paper; if not, he sets the card aside. He continues with each remaining card and then reads the resulting list to an adult. *Word families*

Marie E. Cecchini
West Dundee, IL

Caterpillar Construction
Math Center

To make a caterpillar, decorate a plastic egg half so it resembles a caterpillar head. Then program each of several egg halves with a number in a skip-counting sequence. (To make the activity self-checking, write letters on the underside of the egg halves so that the letters are in order when the caterpillar is assembled correctly.) Place the parts of the caterpillar in a large resealable plastic bag. Make several caterpillars in this manner and place them at a center. A child chooses a bag and takes out the pieces. Then he puts the caterpillar in order and reads the sequence. This versatile activity can also be used to practice number order or alphabetical order. ***Skip-counting***

Kimberly Barnhill
North Highlands Elementary
Shreveport, LA

Sudsy Fun
Literacy Center

To prepare this high-frequency word activity, color a copy of the center mat on page 63. Color and cut apart a copy of the center cards on page 64 and store them in a resealable plastic bag. Place the bag, mat, and writing paper at a center. To complete the activity, a student stacks the word cards and puts the letter cards in rows faceup. Next, she puts a word card on the mat, reads it, and uses the letter cards to spell the word. Then she writes the word on her paper. She continues with each word as time permits. **For an added challenge,** encourage youngsters to write sentences using each word.

Catherine Broome-Kehm
Melbourne Beach, FL

Learning Centers

Word Manes
Literacy Center

When a lion is missing its mane, students are sure to want to help! To make one lion, write a desired word family ending in the center of a paper plate. Then draw a nose around the rime and draw eyes and a mouth. Next, write words, most of which end with the featured rime, on individual clothespins. Place the lion and clothespins at a center. A child clips each word with the matching rime to the lion so it resembles a mane and sets the remaining clothespins aside. Then he reads the words in the word family. **For an added challenge,** set out more than one lion and corresponding clothespins for youngsters to distinguish words and form word families. *Word families*

Jennifer Willis
Imagine School at Palmer Ranch
Sarasota, FL

Number Kites
Math Center

Students sort various forms of the numbers 7, 10, and 12 on these springtime center mats. To make the mats, attach lengths of yarn and construction paper bows labeled as shown to three kite cutouts. Then cut apart a copy of the cards on page 65. If desired, label the back of the cards for self-checking. Set out the kites and cards. A child takes a card, determines which number it represents, and places the card on the matching kite. She sorts the remaining cards in this manner. *Equivalent forms of a number*

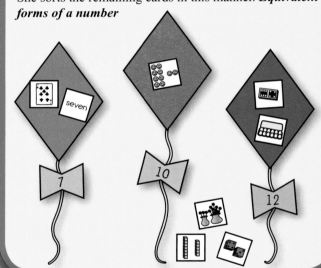

Read and Circle
Literacy Center

This quick-to-prepare center is perfect for reviewing word recognition. On the right side of a folder, glue a copy of a familiar poem or rhyme. On the left side of the folder, glue a list of words for students to find in the poem. Laminate the folder. Place at a center the folder and washable markers. A child reads the poem. Then he draws a line under the first word on the list, reads the word, and circles each occurrence of it in the poem. He continues with different-colored markers for each word on the list. **For a word identification variation,** replace the word list with simple poem-related pictures. Have students name each picture and circle the matching word in the poem. *Word recognition*

Vanessa Rivera
La Luz Elementary
La Luz, NM

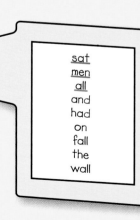

Learning Centers

An -ug Bug
Literacy Center

This bug is the perfect tool for forming an -*ug* word family! Cut out a copy of the bug pattern and onset wheel on page 66. Use a brad to attach the wheel behind the bug where indicated, making sure -*ug* words are formed when the wheel is turned. When a child visits the center, he turns the wheel to make a word, reads it, and writes it on a sheet of paper. He continues in this manner to form an -*ug* word family. **For a take-home activity**, have each child use the patterns to make his own bug and encourage him to read the words to family members as he spins the wheel! *Word family* -ug

Amanda Boyarshinov
Boyarshinov Homeschool
Gainesville, FL

Wyatt

hug
dug
jug

Flower Picking
Math Center

Problem solving is in full bloom during this activity. Program each of several flower cutouts (patterns on page 67) with an addition or a subtraction problem. Attach a craft stick (stem) to each flower and then write the answer to the problem near the bottom of the stem. Poke the stems into a floral foam rectangle so the answers are hidden. Place the flower arrangement and counters at a center. A child writes a problem on a sheet of paper. She determines the answer using the counters as needed and writes to complete the number sentence. Then she removes the flower to check her answer. She continues with each remaining flower as time permits. **For an easier version**, set out two flower arrangements: one for addition and one for subtraction. *Addition and subtraction*

Ashley Rives, Lil Sprouts Kids Day Out, Greenwood, MO

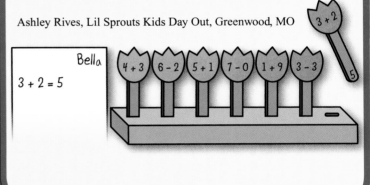

Bella

3 + 2 = 5

4 + 3   6 - 2   5 + 1   7 - 0   1 + 9   3 - 3   3 + 2   5

Sprinkles!
Literacy Center

Youngsters stack scoops of sentence-reading practice with this partner game. Write simple sentences on separate ice cream scoop cutouts (pattern on page 67). On one scoop, draw colorful sprinkles and label it "Sprinkles!" Place all the scoops in a clean, plastic ice cream tub or other container. Set out the tub, two cone cutouts (pattern on page 67), blank paper, and crayons. To play the game, each child places a cone in front of him. In turn, a player takes a scoop, reads the sentence, and puts it at the top of his cone. When a player removes the scoop with sprinkles, each player writes the sentence at the top of his cone and draws a picture to match. If a player does not have a scoop on his cone, he takes a scoop from the tub and writes and illustrates its sentence. *Reading sentences*

Megan Johnson
Dayton, MN

Sprinkles!

The pot is hot.

I have a cat.

Learning Centers

What's in the Net?
Literacy and Math Center

Youngsters catch color and number word skills along with addition practice during this bug-themed center. On the handle of each of several net cutouts, write an addition problem similar to the one shown. Then place at a center the nets, plastic bugs or bug cutouts of corresponding colors, and blank paper. A child chooses a net, reads the handle, and places the matching bugs on the net. Then he writes the matching number sentence on a sheet of paper. He continues with the remaining nets. ***Number and color words, addition number sentences***

adapted from an idea by Marie E. Cecchini
West Dundee, IL

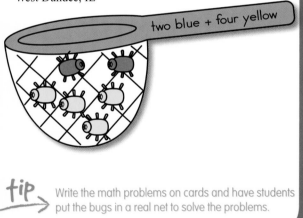

two blue + four yellow

tip → Write the math problems on cards and have students put the bugs in a real net to solve the problems.

Family Members
Literacy Center

This pocket chart activity features *-ick*, *-ack*, and *-ock* words. Cut apart a copy of the picture cards on page 68. For each card, write the name of the picture on a paper strip and cut the card in two, separating the onset and the rime. Write the same word on the back of each picture card to make the activity self-checking. Then put the picture cards, word part strips, and the three heading cards shown in a resealable plastic bag. A child puts the heading cards in the top row of the pocket chart. Next, she names each picture on a card and puts it in the matching column. Then she joins the word part strips to spell each word and puts it next to its picture. To check her work, she flips the picture cards. **For an easier version**, put the word family sets in separate resealable plastic bags. ***Word families***

Vanessa Rivera, La Luz Elementary, La Luz, NM

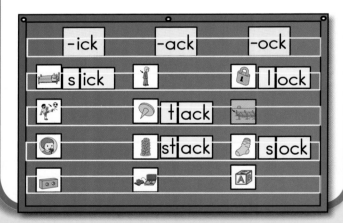

Shapely Flowers
Math Center

Simple pattern block shapes are the perfect manipulative to form larger shapes. Make a work mat by tracing a hexagon block several times near the top of a sheet of paper. Then add a stem, leaves, and desired details. Laminate the mat for durability. A child uses different combinations of pattern blocks to cover each flower on the work mat. **For an added challenge,** make a work mat with a supersize flower for students to cover with pattern blocks. ***Using simple shapes to form larger shapes***

Learning Centers

Word Wall Pockets
Literacy Center

An interactive word wall and envelopes labeled to review a desired skill are all you need to prepare this center. Skills may include two-letter words, three-letter words, and four-letter words; "words I know" and "words I do not know"; or words with one syllable and words with two syllables. A child reads each word and places it in the appropriate pocket. Next, she reads the words in each pocket to an adult and corrects any mistakes. Then she returns the words to the word wall to ready the center for the next child. *High-frequency words*

Colby Mason
Butler Elementary
Butler, IN

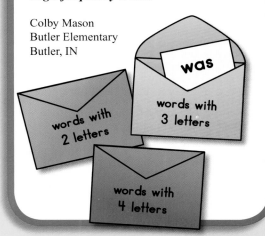

Numbers on the Vine
Math Center

Can these watermelons help your students solve subtraction problems? Yes, indeed! Set out student copies of page 69, a few dried black beans (watermelon seeds), subtraction flash cards, and blank paper. A child writes his name on a copy of page 69 where indicated. Next, he colors, cuts out, and glues the patterns to form a vine number line. Then he takes a card and reads the subtraction problem. To solve, he looks at the first number in the problem and puts a watermelon seed on the same number on the vine. Next he looks at the second number in the problem and moves the seed left that many spaces. Then he writes the corresponding number sentence on a sheet of paper. *Subtraction*

Amber Dingman
Play 'n' Learn Family Child Care and Preschool
Sterling, MI

Shapely Shopping
Math Center

To prepare this geometric sort, color a copy of the center mat on page 70. Color and cut apart a copy of the center cards on page 71 and store them in a resealable plastic bag. Place the bag and mat at a center. To complete the activity, a student stacks the cards faceup. She identifies the two solid figures on the top card, finds the matching shapes on a shopping buggy on the mat, and then puts the card on that buggy. She sorts the remaining cards and then has an adult check her work. *Solid figures*

Catherine Broome-Kehm
Melbourne Beach, FL

Soup Can Label and Recording Sheet
Use with "Soup Sort" on page 50.

Name _____

So Many Noodles!

✏️ Write how many.

Circle.

Which has the **most**?

Which has the **fewest**?

TEC42057

Noodle Cards

Use with "Make 'Chunk-y' Soup!" on page 51.

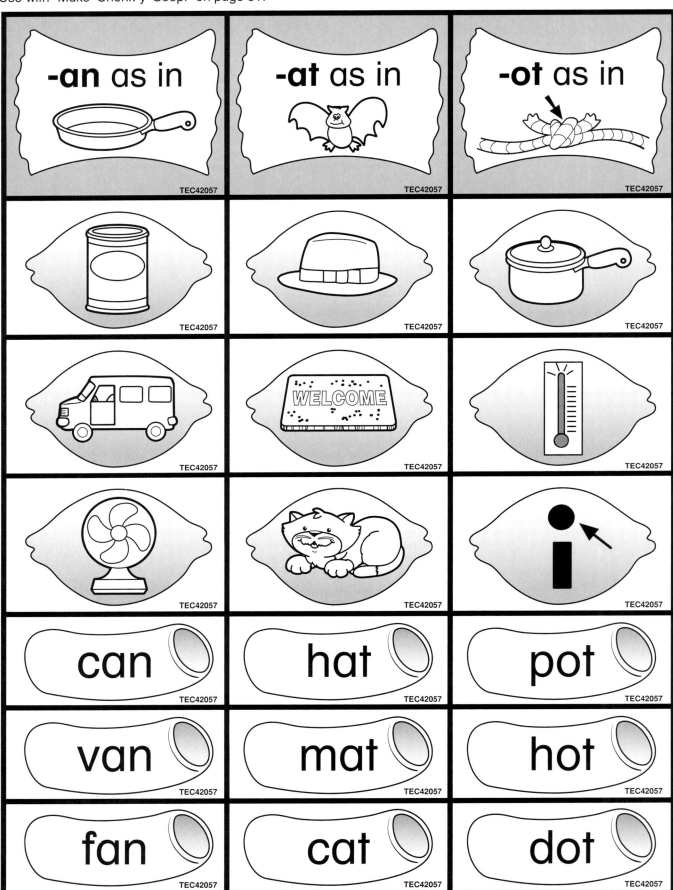

-an as in

-at as in

-ot as in

can

hat

pot

van

mat

hot

fan

cat

dot

How Many Scoops?

✏️ Draw	Estimate ?	Tally Marks 卌	Actual Number
	_____ scoops		_____ scoops
	_____ scoops		_____ scoops
	_____ scoops		_____ scoops
	_____ scoops		_____ scoops

©The Mailbox® • TEC42058 • Dec./Jan. 2011–12

Note to the teacher: Use with "How Many Scoops?" on page 52.

Clothing and Snowpal Patterns
Use with "Dress That Snowpal!" on page 52.

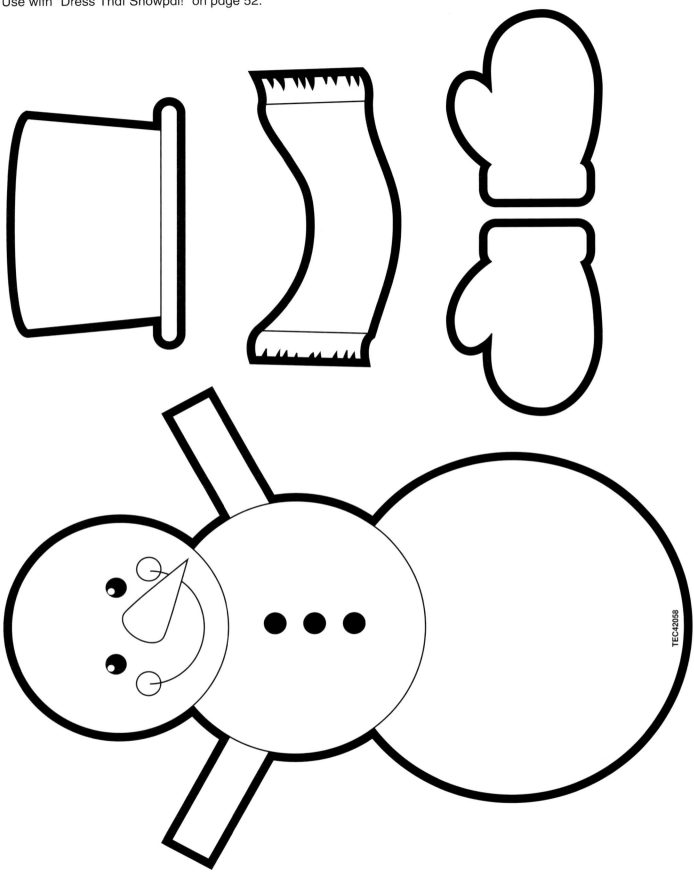

TEC42058

©The Mailbox® • TEC42058 • Dec./Jan. 2011–12

Sudsy Fun

Put. the
Spell. t h e
Write. the

Bubbles a Lot

and	are	good
had	have	let
look	love	one
red	saw	she
soon	the	want

g	k	e	o	w
l	o	t	n	s
d	a	r	h	v

Bug Pattern and Onset Wheel
Use with "An -ug Bug" on page 55.

TEC42060

Flower Patterns
Use with "Flower Picking" on page 55.

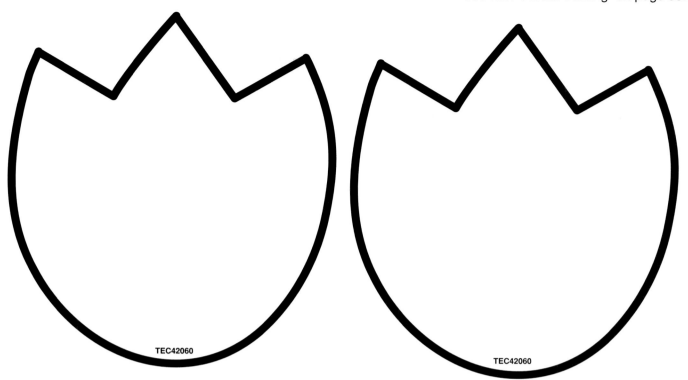

TEC42060

TEC42060

Scoop and Cone Patterns
Use with "Sprinkles!" on page 55 and "Where Am I?" on page 83.

TEC42060

TEC42060

Picture Cards

Use with "Family Members" on page 56.

TEC42061

TEC42061

TEC42061

TEC42061

TEC42061

TEC42061

TEC42061

TEC42061

TEC42061

TEC42061

TEC42061

TEC42061

Glue.

_____'s

Number Vine

Shapely Shopping

Put ☐ to match the shapes.
Check.

Complete the Words!

Initial consonants

un

og

um

at

eb

ib

op

an

ig

©The Mailbox® • TEC42057 • Oct./Nov. 2011

Note to the teacher: Use with the directions on page 73.

To prepare this center activity, remove the center mat on page 72 and cut out the letter cards below. (Make a copy of pages 71 and 74 for your files.) Store the cards in a resealable plastic bag. A child names each picture and uses the cards to complete each word. For an assessment, she completes a copy of the activity below.

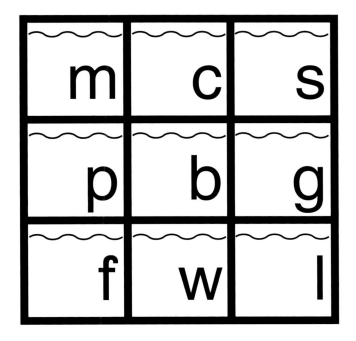

Partner game option: Prepare the activity as described above. Also cut out the scarecrow cards below and then back the letter and scarecrow cards with construction paper. To begin, partners place all the cards facedown. To take a turn, a player flips over a card. If it shows a letter, she places the card on the mat. If it shows a scarecrow, her turn is over. The player who places the last letter card on the mat wins.

Name _____   Initial consonants

Quick Skill Check

✏️ Write the missing letters.

🐟 ___ in	🐻 ___ og	
📦 ___ ag	👄 ___ ip	🥫 ___ an
🥅 ___ et	🦀 ___ at	🍳 ___ ot

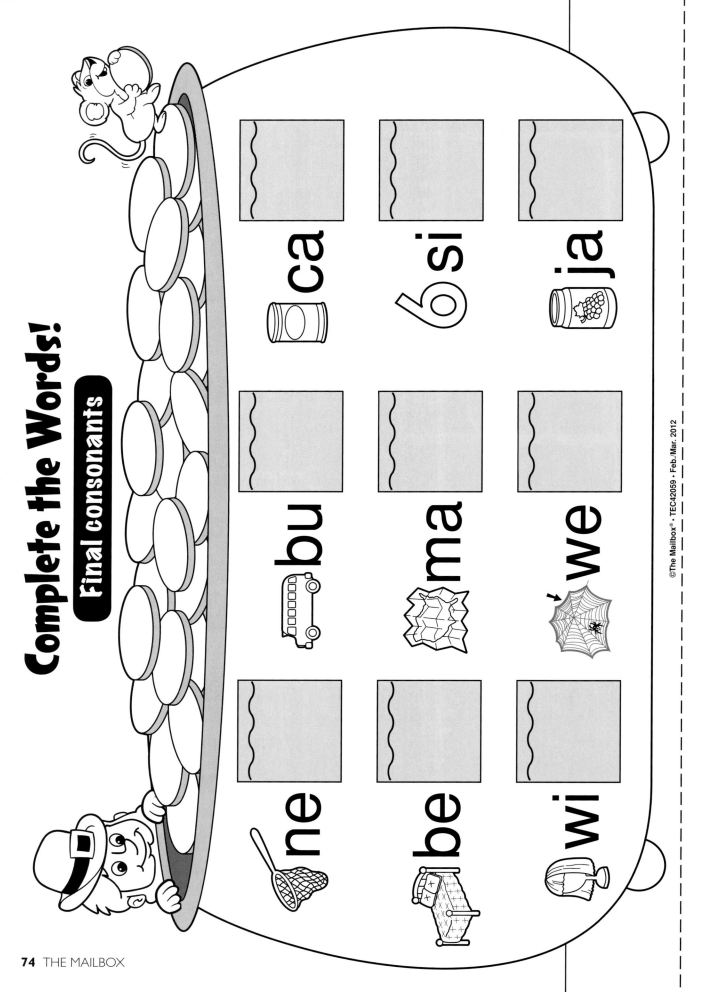

Complete the Words!

Final consonants

ca

si

ja

bu

ma

we

ne

be

wi

©The Mailbox® • TEC42059 • Feb./Mar. 2012

Note to the teacher: Use with the directions on page 75.

Each child cuts apart a copy of the letter cards below. Then she names each picture on a copy of page 74 and uses the cards to complete the words. For an assessment, she completes a copy of the activity below.

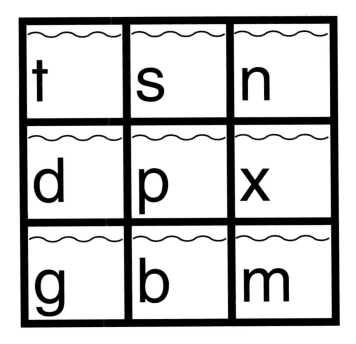

Partner game option: Cut apart a copy of the letter and four-leaf clover cards and back the cards with construction paper. Place the cards by a copy of page 74. To begin, partners place the cards facedown. To take a turn, a player flips over a card. If it shows a "lucky" clover, she puts the card on any open letter space and names the missing letter. If the card shows a letter, she places the card on the mat; if the corresponding space is covered by a clover card, she sets the letter card aside and her turn is over. The player who places the last card on the mat wins.

Name_____

Final consonants

Quick Skill Check

Write the missing letters.

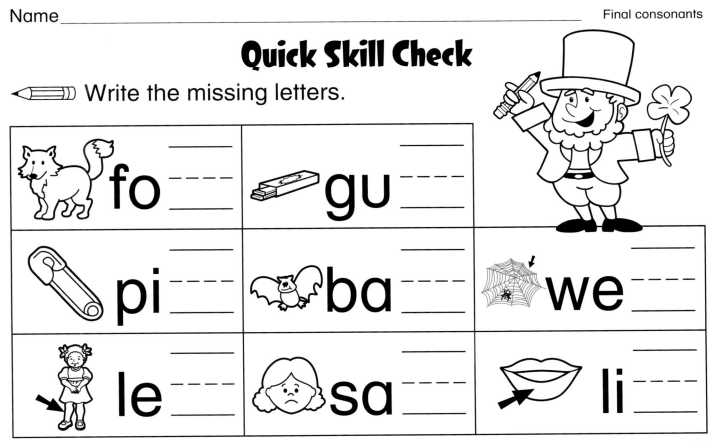

fo___ gu___

pi___ ba___ we___

le___ sa___ li___

Making Pairs

What You Need

2 dice

12 linking cubes

paper

① Toss.

② Count. Write.

7

③ Take.

④ Make pairs.

⑤ Write **odd** or **even**.

7 is odd.

⑥ Do Steps 1–5 again.

"2" is even!

Two socks make a pair.

Step-by-step center activity: Put the activity card and the needed materials at a center.

What's in the Family?

What You Need

7 letter cards

| l | r | s | t |

| bl | st | sh |

paper like this

1 Pick 1.

ack

ock

2 Write.

___ack

3 Put.

s | ack

4 Write.

s | ack
sack

5 Do Steps 3 and 4 for each card.

r | ack
sack
rack

6 Do Steps 1–5 again.

___ack
sack
rack

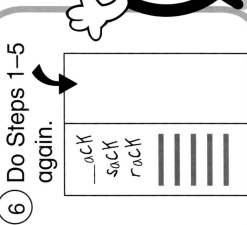

I am a black clock!

©The Mailbox® • TEC42060 • April/May 2012

Step-by-step center activity: Put the activity card and the needed materials at a center.

Farm-Fresh Eggs

What You Need

prepared egg carton
6 white pom-poms
9 brown pom-poms
die
paper

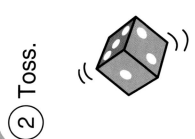

① Write.

___ plus ___ makes 10.

② Toss.

③ Put.

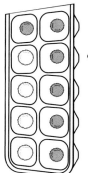

④ Write.

4 plus ___ makes 10.

⑤ Put to make 10.

⑥ Write.

4 plus ___ makes 10.

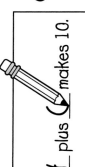

Do Steps 1–6 again.

Step-by-step center activity: Sterilize an egg carton and trim it to ten cups. Then put the activity card and the needed materials at a center.

Let's Do Social Studies!

Let's Do
Social Studies!

Kindergarten Road
Knowledge of home and family

This neighborly project is a great way to welcome students' families for a visit or a conference. Have each youngster draw a picture of her home on a sheet of construction paper. Next, have her draw and write about the people and pets that she lives with on a sheet of story paper. Staple the top of each child's home drawing to her story paper and put it on a long strip of black bulletin board paper (road). Add details as desired to complete your class's road of homes.

Jennifer Cummings
Lomax Elementary
La Porte, TX

Kindergarten Road

Which Is It?
Wants and needs

This toe-tapping tune prompts students to name a want or a need. Lead youngsters in singing the song shown. Then invite a child to respond. Guide kindergartners to determine whether the named item is a want or a need and say either "Want it!" or "Need it to live!" Continue as time permits. **For a vocabulary connection**, write each child's response on a T-chart labeled *wants* and *needs*.

(sung to the tune of "The Muffin Man")

Oh, can you name a want or need,
A want or need,
A want or need?
Oh, can you name a want or need
Of people here on Earth?

Water.

Need it to live!

A Pleasing Planet
Identifying land and water

These student-made projects help youngsters make connections to Earth on a globe. Explain how most maps and globes use green to show land and blue to show water. Then instruct each child to brush diluted glue on a tagboard circle. Direct her to place green tissue paper squares (land) and blue tissue paper squares (water) atop the glue to create her own land-and-water map. Next, have her brush a thin layer of diluted glue over her map. When the glue is dry, help each child use a permanent marker to label the land and water areas. To make connections to our planet, have youngsters use their projects to help them identify land and water areas on a globe.

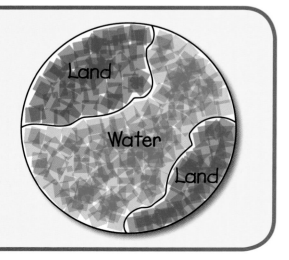

Let's Do Social Studies!

Wally Wants It All!

This poster activity is sure to show one's wants exceed one's needs. Glue a copy of the Wally pattern on page 85 to a piece of bulletin board paper. Then have each child draw on a paper square a picture of her choice that shows either a need or a want. In turn, ask each youngster to glue her square to the bulletin board paper and name her drawing. Have the class respond, "Wally wants it!" Then ask, "But does Wally need it?" Help youngsters discern if the drawing depicts a need or a want. If it is a need, circle the paper square. After every child has a turn, look at the circled drawings and lead youngsters to determine if Wally has all he needs to live. If not, guide youngsters to name the missing essential needs. *Needs and wants*

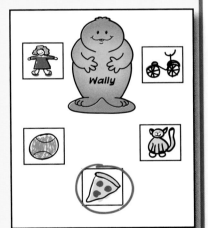

Gerri Primak
Charlotte, NC

Hand in Hand

Students lend a hand to create this visual display that honors Dr. Martin Luther King Jr.'s dream. Have each child draw a self-likeness on a copy of the person pattern on page 85 and then cut it out. Glue the cutouts hand over hand across a large map. Before putting the project on display, attach a copy of the poem shown. Over the next several days, chant the rhyme with youngsters and discuss its meaning. *Understanding Martin Luther King Jr.'s dream*

Sarah Garbett, Harvie Elementary, Richmond, VA

Hand in hand, across the land,
For Martin's dream we choose to stand.
We say it loud. We say it clear.
Peace and love throughout the year!

On the Job

The result of this idea is a class book featuring your young community helpers! In advance, invite each youngster to choose a community helper she would like to represent. Send home a note asking that each student bring in a costume or props that correspond with the helper. (If needed, help the student draw a costume on a large paper grocery bag.) On the predetermined day, take a photograph of each child wearing her costume or holding her props. Then invite her classmates to guess what type of helper she is. Later, glue each photo to a sheet of paper and add a label. Bind the pages together to make a class book. **To extend the activity**, lead students in a discussion about the tools each helper needs and the goods or services he provides. *Community helpers*

Kaitlyn the Doctor

Jeanne-Marie Peterson, Charlottesville, VA

Let's Do Social Studies!

How Many States?
Map awareness

Invite students to name friends or family members who live in other states. Help each child place a personalized sticky dot on a corresponding state on a map. Then lead students in a discussion about the different states where people they know live. **For a letter-writing connection,** have each child write a letter to a friend or family member who lives out of state. If he receives a response, invite him to share the envelope with the group, identify the state in the return address, and mark the state on the map.

adapted by an idea from Brenda Teal
Maxwell Air Force Base Elementary
Maxwell Air Force Base, AL

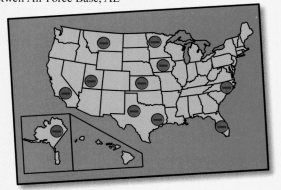

Inventive Americans
Black History Month

Applaud famous African American inventors as you celebrate Black History Month. Share with students information about several African American inventors and their inventions. Discuss with youngsters how people's lives would be different if these inventions had not been created. Then ask students to brainstorm a list of existing inconveniences or problems. Invite each child to choose a problem and design an invention to solve it. Have her draw a picture of her invention and then help her write to describe its function.

Famous African American Inventors

George Crum—invented the potato chip

Garrett Morgan—developed versions of the traffic light

George Washington Carver—300 uses for peanuts, including cooking oil

Madam C. J. Walker—developed a line of hair-care products

Frederick McKinley Jones—invented a cooling system for trucks

Benjamin Banneker—made one of the first watches in America, a wooden pocket watch

This is a room cleaner. It cleans your bedroom.

Abraham Lincoln
Presidents' Day

Celebrate this presidential holiday with a booklet about Abraham Lincoln. Have each child cut apart a copy of pages 86 and 87. Next, have her stack booklet pages 1–5 in order behind the cover and staple them atop the booklet backing (page 6). Then lead students in reading each page and discussing the illustrations. **To extend the activity**, explain to youngsters that Mr. Lincoln had the nickname Honest Abe. Then ask students to share different nicknames they would be proud to earn.

Catherine Broome-Kehm
Melbourne Beach, FL

Let's Do Social Studies!

Mark the Spot
Mapping skills

Students' sticky notes show where their seat assignments are on this supersize map. On a length of bulletin board paper, draw a simple map of your classroom that labels everything but students' seats. Display the map in a student-accessible location and guide youngsters to notice that the seat markers are missing from the map. Then have each child put a personalized sticky note on the map to show where she sits in the classroom. If students' seat assignments change, the notes are easy to move for more mapping practice.

Beth Parry, Zane North Elementary, Collingswood, NJ

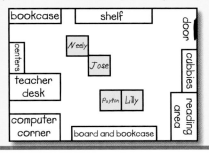

Where Am I?
Understanding one's location

These ice cream scoops are a perfect visual reminder of one's location in the world. Discuss with youngsters how they not only live in a city but also in a state, country, and continent and on a planet. Then write the name of the school on a supersize cone cutout. Guide youngsters to name each place, from the city to the planet, and write each response on a large ice cream scoop cutout. To review, lead the group in ordering the scoops so the planet scoop is farthest from the cone. **For a center option**, post the supersize craft as a reference and have each child make a smaller cone (patterns on page 67) that features the city in which he lives all the way to Earth. For added fun, provide a small student photo for him to use to personalize his cone.

Christy Bailey
Marion Primary School
Marion, VA

tip > Enlarge the patterns on page 67 to make this ice cream cone display.

A Presidential Tune
Leaders of the United States

This toe-tapping ditty helps youngsters remember the names of the president and vice president of the United States. After sharing information about these men, lead students in singing the song shown.

(sung to the tune of "Bingo")

Barack Obama's the president
Of the USA.
O-B-A-M-A,
O-B-A-M-A,
O-B-A-M-A.
He is the nation's leader.

Joe Biden's the vice president
Of the USA.
B-I-D-E-N,
B-I-D-E-N,
B-I-D-E-N.
He helps the nation's leader.

adapted from an idea by Jeanne-Marie Peterson
Crozet, VA

Let's Do Social Studies!

The Red, White, and Blue
American flag

To celebrate America's Flag Day on June 14, showcase a United States flag and discuss the symbolism of the 13 stripes and 50 stars. Then lead youngsters in singing this toe-tapping tune.

(sung to the tune of "Row, Row, Row Your Boat")

Look at the country's flag,
Three colors that we see.
America is where we live.
It's home for you and me.

See the 13 stripes;
They are red and white.
On the blue are 50 stars.
It's really quite a sight!

adapted from an idea by Cynthia Singletary
York, PA

All Around the Classroom
Map skills

Students make milk-carton props to create this three-dimensional map. On a length of bulletin board paper, draw or make structures to show classroom landmarks, such as your desk, bookshelves, the door, and the board. To begin, have each child use craft materials to personalize a clean, dry milk carton. Then have him use the landmarks on the map to position his craft to show where he sits in the classroom. Guide students to use the completed map to answer map-related questions. To incorporate directionality, label the map "north," "south," "east," and "west" for students to use as a reference.

adapted from an idea by Ivet Alonso
West Hollywood Elementary
Hollywood, FL

A Patriotic Prop
National symbols

Discuss with youngsters some national symbols and their locations with this American bald eagle activity. On a class supply of page 88, cut out the window boxes on the eagles. Next, have each child color and cut out her copy of the page. Help her attach the wheel cutout behind the eagle with a brad. Then lead youngsters in singing the song shown and have them move the wheel to match the named symbol and the state in which it is located for each verse.

(sung to the tune of "London Bridge")

We know where to find the [White House],
Find the [White House], find the [White House].
We know where to find the [White House]—
[Washington, DC] !

Continue with the following: *Statue of Liberty, New York Harbor;*
Liberty Bell, Pennsylvania

adapted from an idea by Jennifer Reidy, Halifax Elementary
Halifax, MA

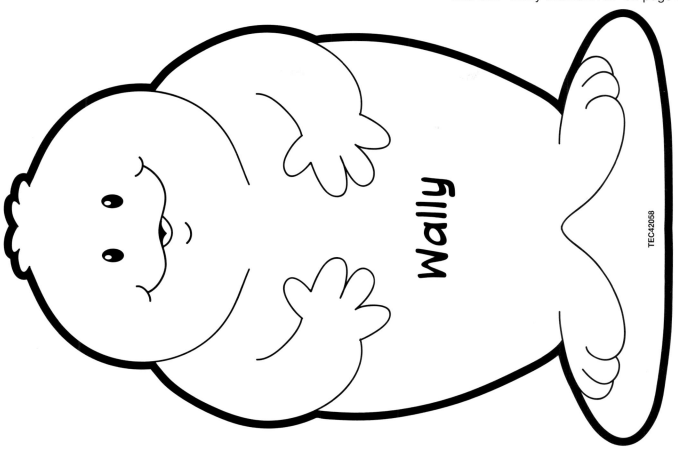

Wally

TEC42058

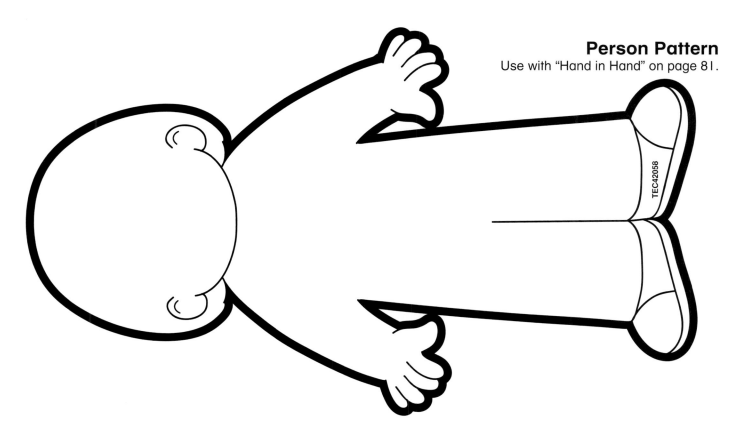

TEC42058

February 2012

Sun	Mon	Tues	Wed	Thurs	Fri	Sat
			1	2	3	4
5	6	7	8	9	10	11
12	13	14	15	16	17	18
19	20	21	22	23	24	25
26	27	28	29			

Abraham Lincoln was born on February 12, 1809.

1

Lincoln loved to read books. He became a lawyer.

3

Abraham Lincoln

He lived in a log cabin.

2

Abraham Lincoln Booklet Use with "Abraham Lincoln" on page 82.

4

16

Lincoln became the 16th president of the United States.

5

one cent

1¢

IN GOD WE TRUST

LIBERTY

2001

We see a picture of his face on a penny.

We honor Lincoln and all the US presidents on Presidents' Day.

6

by _____

©The Mailbox® • TEC42059 • Feb./Mar. 2012

Bald Eagle and Wheel Patterns
Use with "A Patriotic Prop" on page 84.

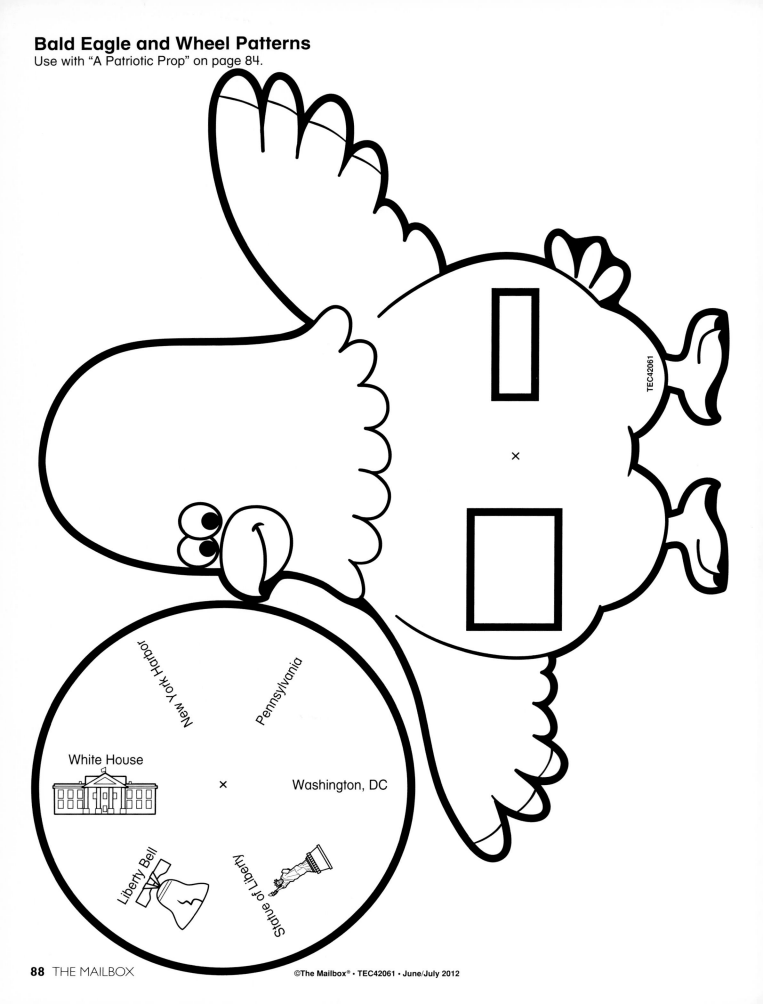

White House

New York Harbor

Pennsylvania

Washington, DC

Liberty Bell

Statue of Liberty

TEC42061

Management Tips
& Timesavers

Management Tips & Timesavers

Less Mess!

Looking for a mess-free way to **clean paintbrushes**? Use an empty wipes container! Partially fill the container with water and replace the lid. Youngsters simply slip used paintbrushes (brush-side down) through the lid. The brushes get clean without dirtying the sink! *Dr. Ashlei Haskell, Rosebud Elementary, Loganville, GA*

Join the Parade

Avoid noisy **pencil sharpening** interruptions with this idea! During a transition time, call out, "Pencil parade!" and have students who need to sharpen their pencils get in line behind you. Lead the line to the sharpener and have each child sharpen his pencil. When there is one child left in line, call out, "Going once, going twice—last call to make your pencils nice!" Encourage students who need additional pencils sharpened to get in line. *Amy Hart, Saint Sylvester School, Pittsburgh, PA*

Game Binder

Organize your **collection of games** from *The Mailbox*® magazine and The Mailbox Companion® with a three-ring binder. Put the gameboards and directions in separate sheet protectors. Then place the materials needed to play the games in a plastic pencil pouch in the front of the binder. Now, all the games and supplies are in one place and are ready to be used. *Cheryl Kulp, Grace Christian School, Telford, PA*

A Sweet Break

Put a **positive spin on your time-out chair** by calling it a sugar chair. If a child is sent to the sugar chair, encourage her to think about sweeter choices. When appropriate, invite her to rejoin the group to show off her sweeter attitude. *Ahnice Pierce, New Deal Elementary, New Deal, TX*

Ready to Read

Use this variation of the familiar chant "We're Going on a Bear Hunt" to help youngsters quickly **transition to story-time**. Say the chant shown, pausing for youngsters to repeat each line as they gather in your storytime area. If desired, invite children to pat their legs to the beat as they chant. *Patrice Lincoln, Lakeview Elementary, Ridley Park, PA*

> We are having a read-aloud!
> We're starting right away!
> So let's all listen carefully
> To this story here today!

Management Tips & Timesavers

Parallel Parking

Here's a fun way to manage class **bathroom breaks**! While students are waiting to use the restrooms, encourage them to pretend to be cars and "parallel park" in the hallway against a wall. Once each child is seated on the floor, remind him that his doors should be closed (hands in lap) and his radio off (voice silent). Youngsters love pretending to be cars, and the resulting quiet is the perfect time to review letters, numbers, and shapes! *Gina Thornton, Glenwood Elementary, Enid, OK*

Label It!

To label baskets and other containers, use **clip-on name badges**! Simply make the desired label, cut it to size, and slip it into the name badge. Then clip the badge to the basket. It's easy to remove the badge, clip it to a new container, or replace the label! *Stacey Pellicano, Lockport, NY*

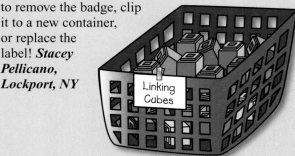

Time to Think

Encourage a child to think about **behaving in a positive way** with this tip! Label a chair "The Thinking Chair" and place it in a quiet area of the room. When a child breaks a classroom rule, encourage her to sit in the chair and draw a picture that shows how she should have behaved. Discuss the illustration and write her description on the paper. Then make a copy of the page for your records and send the original home with the youngster. *Laura Ives, Daniels Farm School, Trumbull, CT*

Clipped Copies

Constantly forgetting **paper clips** when you go to the copy room? Simply mark the pages you want to copy with paper clips! Remove a clip, copy the page for your students, and then clip the copies together! *Rebecca Henry, Windsor Elementary, Windsor, ME*

Book Baskets

Early finishers know where to go with this simple idea. Place baskets of books in strategic places around the room. Then if a child finishes his work early, he sits next to a basket, chooses a book, and reads. Each book basket can have four visitors—one for each side of the basket. *Laurie Block, Cabool Elementary, Cabool, MO*

Management Tips & Timesavers

"Beary" Good Behavior

Make a supply of simple play money (bear bucks) similar to the ones shown. When a child is caught exhibiting good behavior, give him a bear buck. Youngsters can trade in their bear bucks at the end of each week for special privileges, such as extra computer time.

Laura Baynard, Freeman's Mill Elementary, Lawrenceville, GA

Who's Listening?

Recognize a good listener with this engaging song!

(sung to the tune of "My Bonnie Lies Over the Ocean")

I'm proud of somebody who's listening.
I'm proud of somebody right here!   *Point to a child.*
I'm proud of somebody who's listening.
Let's all give our classmate a cheer!
Thank you, thank you,
Oh, thank you for being so nice, so nice!
Thank you, thank you,
Oh, thank you for being so nice!

Lucille Iscaro, PS 257, Bronx, NY

Form Groups

Tuck in a bit of skill review with this simple grouping method. For each pair or small group of students, write the same word—such as a color, high-frequency, number, or spelling word—on a card for each child. To form groups, give each child a card. Then have youngsters with matching word cards stand together. To review different skills, program the cards with letters, numbers, or shapes. *Mary Amoson, Moreland Elementary, Moreland, GA*

Easy Bulletin Boards

Take a picture of each bulletin board and wall display in your classroom. When it's time to change the display, store the photo in a large resealable plastic bag with all the corresponding pieces. For quick reassembly, simply give the bag to a parent volunteer and ask her to re-create the display. *Leslie Wright, Aviara Oaks Elementary, Carlsbad, CA*

Shhhh!

Encourage students to travel or work quietly in zero-talking zones! Attach die-cut zeros in locations where talking isn't allowed, such as in the hallway or in reading areas. Then, each time students respect the zero-talking zones, attach a hole reinforcer (zero) to a chart. When youngsters reach a predetermined number of zeros, reward their behavior with a zero-shaped treat! *Jodi Darter, Cabool Elementary, Cabool, MO*

OUR READERS WRITE

Our Readers WRITE...
(and EMAIL and BLOG and TWEET and POST)

First-Day Goody Bags

Ease youngsters' fears of starting kindergarten with a first-day surprise. For each child, I put a few items—such as a fun pencil, an eraser, a lollipop, and a small toy—in a personalized lunch bag. I display the bags at our meet-the-teacher day. When students and families visit the classroom, I point out the bags and explain that they will be sent home on the first day of school. In many cases youngsters are so excited to come to school to receive their prizes that they forget about their fears! *Brook Baglini, Main Elementary, Athens, PA*

"I LOVE your magazine. I have been using it in my classroom since 1990."—*Cajsa Howland Sheen via Facebook*

"Great teaching ideas! My students love them all!"—*Jennifer Marcinkus Chumbley via Facebook*

Glue Monsters

To remind students to handle glue properly, I often say the poem, "Just a dot, not a lot, of glue will do." Then I show youngsters how the top of the glue can be turned on and off just like a faucet. We pretend that if the glue comes out too fast, then glue monsters will make a mess of students' projects. My class enjoys avoiding sticky globs of glue to be free of those messy monsters! *Nikole Zegunis, Cedar Creek Elementary, Olathe, KS*

NIFTY NAMETAGS

These durable nametags are perfect for students to wear during the first week of school. To make a nametag, I glue an uppercase craft foam letter that matches the first letter of the child's name to the left side of a craft foam rectangle. Then I use a marker to write the rest of the child's name. Finally, I punch two holes near the top of the nametag and attach a length of yarn to make a necklace. *Jodi Darter, Cabool Elementary, Cabool, MO*

The MAILBOX® BLOG

"Thank you for the wonderful ideas that you provide every month! I look forward to my new edition like it's Christmas morning!"—*Rolanda Staley, Aiken, SC, via The Mailbox® Blog*

Our Readers WRITE...
(and EMAIL and BLOG and TWEET and POST)

OUR DAY IN K

To show parents what goes on in the classroom, I make this class book. During the school day, I take photographs of students while they are at centers, lunch, storytime, calendar time, special classes, and recess. I print the photos on copy paper, leaving room at the bottom of each paper for a caption. With students' help, I write a caption below each photo. Then I slide the papers into separate plastic sheet protectors and place the resulting pages in a binder. Each night a different child takes the book home to share with his family. *Suzanne Ward, Seneca Unity Public School, Caledonia, Ontario, Canada*

Stay on the Road

To teach youngsters to follow the lines when cutting, I tell a child to pretend that the cut line is a road and his scissors are a car. Then I remind him to stay on the road and go slowly around curves so that he does not have a wreck. Vroom, vroom! *Annette Warren, First Baptist Child Development Center, Taylorsville, NC*

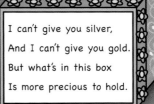

Cherished Keepsakes

I can't give you silver,
And I can't give you gold.
But what's in this box
Is more precious to hold.

Students box up some love for special grandparents with this gift idea. In advance, I ask parents and coworkers to donate new or gently used small boxes. I glue a copy of the poem shown to the box lid; then I give each child a box to decorate. On the inside of the lid, each student writes "Me." Next, each child glues a photo of herself to the inside of the box and replaces the lid. She gives her special gift to a grandparent for Grandparents Day. *Janice Burch, Tri-Valley Elementary, Downs, IL*

Happy Birthday!

BIRTHDAY CHAIR

I use a birthday chair cover to make each child's birthday special. To make a cover, I use glitter and felt to decorate an inexpensive pillowcase. Prior to the child arriving on her birthday, I slip the cover on the back of her chair. If desired, invite the child to take the chair cover with her to other places she visits during the day and place it on the back of any chair in which she sits. *Barbara Hollis, Las Flores Elementary, Rancho Santa Margarita, CA*

Our Readers WRITE...
(and EMAIL and BLOG and TWEET and POST)

Luggage Learning

This home-school connection is always a hit for my class! I pack a suitcase of skill-related and craft activities for youngsters to do with family members. Along with the take-home activities, I pack a note to parents explaining what I would like them to do and when to return the suitcase to school. I also include a notepad for parent comments. Parents and students alike look forward to the opportunity to bring the suitcase home. *Karen Nelson, Lordstown Elementary, Warren, OH*

"I love *The Mailbox*!!! I have been a subscriber for nine years!"—*Diana Oldham via Facebook*

A Class of "Friend-ensteins"!

My seasonal door display is a first-place prizewinner! I have each child add details to a Frankenstein's monster head–shaped cutout. Then I help her write her name with the suffix *-enstein* (for example, Lizenstein) on a paper strip and have her glue it to her craft. I post the completed crafts on my door; the display is perfect for Halloween! *Michele Atlas, Eagle Point Elementary, Weston, FL*

Lizenstein

Carlenstein

PUZZLE TREES

I recycle extra puzzle pieces to make an attractive fall display. I give each child a sheet of card stock and ask him to draw a tree trunk on the bottom half. Then I have him glue puzzle pieces on his paper to form the top of his tree. When the glue is dry, I use the trees to create a colorful hall display. **Paula Staffeld, Westwood Elementary, Wellington, OH**

Neat and Tidy

A visit from a special guest encourages my class to keep our room clean. I invite the custodian to talk with my students. I have him tell the group about his job and invite them to ask him questions. After the custodian leaves, I lead students in a discussion about how they can make his job easier by cleaning up after themselves. My youngsters enjoy helping out their new friend! *Clare Cox, Homer Davis Elementary, Tucson, AZ*

The **MAILBOX** BLOG

"I am so thankful for *The Mailbox* and all the teachers who share their ideas."—*Ruth Zabelin, Kingsville, TX, via The Mailbox Blog*

Our Readers WRITE...

Sort It Out

I grab a stack of reading books from our classroom library for a ready-to-go math activity. I show the books to my youngsters and discuss different ways the books can be sorted, such as fiction and nonfiction, big books and small books, or books about animals and books that are not about animals. After we sort the books one way, we sort them using a different attribute. It is amazing how many ways one group of books can be sorted! *Vanessa Rivera, La Luz Elementary, La Luz, NM*

Follow Along With Me

To help a student complete a worksheet, I slip a copy of the matching page into a plastic sheet protector. I use wipe-off markers to write on the sheet protector as I model what to do on the page. To clear the page for a different student or small group, I simply wipe it clean. It's not only helpful and quick, but I save paper too! *Carol Schafer, Trinity Lutheran School, Joppa, MD*

The MAILBOX. BLOG

"Thank you for the ideas I have gotten from *The Mailbox* magazine over the years. My fellow teachers think I am so smart—even when I tell them my idea is from *The Mailbox*." —*Linda Jones, Austin, TX, via The Mailbox Blog*

f "I love *The Mailbox* magazine. It has enhanced my classrooms since the 1980s."—*Lisa Parks Reed via Facebook*

On Our Way to 100

The kindergarten classrooms at my school celebrate the 50th day of school as well as the 100th day of school. Each kindergarten teacher plans an activity related to the number 50. On the 50th day of school, the kindergarten classes rotate from room to room to participate in each activity. Some of our experiences include a scavenger hunt for 50 paper shapes, counting by 5s to 50 by stacking paper ice cream scoops on a paper cone, and using craft materials to decorate a 5 and a 0 to make a fashionable 50. *Lindsay Davis, Rosehill Elementary, Lenexa, KS*

BUY NOW, USE LATER!

I plan ahead with this money-saving tip. I ask parents to donate unwanted Halloween candy. I store the candy until I am ready to make gingerbread houses with my students in December. Then I pull out the candy and we use it to decorate the houses. *Nancy Schneider, Saint Charles, MO*

Our Readers WRITE...

(and EMAIL and BLOG and TWEET and POST)

A Supersize Wreath

Each year during the holidays, my class visits a local nursing home. Along with our gifts of songs and homemade cards, we make an enormous wreath for the residents to enjoy in their common area. To make a wreath, I have each of my students trace, cut out, and glue handprints (holly leaves) to a large cardboard wreath shape for several mornings. When the cardboard is covered, we glue red paper circles (berries) and a holiday bow to the holly leaves. For added personalization, we each sign the back. The huge wreath is always a big hit! *Faith Best, Hampton Academy, Courtland, VA*

> f *"The Mailbox* is an **excellent resource** for my teaching plans. Thank you for helping me find great ideas to implement in my lessons each and every week."— *Cathy Jo McCall via Facebook*

Sentence Highway

Guide youngsters down the road of great sentence writing with this cool comparison. I explain to youngsters that the lines on a paper are the roads, the words are cars, and the end punctuation serves as stop signs. I tell students to think of the letters that make up each word as passengers in the car, which means they would sit close together. To remind youngsters to leave spaces between words, I tell them to keep some distance between the cars to prevent a crash! *Jodi Darter, Cabool Elementary, Cabool, MO*

IN THE BAG

I reuse gift bags of various sizes and themes to add a unique twist to show-and-tell. I give each child a bag and instruct him to find something for show-and-tell that will fit inside the bag and also relates to the theme featured on the bag. When it is time to share, it is a lot of fun to see what creative things my students bring in. *Maribel M. Mohr, The Peck School, Morristown, NJ*

The MAILBOX BLOG

> 🔊 *"I totally love The Mailbox* website and magazines!"—*Karen Lesmerises, Allenstown, NH, via The Mailbox Blog*

Our Readers WRITE...

(and EMAIL and BLOG and TWEET and POST)

A BOX FOR BORDERS

I have found that the perfect place to store display borders is in a wreath box. (Search after holiday sales to find one at a great price.) Now finding the border I want is a snap, and my borders are no longer ripped, curled, or tangled. **Erica Atchison, Sonoma Ranch Elementary, Gilbert, AZ**

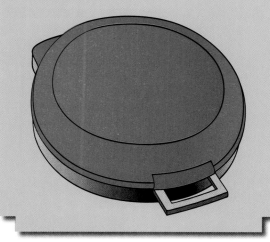

Tic-Tac-Write!

My youngsters are eager for me to say "Flip your paper!" for more letter-writing practice! After reviewing letter formation for several letters, I encourage student pairs to play a modified version of tic-tac-toe on the back of their papers. Instead of using Xs and Os to claim boxes on the grid, youngsters play each of several rounds using two letters that we have been practicing. Not only do I get to monitor correct letter formation, the kids have loads of fun while working on their letters! *Susan Brown, Central Elementary, Palmyra, VA*

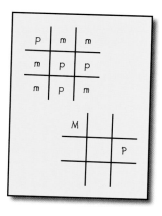

f "I love the various types of activities in *The Mailbox* magazine. It's really a pleasure to have it!"—*Rola Abou Dargham via Facebook*

The MAILBOX BLOG

I have made many games and activities from ideas in *The Mailbox*. I love this magazine!"—*Cindy MacDonald, Raynham, MA, via The Mailbox Blog*

STARS FOR STUDENTS

A star-shaped hole puncher is a great tool for motivating students to do their best work. When I check a child's paper, I punch up to five stars along the top. A youngster earns stars for a pre-established set of skills, such as writing her name neatly, taking time with her coloring, cutting on the lines, and using the correct amount of glue. **Jodi Darter, Cabool Elementary, Cabool, MO**

Admit One
Polar Express

Tickets, Please!

Reading a simple book to a parent earns a ticket to our Polar Express Party! I send home with each child a note explaining the special activity and a book I want the child to read. When I receive a signed note verifying the child read the book, he earns a ticket to attend the party. On Polar Express Day, ticketholders wear their bathrobes and slippers during a reading of *The Polar Express* by Chris Van Allsburg and a viewing of the movie. For added fun, I serve small doughnuts and hot chocolate. Yum! *Denise Bessemer, Stillwater Township Elementary, Stillwater, NJ*

Our Readers WRITE...

Learning on the Go!

My students are prepared for a quick sorting activity when I pick them up from recess, lunch, or a special class. In separate resealable bags, I keep sets of skill-based cards we've sorted during group-time lessons. Before I leave, I choose a set of cards and put the headings in a pocket chart. When I pick up my youngsters, I hand each child a card and name the skill—such as initial consonants, ending sounds, short vowels, or addition. By the time we return to the classroom, each child is eager to put her card below the matching heading. Then we check the chart for accuracy. *Vanessa Rivera, La Luz Elementary, La Luz, NM*

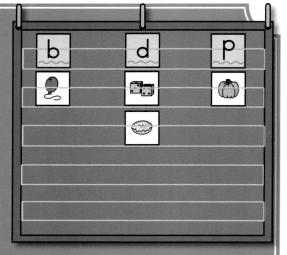

"I love the new layout of *The Mailbox* magazine. It's easy to find what you need, and the latest tweets and messages from Facebook get published. I can't wait to use it!"—*Nicole DeVincenzo via Facebook*

Storage Trays

Looking for a way to organize small objects in your classroom? Try using flat-ware trays! I use the trays in the art area for storing markers, colored pencils, and paint-brushes; in the math center for storing and sorting math manipulatives; and in the literacy area for storing letter manipulatives. The trays are functional, come in a variety of colors, and can be found at most discount stores. *Michelle Devey, Londonderry Elementary, Middletown, PA*

The MAILBOX BLOG

"Thanks so much for striving to make learning fun!"—*Sarah Chestnut via The Mailbox Blog*

TOOTHBRUSHES OR PAINTBRUSHES?

To add a fun twist to painting projects, I stock my art center with a supply of toothbrushes. The kids think it is really neat to paint with the toothbrushes, they experience a different style of painting, and the toothbrush sets from a dollar store are perfectly suitable and inexpensive! *Tonya Ellis, Dekalb West Elementary, Liberty, TN*

Make a Match

I use boxes of valentine cards to create a visual discrimination small-group game. I laminate matching pairs of cards and store them in a Valentine's Day gift bag. To play, each child puts three different cards in front of her. To take a turn, a child removes a card from the bag without looking. If the card matches one of her cards, she places it on top to make a match. If the card is not a match or the card already has a perfect pair, she returns it to the bag. Play continues until one player matches all of her cards. **Sarah Link, Wells Elementary, East Moline, IL**

The MAILBOX BLOG

"I love this magazine. I have used it most of my 28 years of teaching and will continue to use it until I retire! Thank you for all the wonderful 'tools' you have given me over the years!"—*Lisa Reed via The Mailbox Blog*

CLIP IT ON!

A plastic link chain makes it easy for me to display students' artwork. When a child completes a project, I simply clip the paper to the chain so it can be admired by all. **Angie Kozeal, Tri-Center Community Schools, Neola, IA**

Create-a-Cube

When I want my students to play a math game with number cubes and want to include numbers higher than six, I use my Unifix number cube! To make one, simply write each number from 7 to 10 on a different flat side of the cube. The blank sides of the cube add a little excitement to the game, because when a number does not land faceup, the player loses a turn! *Melissa McMurray, Meadow View Elementary, Alabaster, AL*

The MAILBOX BLOG

"Thank you, *Mailbox*. I have subscribed to this magazine for more than a decade, and I love how it has continued to evolve with the changes in education."—*Theresa Clevenstine via The Mailbox Blog*

Connecting With Words

I incorporate high-frequency word practice with traditional store-bought games such as Connect Four. For each game piece, I write the same word on two sticky dots. I put the matching dots on each side of the piece. To play, partners take turns reading a word on a game piece before dropping it into the grid. The opponent also reads each word to make sure his partner is correct. When a player gets four in a row, partners reread the words together. Other skills I review in this manner include letter-sound associations, number recognition, and addition. **Bernadette Todaro, Kadimah School of Buffalo, Amherst, NY**

Our Readers WRITE...

(and EMAIL and BLOG and TWEET and POST)

Tally Mark Help

Craft sticks make the perfect visual aid to remind students how to make tally marks! I have each student place four plain craft sticks side by side and a colored craft stick diagonally across the top so they look like five tally marks. Then I glue each set together and display the sets for students to use as references. **Helen Moen, Maternity B. V. M., Chicago, IL**

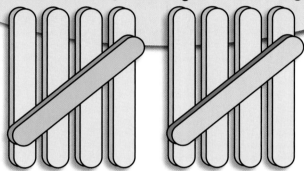

f "My favorite magazine!"
—*Julie Viano via Facebook*

Lights Out

My youngsters know they can help our planet on Earth Day and every day! During our discussion about ways to help Earth, I guide students to think about how much energy is used to keep lights on all day. Then we start a school campaign to encourage teachers and students to celebrate Earth Day by spending part of the day with the lights off and by turning off all lights when leaving a room. I invite students to make posters to promote the idea and even make an announcement on the loudspeaker. *Kate Wonders, Carlisle Elementary, Carlisle, IA*

The MAILBOX. BLOG

"I really love reading all the tips and ideas from my fellow teachers. *The Mailbox* magazines are great!"— *Linda Stoffan, Rio Rancho, NM, via The Mailbox Blog*

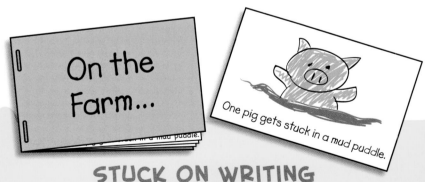

On the Farm...

One pig gets stuck in a mud puddle.

STUCK ON WRITING

I use the story format in *One Duck Stuck* by Phyllis Root to practice creative writing and review animal habitats. After a lesson on any habitat, I have each child choose an animal in the habitat and write about it getting stuck somewhere in the environment. Then I bind students' completed pages between construction paper covers and feature the habitat on the front cover. **Cathy Collier, Portlock Primary, Chesapeake, VA**

Our Readers WRITE...

(and EMAIL and BLOG and TWEET and POST)

QUICKER MEMORY GAMES

I use two different sets of die cuts or two colors of construction paper squares to make Concentration-style games easier to play. I write one half of each matching pair on one set and write the other half on the second set. To play, students put each set together in rows, skill-side down. Then players take turns to find each match. Now my games are quicker to play, and my students are more focused on the skill I set out for them to review! **Vanessa Rivera, La Luz Elementary, La Luz, NM**

Weather, Word Families, and More!

During our morning meeting when we discuss the calendar and weather, I use a related word to jumpstart a word family review. For example, I might write hot on a hot day and ask, "If you can spell *hot*, what else can you spell?" It takes about five minutes, and youngsters are thrilled each time a word is added to the list! *Janice Shuman, Saint Brigid School, South Boston, MA*

The MAILBOX BLOG

"I love *The Mailbox*. The activities are so colorful and creative."—Nancy C. Allen, Glen Allen, VA

Mustard, Pickle, Pickle...

Here's a great way to add a fun twist to patterning practice. After creating a pattern with colorful manipulatives, I encourage students to think of real-life objects that match the pattern's colors. Then we read our pattern using those objects. For example, if we have a yellow, green, green pattern, we might change it to mustard, pickle, pickle! My students love coming up with fun ways to read our patterns. *Jodi Darter, Cabool Elementary, Cabool, MO*

Spotted: A Great Mom!

This cute ladybug clip makes a wonderful Mother's Day gift. I give each child a clothespin, a large black pom-pom (head), a three-inch red craft foam circle (wings), and paper eyes. I help her glue the head and wings to the clothespin. Then I direct her to glue the eyes to the head. Next, I have her dip a cotton swab into black paint and add dots to the wings. When the paint is dry, I attach a magnet to the back of the clothespin and clip the completed ladybug to a message the child has written for her mom. **Roxanne Chance Northwest Elementary Dodge City, KS**

You are the best mom!
Love,
Adalyn

"Love *The Mailbox*. It's been a big part of my classroom for many years!"—*Lynn McMinds Harrell via Facebook*

Our Readers WRITE...

(and EMAIL and BLOG and TWEET and POST)

Soda Bottle Terrariums

These real-world habitats give youngsters up-close experiences with the growth of living things. For each child, I cut around the top portion of a two-liter soda bottle, leaving a two-inch section intact to act as a hinge. (This keeps the terrariums moist and allows students easy access.) I take the class outside and direct each child to gather small rocks, soil, worms, and weeds with roots. After we assemble the terrariums, we place them by a sunny window. As we check our terrariums, we share observations and draw conclusions about the minihabitats. *Suzanne Clark, Edmunds Elementary, Burlington, VT*

TWO GAMES IN ONE

Students double their fun while reviewing skills with this combination of the classic games concentration and bingo. For each pair of students, I prepare two identical bingo-style cards and a corresponding set of matching concentration cards to review a desired skill. I give the partners the bingo and concentration cards along with a supply of bingo chips. Each child takes a bingo card and the partners place the concentration cards facedown. In turn, each player turns over two cards. If the cards match, that player takes the cards and both players cover the matching space on their bingo cards. If the cards do not match, they are turned back over and play resumes. When all the matches are made and the bingo cards are covered, each player counts her total number of cards and the child with more is the winner. *Mary Ann Craven, Fallbrook United Methodist Christian School, Fallbrook, CA*

From Placemat to Math Mat

Here's a quick way to create durable math mats for any theme. I purchase several inexpensive foam placemats. Then I use my school's die-cutting machine to cut the mats into large shapes. I have students use the mats for a variety of math activities, such as sorting, patterning, counting, addition, and subtraction. Students enjoy using the mats, and I like the ease of keeping the mats clean by simply wiping them with a cloth! *Debra K. Santa, Oceanway Elementary, Jacksonville, FL*

The MAILBOX® BLOG

PARTNER GAMES

Fine-Tuned Friends

Partner Game Use with the directions on page 108.

Woo Hoo!

Fine-Tuned Friends

Skill: Plane shapes

How to play:

1. Play with a partner. Pick a crayon.

2. When it is your turn, spin the spinner. Name the plane shape.

3. Look inside the large square for a matching shape. If you find one, trace it. If you do not find one, your turn is over.

4. Play until every shape is traced. The player who traces more shapes wins.

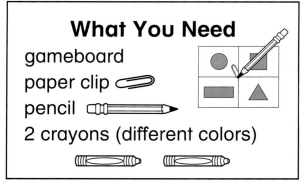

What You Need
gameboard
paper clip
pencil
2 crayons (different colors)

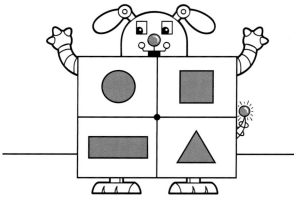

©The Mailbox® • TEC42057 • Oct./Nov. 2011

Woo Hoo!

Skill: Initial consonants

How to play:

1. Play with a partner. Put your game marker on any game space.

2. When it is your turn, roll the die and move your marker.

3. Name the picture and the beginning letter. Look for the letter in a balloon. If you find it, color the balloon. If it is already colored, your turn is over.

4. Play until one player colors every balloon or time runs out. The player who colors more balloons wins. If both players color the same number of balloons, the game is a tie.

What You Need
2 gameboards
2 game markers
die
2 crayons

©The Mailbox® • TEC42057 • Oct./Nov. 2011

Note to the teacher: Use with the gameboards on pages 106 and 107.

Gumballs Galore!

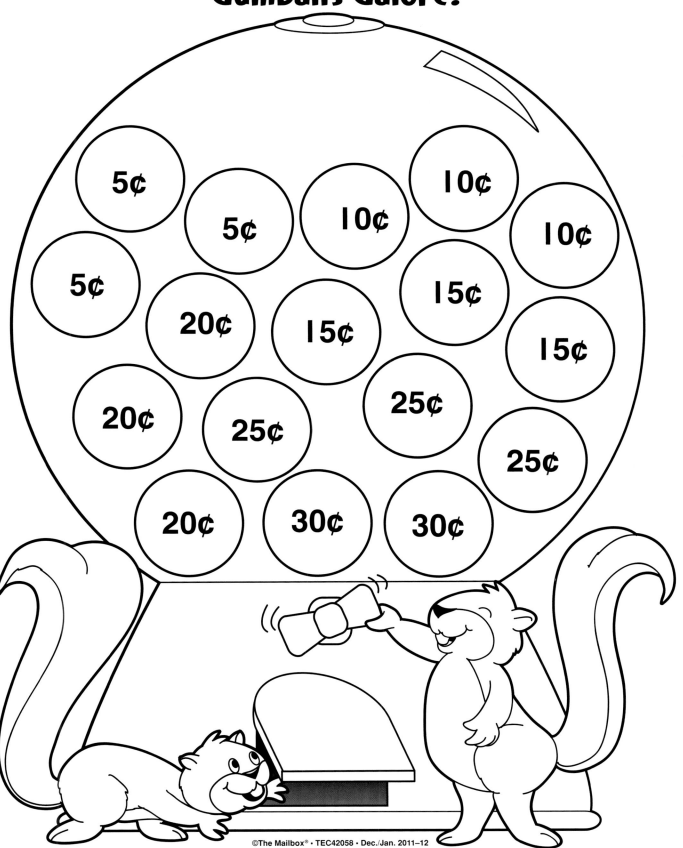

Now Boarding!

ends like →

START

FINISH

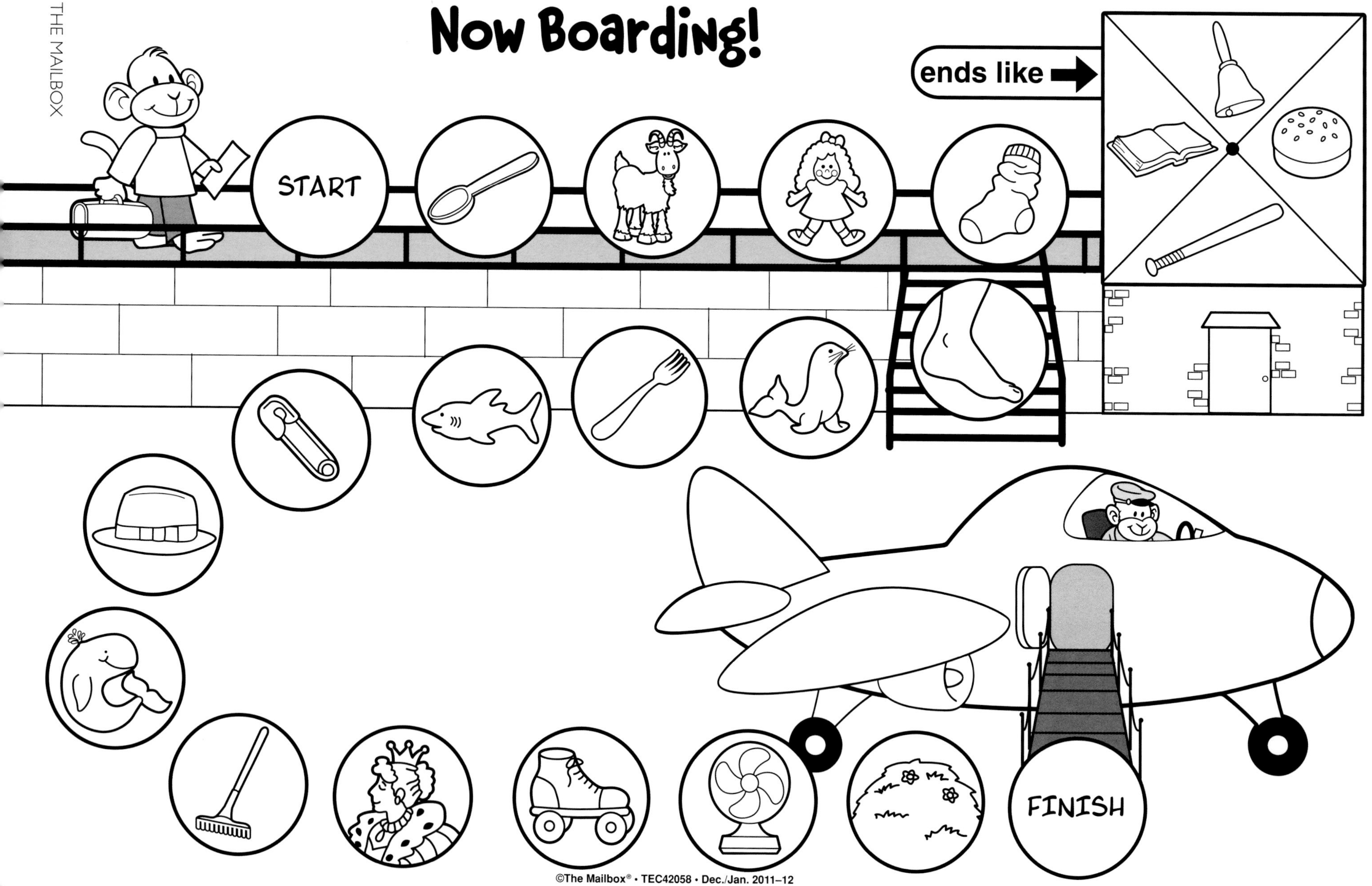

©The Mailbox® • TEC42058 • Dec./Jan. 2011–12

Partner Game Use with the directions on page 111.

Gumballs Galore!

Skill: Counting by fives

How to play:

1. Play with a partner. Pick a crayon.

2. When it is your turn, roll the die. Take a matching number of nickels.

3. Count the nickels by fives. Look for the matching amount on a gumball.
   - If you find the amount, color the gumball.
   - If you do not, your turn is over.

4. Play until each gumball is colored or time runs out. The player who colors more gumballs wins. If both players color the same number of gumballs, the game is a tie.

What You Need
gameboard
6 play nickels
die
2 crayons (different colors)

©The Mailbox® • TEC42058 • Dec./Jan. 2011–12

Now Boarding!

Skill: Ending sounds

How to play:

1. Play with a partner. Place your markers on START.

2. When it is your turn, spin the spinner. Name the picture.

3. Move your marker to the first picture on the gameboard whose name has the same ending sound.

4. The first player to reach FINISH wins.

What You Need
gameboard
2 game markers
paper clip
pencil

©The Mailbox® • TEC42058 • Dec./Jan. 2011–12

Star of the Show

PIZZA

COLA

A B

©The Mailbox® • TEC42059 • Feb./Mar. 2012

112 THE MAILBOX   Partner Game   Use with the directions on page 114.

Fetch!

pig	pin	hit	ring
I or 2	**3**	**4**	**5 or 6**
dig	win	sit	king
wig	fin	kit	sing
jig	bin	fit	zing
big	tin	lit	wing

©The Mailbox® • TEC42059 • Feb./Mar. 2012

Partner Game Use with the directions on page 114.

113

Star of the Show

Skill: Surfaces of solid figures

What You Need

gameboard
paper clip
pencil
15 two-color counters

How to play:

1. Play with a partner. Pick a counter color.

2. When it is your turn, spin the spinner. Name the shape.

3. Look for a matching shape. If you find one, put a counter on it. If you do not find one, your turn is over.

4. The player who marks more shapes wins.

©The Mailbox® • TEC42059 • Feb./Mar. 2012

Fetch!

Skill: Word families -ig, -in, -it, -ing

What You Need

gameboard
number cube
15 two-color counters

How to play:

1. Play with a partner. Pick a counter color.

2. When it is your turn, toss the number cube. Find that number on the gameboard.

3. Look for a word below the number, read the word aloud (use the picture and word above the number to help you), and put a counter on it. If you do not find a word, your turn is over.

4. The player who marks more words wins.

©The Mailbox® • TEC42059 • Feb./Mar. 2012

Lions on the Go!

cup ___

key ___

pen ___

bell ___

hat ___

fork ___

tree ___

egg ___

pot ___

nut ___

kite ___

dot ___

pin ___

sock ___

log ___

mug ___

ball ___

star ___

©The Mailbox® • TEC42060 • April/May 2012

Partner Game Use with the directions on page 117.

Sweet Strawberries!

5 – =

5 – =

5 – =

5 – =

5 – =

5 – =

©The Mailbox® • TEC42060 • April/May 2012

Partner Game   Use with the directions on page 117.

Lions on the Go!

Skill: Plurals with *s*

How to play:

1. Play with a partner. Pick a colored pencil.

2. Pick a suitcase. Play like Tic-Tac-Toe.

3. When it is your turn, read the word. Draw a picture to make two of the object. Then write **s** in the blank. Read the new word.

4. The first player to make three plural words in a row wins. If no player gets three in a row, the game is a tie.

5. Do Steps 2–4 for the other suitcase.

What You Need
gameboard
2 different-colored pencils

©The Mailbox® • TEC42060 • April/May 2012

Sweet Strawberries!

Skill: Subtracting from five

How to play:

1. Play with a partner.

2. When it is your turn, spin. Use the green crayon to cross out the matching number of strawberries in the first box.

3. Write a subtraction sentence to match.

4. Do Steps 2 and 3 for each box of strawberries.

5. Use a red crayon to color the strawberries that are left. The player with more red strawberries wins.

What You Need
2 gameboards
green crayon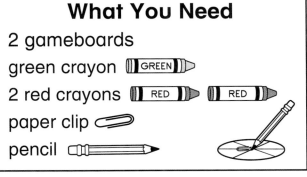
2 red crayons
paper clip
pencil

©The Mailbox® • TEC42060 • April/May 2012

Partner Game Use with the directions on page 120.

Peanut Treasure

ŏ as in log

ĭ as in fish

ŭ as in bug

©The Mailbox® • TEC42061 • June/July 2012

Buzz!

Skill: Addition to 10

What You Need

gameboard
2 game markers
10 counters
die

How to play:

1. Play with a partner. Put your markers on START.

2. When it is your turn, roll the die. Put a matching number of counters on the hive.

3. Decide how many more counters are needed to make ten. Move your marker to the first gameboard space showing this number.

4. The first player to go around the hive and buzz by START wins.

©The Mailbox® • TEC42061 • June/July 2012

Peanut Treasure

Skill: short vowel sounds: *i, o, u*

What You Need

gameboard
15 two-color counters
paper clip
pencil

How to play:

1. Play with a partner. Pick a color of counter.

2. When it is your turn, spin the spinner. Name the vowel sound.

3. Find a picture with the same vowel sound. Name the picture and cover it with a counter. If there are no pictures left with the sound, your turn is over.

4. Play until all pictures are covered or time runs out. The player with more pictures covered wins.

©The Mailbox® • TEC42061 • June/July 2012

Note to the teacher: Use with the gameboards on pages 118 and 119.

Problem Solved!

Problem Solved!

Your Solutions to Classroom Challenges

I have one classroom helper per day, so I create a **helper-of-the-day book**. To make the book, I write each child's name on a separate sheet of construction paper. Then I bind the pages with a metal ring. Each morning I thank the classroom helper from yesterday before turning the page to reveal the current day's helper.

Beverly Brown, Ninety Six Elementary, Ninety, SC

85% of kindergarten teachers assign classroom jobs.

Source: The Mailbox® online poll

I've found that Velcro hook and loop fasteners are the perfect tools for my classroom helpers display. First, I label each of several **thematic cutouts** with a different job. I attach a Velcro fastener strip to the front of each cutout and then display the cutouts on one of my bulletin boards. Then I label a name card for each child and attach a Velcro fastener strip on the back. To assign jobs, I fasten a name card to each cutout. For added fun, I use thematic cutouts for both the helper label and the name card. This year, I'm using frogs and lily pads!

Tammy Vincent, Northern Valley Schools, Almena, KS

How do you keep track of *classroom jobs?*

I label **library card pockets** with classroom jobs and then glue the pockets to a sheet of tagboard. Then I glue a photo of each student to the end of a separate craft stick. I display the poster in my circle-time area and set the craft sticks nearby. To assign jobs, I simply slide a stick into each pocket.

Lindsey Vail, Braintree, MA

tip Use name cards in place of student photos and craft sticks.

It's your turn! We're always looking for your tips, ideas, and suggestions. **Go to TheMailbox.com to share!**

Your Solutions to Classroom Challenges

I spell a color word. Students identify the word and then youngsters **wearing that color** get in line. I continue with other colors until all my students are lined up!

Linda Donald, Austell Primary School, Austell, GA

R-e-d.

I call on a child and hold up a number card from 0 to 10. The child then **holds up a matching number of fingers** as a password to get in line.

Suzanne Ward, Seneca Unity Public School, Caledonia, Ontario, Canada

8

How do you help your students *line up* successfully?

I squeeze in phonological awareness practice when it's time to line up. I say a child's name. Then I lead students to repeat the name and **clap the matching number of syllables** while the featured child gets in line.

*Pam Marks
Stough Elementary
Raleigh, NC*

I write a different number on separate tags to have one per student. Each of my youngsters randomly selects a number tag to wear each day. Then, to line up, each child **gets into number order**.

Jan Georgson, St. Paul's Lutheran School, Ixonia, WI

To establish a defined area for each child to stand on when in line, I tape **footprint cutouts** to the floor. When a child is asked to line up, he simply steps on the next available pair of prints. Crowding in line is no longer an issue!

Sue Frederick, W. W. Evans Elementary, Bloomsburg, PA

The Three Steps to Teaching Procedures
1. Explain
2. Rehearse
3. Reinforce
—*Harry K. Wong and Rosemary T. Wong*

It's your turn! We're always looking for your tips, ideas, and suggestions. **Go to TheMailbox.com to share!**

Your Solutions to Classroom Challenges

I have each child involved **draw a picture** of the problem and a proposed resolution. Youngsters appreciate the opportunity to express themselves and often turn the negative situation into a positive problem-solving experience. Then we all appreciate the happy ending!

Lynn Hayden, Cincinnati, Ohio

I teach my students to say, **"Stop that! I don't like that"** when they are being bothered. Then I expect the speaker to give the person a chance to be respectful and stop the behavior. If the problem persists, the youngster is encouraged to bring it to my attention. This has cut down on a lot of tattling in my classroom!

Jennie Kennedy, Discovery Plus, Pima, AZ

How do you tackle *tattling in your classroom?*

I have kindergartners tell their grievances to the **tattling phone**! I keep a play phone in our classroom. When a youngster has a small issue to tattle about, I direct him to pick up the phone and voice his issue.

Susan Fry, St. Mary School, Schwenksville, PA

From the Editor
Talk to the Frog!

Try using a large stuffed animal to serve as your problem solver. Use the animal as a puppet to model problem-solving skills and then set it out in a child-friendly location. A child who is eager to tattle should first tell the tale to the critter and ask for its advice. More often than not, the problem is resolved!

When a youngster tattles, I ask, "How are you going to work it out?" This reminds my students to try resolving the conflict with **solutions they can use on their own**, such as walking away, talking nicely about the problem, sharing the object in question, or waiting their turn.

Clare Cox, Homer Davis Elementary, Tucson, AZ

It's your turn! We're always looking for your tips, ideas, and suggestions. **Go to TheMailbox.com to share!**

Problem Solved!

Your Solutions to Classroom Challenges

56% of simple three- to four-letter words contain one or more of the letters b, d, and p. A recent study showed about 94% of superior and average readers had mastered b, d, and p confusions by the age of 8.

—Byron Harrison and Jean Clyde

"Little *b* in a big *B*." This nifty saying helps my students recognize and remember that the lowercase *b* can be seen in an uppercase *B*.

Millie Morris, Berkmar United Methodist, Lilburn, GA

To form ***b* and *d* eyeglasses**, I have my kindergartners use their hands to pretend to look through binoculars. Then I guide them to raise the back three fingers on each hand to form unique eyeglasses; when students lower the glasses, they have a *b* and *d* in alphabetical order right in front of them. It's a "hand-y" reference!

Susan Schmidt, Jessamine Early Learning Village, Wilmore, KY

How do you handle b *and* d reversals?

I tell my youngsters that ***D* and *d* face each other**. Then I add details to each letter for youngsters to see a daddy *D* facing its little *d*. For added fun, feathers and duck feet can be drawn to show a daddy duck dancing with its little duckling.

Donna Folwell, Chatsworth Elementary, Chatsworth, IL

I write the letters *a*, *b*, and *c* on the board. To get past *c*, we agree the next letter is *d*. Then I form another *c* and **close the *c* to make a *d*.** For added visual support, I show how this does not work with the letter *b*. In a short while, my students are forming both lowercase *b* and *d* correctly!

Linda Lundgren, Immanuel Lutheran School, Valparaiso, IN

Bat or doughnut? My picture-clue poster helps my students correct letter reversals and make letter-sound associations. I use a baseball bat drawing to form the "stick" on the letter *b* and a doughnut drawing to form the "ball" on the letter *d*. Then I simply ask, "Do you need a /b/, /b/, bat or a /d/, /d/, doughnut?" It works wonders!

Andrea Day, Wabasha-Kellogg Public School, Wabasha, MN

It's your turn! We're always looking for your tips, ideas, and suggestions. **Go to TheMailbox.com to share!**

Q&A

Problem Solved!

Your Solutions to Classroom Challenges

 I store a **variety of flash cards** in my apron's pockets! I've used cards to review letters, sight words, oral segmentation skills, and beginning sounds. When there are a few available minutes between activities, I pull out the flash cards for some quick practice!

Sarah Seitz, J. Larry Newton Elementary, Fairhope, AL

A typical school day often involves more than 30 transitions, including taking bathroom breaks, switching subjects, and going out for recess and fire drills, to name just a few.

—American Psychological Association

 We play a quick game of **storybook charades**! I act out the title of a familiar book or popular story event and youngsters try to guess the title. After we've played a few times, students are eager to take over my acting role. This time filler is a great way to review books, and we have fun too!

Beth Marquardt, St. Paul's School of Early Learning, Muskego, WI

How do you make the most of the *time between activities?*

 When we have extra time waiting in the hallway, I take an **assessment**. For an ordinal numbers assessment, I tap the first child in line and prompt her to say "first." Then I continue down the line, having each child name the next ordinal number. I do similar time-filling activities with months of the year, days of the week, counting up, and counting backward!

Jana Pennock, Council Grove Elementary, Oklahoma City, OK

 To eliminate wasted time during bathroom breaks, I give each child two cards (or one) programmed with **CVC words**. When a child correctly reads his words to me, I take the cards and give him two more. Since we started reading "bathroom words," I've noticed an increased enthusiasm to read words, and my students' reading skills have improved dramatically!

Jana Pennock

It's your turn! We're always looking for your tips, ideas, and suggestions. **Go to TheMailbox.com to share!**

READING TIPS & TOOLS

Apples, apples, one, two, three.
Apples, apples for you and me!

Bananas, bananas, one, two, three.
Bananas, bananas for you and me!

I see a red bird looking at me.

From A to Z!
Letter knowledge

Looking for a fresh look for an annual alphabet book? Try this! Select a theme for the book along with a simple poem or repetitive text. Each time a letter is introduced, share with youngsters a letter-sound association that corresponds with the theme. Then have each child complete a book page that features the letter, relevant text, and a corresponding craft or drawing. At the end of the year, bind each student's completed pages between construction paper covers to make a memorable kindergarten keepsake. If desired, assemble teacher-made pages to make a book for your classroom library.

Sheila Wilcox
St. Matthew Cathedral School
South Bend, IN

Dot That Word!
Concepts of print

This dot-to-dot trick helps to develop the concept of a word when reading sentences. Give each child a copy of a sentence or familiar rhyme. Prior to reading, instruct her to make a dot beneath each word. If needed, guide her to use the spaces between words to help her. Then have each child touch the dot as she reads each word in the sentence. For added fun, tell youngsters the dots are the words' buttons and they must push the button when each word is read. With increased proficiency, foster fluency by encouraging each child to slide a finger across the dot, moving from left to right as she reads.

Vanessa Rivera
La Luz Elementary
La Luz, NM

READING
tips & tools

P Is for *Pizza*
Discriminating sound /p/

Putting pepperoni on this pizza is perfect /p/ practice! Give each child a copy of page 148 and a piece of yellow construction paper. Have her color each pepperoni slice that shows a picture that begins with /p/ and cross out each pepperoni slice that shows a picture that does not begin with /p/. Then instruct her to color the pizza crust brown and the top of the pizza (sauce) red. To assemble the pizza slice, have her cut out the patterns, cut yellow strips (cheese) to glue atop the sauce, and then glue the colored pepperoni slices atop the cheese. **For a writing connection**, have each child write a sentence that tells about her pizza slice.

Ashley N. Sorice
Yavapai Elementary
Scottsdale, AZ

Guess!
Letter-sound associations

This show-and-tell activity is sure to inspire students to find objects that begin with a designated sound. Lead youngsters to name words that begin with a chosen letter's sound. Next, instruct each child to bring from home an object whose name begins with the featured letter-sound combination. If desired, provide a personalized paper bag for each student to use to keep the object hidden as well as to limit the size of her object. On a predetermined day, invite each child to give clues about what she selected, guiding classmates to name the hidden object. Be sure to praise students' guesses that begin with the featured sound until the object is named.

Christy Bentley-Dye
Eastminster School
Conyers, GA

When I forget to put the cap on, it makes a mess.

What's the Password?
Word recognition

Foster reading-word mastery with a door sign. Write "Password" on a sheet of decorative paper to make a sign, laminate the sign for durability, and post it on the door. Each day, tape a different high-frequency word or vocabulary word on the sign. Whenever a child passes through the door, have him whisper the word of the day.

For a letter-sound variation, feature a letter on the sign for youngsters to whisper its associated sound as the password.

For a more advanced version, feature more than one word on the sign and point to a specific word for each child to whisper.

Cheryl Latil
Magnolia Park Elementary
Ocean Spring, MS

See.

Password
see

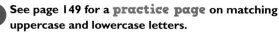
See page 149 for a *practice page* on matching uppercase and lowercase letters.

Syllable Stomp
Phonological awareness

No materials necessary! Just incorporate action with segmenting syllables and you'll have an activity that is sure to be a hit. Announce an action such as stomping, frog hopping, knee bends, or supersize steps. Then say a word. Have youngsters slowly repeat the word as they do the action with each syllable. For added fun, invite volunteers to provide the action for each round.

Jennifer Willis
Imagine School at Palmer Ranch
Sarasota, FL

See page 150 for a **practice page** on counting syllables.

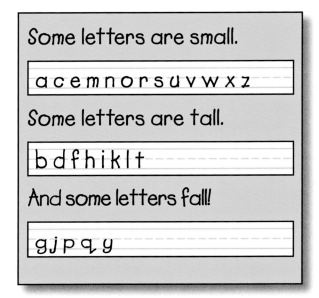

Letter Limbo!
Letter knowledge

What do lowercase letters and exercises have in common? Read this! Display a copy of the poem shown. Have youngsters practice crouching into a little ball (small letters), stretching high to the sky (tall letters), and falling to the floor (letters that dip below the baseline). Then read the poem and have students maintain the practiced position as you name each set of letters. To continue, name a letter and have youngsters respond with the appropriate action. Students will not only learn to recognize and form letters, but they'll have loads of fun too!

Barb Starkey
Boys' Latin School
Baltimore, MD

READING
tips & tools

T Is for *Turtle*
Letter-sound association

This supersize reptile doubles as a vocabulary poster. On a large turtle shape, draw desired details and write the sentence starter shown. Then have each child cut out a picture from a magazine or draw a picture whose name begins with /t/. If correct, help her glue the picture below the sentence starter and label it with the corresponding word. After all students have contributed to the poster, lead the class in reading it. **For a writing connection**, put the poster at a center for youngsters to write and illustrate sentences using one or more of the words.

Marie E. Cecchini
West Dundee, IL

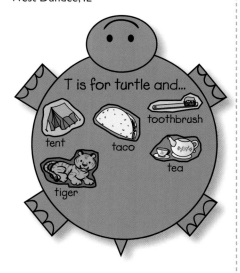

Word Wallets
Word recognition

With this simple organizer, students have a place to store reading word cards. To make one wallet, fold a horizontal sheet of paper in half. Tape the left and right edges and then fold the paper in half again, from left to right this time. Staple the fold line to make left and right pockets. Label the front and inside halves of the resulting wallet as shown and laminate it for durability. To use the wallet, have each child write each new word on an appropriate-size card and slide it into the left pocket. Once he recognizes the word and reads it with ease, direct him to move the card to the right side of his wallet. At the end of each month, send the familiar words home to make room for more word mastery. **For a home-school connection**, have each child read his complete collection of words to a family member at the end of every month.

Maria Berger
Keys Gate Charter School
Homestead, FL

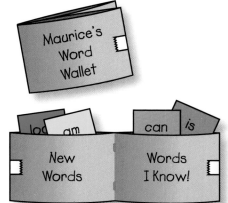

Where's the Mouse?
Predictable text

Develop students' reading skills with a class-made book. Ask youngsters to imagine that a mouse has been spotted at the school. Guide each child to complete the sentence starter "The mouse is…" to tell the mouse's location. Help him write the sentence and then have him draw a picture to match. To assemble the book, bind the pages between construction paper covers with the title "Where's the Mouse?" Then read the book aloud, inviting the author of each page to point to the mouse in his drawing. **For fluency practice**, encourage youngsters to read the pages along with you; if desired, set the book in your reading area for students to reread when time permits.

The mouse is on the fence.

tip → Change the critter and repeat the activity to make a different book with the same style.

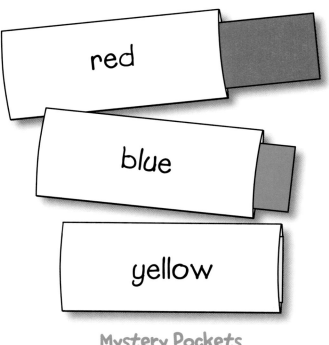

Wintry Helpers
Concepts of print

The fingers of a white glove are perfect for making five snowpal pointers! To make one, cut a finger from a glove and drape it over a craft stick. Then stuff the fingertip with cotton batting and twist half of a pipe cleaner (scarf) around the tip to make the head. Then fill the rest of the finger (body) with more cotton batting and wrap a two-inch length of white pipe cleaner around the bottom. To complete the snowpal, glue wiggle eyes to the head and draw a mouth. Encourage youngsters to use the snowpal pointers to track print when reading. **For a craft variation**, paint a craft stick white, twist on a pipe-cleaner scarf, and add facial details as desired.

adapted from an idea by Lindsey Hall
W. E. Cundiff Elementary
Vinton, VA

Mystery Pockets
Color words

What colors are hidden inside these envelopes? Students read words to find out! Seal each of several envelopes. Then trim the right short edges to create horizontal pockets. Write on each envelope a different color word and slide a corresponding color strip inside the matching pocket. Be sure the strip is short enough to hide the color and long enough to easily pull out of the pocket. To begin, hold up an envelope and ask a student to read the word. Instruct the remaining students to give thumbs-up or thumbs-down to show agreement. Then have a child pull out the hidden color card to check for accuracy. Continue with each remaining envelope.

Jodi Darter
Cabool Elementary
Cabool, MO

tip Use colorful gloves to make bright, buggy pointers in the spring!

READING
tips & tools

READING
tips & tools

Letters on the Line
CVC words

At this center, youngsters use a color-coded line to help isolate phonemes in words. Draw horizontal green, yellow, and red lines across the bottom of a paper as shown. Cut apart a copy of the picture cards on page 151 and write each picture name on the back of the card to make the activity self-checking. Then write on cards the letters needed for students to spell each word. A child names a picture card and puts it near her paper. Then she places a consonant card on the green line to show the first letter in the word, a vowel card on the yellow line, and a card on the red line to show the final consonant. Then she flips the picture card to check her spelling.

Debbie Hutchins
Grenada Lower Elementary
Grenada, MS

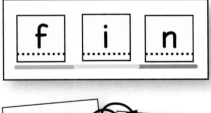

Green means go, and red means stop!

Let's Predict!
Reading comprehension

Jumpstart storytime with this prediction song! After singing, invite youngsters to share their predictions before settling in for a read-aloud of a featured tale.

(sung to the tune of "Mary Had a Little Lamb")

Predict what the book's about,
Book's about, book's about.
Predict what the book's about.
Yes, let's make a smart guess.

Use the title and the cover;
These two things can help us.
Use the title and the cover
To make a prediction.

(Repeat verse 1.)

Doria Owen
William Paca Old Post Road Elementary
Abingdon, MD

A Hunt at Home
Letter review

This sound-related scavenger hunt doubles as a show-and-tell activity. For each child, staple a list of letters you would like to review to a paper bag. Staple a note on the reverse side of the bag asking family members to help their child find objects that begin with the sound associated with each assigned letter; then send the bags home. When the bags are returned, name a letter and its corresponding sound. Have each child remove from her collection an object whose name begins with the featured letter. Then invite her to take a turn naming the object and showing it to the group. For extra letter-sound practice, lead students to say the letter and repeat the object's name, emphasizing the initial sound.

Esther Vanderlick
Forest Hill Elementary
Forest Hill, LA

B, /b/, /b/, ball.

A Scavenger Hunt!

Bb	Ll
Ff	Rr
Hh	Ww

Sounds Like Fun!
Phonological awareness

What do beginning sound practice, rhyming, and giggles have to do with students' names? Check this out! Swap the initial sound of a child's name with a featured sound. To address the student, call her by her modified name, such as *Melsey* for *Kelsey*. Encourage the group to respond with, "Not Melsey, Kelsey!" Continue with other names throughout the day.

Pam Blodgett
Briargate Elementary
Cary, IL

Lights On!
Word families

These word family apartments are perfect for reading, writing, and assessment. Draw a simple building and label the roof with a word family ending of your choice. Also label each window with words to form a word family. Make a class supply of the prepared page. A child reads the words and then writes each one in the window. To assess, ask him to read the words to you. For each correct word, have the child use a yellow crayon to color the window as if to flip on the lights. He continues to practice his words until each window is illuminated. **For a home-school connection,** encourage each child to practice reading the words at home prior to assessment.

Amanda Boyarshinov
Gainesville, FL

READING
tips & tools

For practice **reading sentences**, see page 152.

Tic-Tac-Toe Teamwork
High-frequency words

For this group game, gather a set of high-frequency word cards and draw a tic-tac-toe grid on the board. Arrange youngsters in two teams. To play, show a word card. Instruct a player on Team 1 to read the word aloud. If needed, encourage him to seek help from team members. If he is correct, he puts an *X* on a tic-tac-toe grid. If he is incorrect, the players on Team 2 attempt to read the word aloud to erase an *X* on the grid. If the players on Team 2 are unable to read the word, review the word with both teams. Then Team 2 takes a turn, using an *O* to mark their game space. Play continues until one team marks three spaces in a row.

Stephanie Karolewski
Goodrich Elementary
Milwaukee, WI

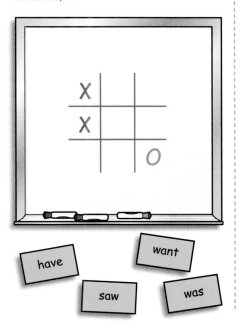

Pass the Letters
Letter-sound associations

Review three or more letters with this little ditty. Write letters of your choice on individual cards to have one card for each child. Have youngsters sit in a circle and pass the letter cards around, one by one, as you lead them in singing the song shown. For a second verse, lead the group to repeat the melody using only the sound associated with the letter named. Next, have each child who stood after the first verse take a turn naming a word that begins with the featured letter; then have her sit down. Continue singing the tune and naming words until each letter has been reviewed.

 (sung to the tune of "Row, Row, Row Your Boat")

Pass, pass, pass the letters.
Pass them all around.
If you have the letter [*m*],
Stand up without a sound.

[/m/, /m/, /m/, /m/, /m/.]
[/m/, /m/, /m/, /m/, /m/.]
[/m/, /m/, /m/, /m/, /m/, /m/, /m/,]
[/m/, /m/, /m/, /m/, /m/.]

adapted from an idea by Kristin Priola
Hickory Day School
Hickory, NC

m

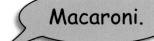
Macaroni.

Out to Sea?
Main idea and details

Reel in comprehension success when students pretend to go fishing! Label a bucket with the main idea of a preselected story. Then write corresponding details on individual fish cutouts. On several additional fish, write details that are unrelated to the story. Spread out the fish in your group-time area. After reading the story aloud, invite students to sit in a circle around the fish, show the bucket, and read aloud the main idea. Next, invite a child to go fishing and help him read the detail shown on his fish. If the detail is related to the story, encourage the group to say, "It's a keeper!" signaling the fisherman to put it in the bucket. If the detail is unrelated to the story, have the group say, "Throw it out to sea!" for the fisherman to gently toss the fish outside the circle. Continue with a different fisherman for each fish.

It's a keeper!

A wolf gives a pig a backrub.

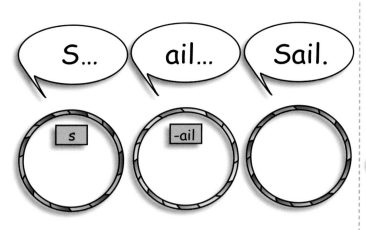

Hoop Hoppin'
Blending words

Use movement to put extra emphasis on skill work for these phonics activities! Put three hula hoops (or yarn loops) side by side on the floor. Then choose one or both of the options below.

Word families: Write a word family ending on a card and put it in the middle hoop. Write on separate cards different onsets, most of which form real words with the featured rime. Put an onset card in the first hoop. A child hops from hoop to hoop, naming the onset; rime; and, finally, the whole word. If it is a real word, classmates respond by hopping and repeating the word; if it is not a real word, students stay still and remain silent. Continue with each onset card.

CVC words: Write CVC words on individual cards. For each card, a child says the first, middle, and last sound for each letter in the word as he hops from hoop to hoop. Then he hops out of the last hoop. When he lands, all students name the word.

Valerie Lewis, Mexico Elementary, Mexico, NY

 See page 154 for a practice page on word families.

"Egg-cellent" Baskets
Making words by changing the last letter

Your young chicks are sure to cheep during this springtime activity. On each of several plastic eggs, write all but the last letter of a decodable word on the left half and the last letter on the right half. (The activity works well if several words can be formed with the different egg halves; for example, the letters in *cap*, *pen*, *fit*, *hog*, and *cub* can make 18 familiar words.) Put the left halves in one basket and the right halves in a different basket. To make a word, invite two students to each remove an egg half from a different basket. Have them put the egg halves together and read the word. For each real word, lead students to cheep like chicks and scurry around the room.

Beth Parry
Zane North Elementary
Collingsworth, NJ

READING
tips & tools

Name That Word!
High-frequency words

Give the traditional Hangman game a whole new look with a Mr. Potato Head character! Write letters that students name on letter lines as with the traditional game. For each letter guessed that is not a part of the featured word, put a part on the Mr. Potato Head toy. If the toy is assembled before the word is named, the character earns a point. If the children name the word before the toy is assembled, they earn a point. The first to earn five points is declared the winner.

Kim Criswell
Wilson Elementary
Wilson, KS

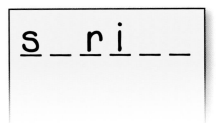

s _ r i _ _

tip For added fun, use a seasonal or theme-related Mr. Potato Head toy.

Toot, Toot!
Days of the week

For this partner game, write the names of the weekdays on separate cards and put the cards in a bag. Also, set out a supply of paper rectangles (train cars). Have each child personalize a copy of the engine pattern on page 153. To build a train, each player takes a card from the bag, writes the word on a train car, and puts the train car to the right of her engine. Players return the cards to the bag and then Player 1 takes a card. If her train does not have the weekday shown on the card, she writes it on a train car and puts the car in order to the right of the engine. If the word is already a part of her train, her turn is over. Then the card is returned to the bag and Player 2 takes a turn. The first player to add all seven train cars to her engine, in order, is named the engineer. The engineer then encourages her partner to finish. To complete the trains, players glue paper wheels to the train cars and glue the engine and cars together.

Barbara Mason Worobey
Deposit Elementary
Deposit, NY

A Reading Highway
Compound words

Your youngsters create the cars that travel on this highway! For each student, write the two words of a compound word on individual paper circles (wheels). Give each child his wheels and a copy of the car pattern on page 153. Help him read the words on the wheels and then guide him to name the compound word. Next, have him cut out the car pattern, write the compound word on the car, and glue the wheels to his car. Then, above the word, have him draw a picture that matches his compound word. Arrange the completed cars on a length of black paper and lead youngsters to read their words on the resulting highway.

Jeanne Wagner
Richboro Elementary
Richboro, PA

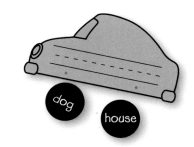

Pickup Sticks
Discriminating sounds: short i

Each round of this whole-group activity engages all your young learners. Cut apart a copy of the cards on page 156 and tape them to craft sticks as shown. To play, gather youngsters in a circle, stand in the center of the circle, and gently drop the cards (sticks). Invite a child to pick up a stick without disturbing any other stick. As she gets a stick, lead youngsters in chanting the rhyme shown. Then have her respond by naming the picture on the card and telling if it has the short *i* sound. If it has /i/, she keeps the stick; if it does not have /i/, the teacher gets the stick. Play continues until students win with six sticks or the teacher gets three sticks and ends the game. For more practice, simply gather and drop the sticks to begin again.

> /i/, /i/, /i/, /i/,
> **Pick a stick.**
> **Does it have /i/?**
> **Tell me quick!**

Sarah Huntley, Kelleytown Baptist Kindergarten
Hartsville, SC

Cool Caterpillars!
Writing word families

The lengths of these legible caterpillars will vary! Write different rimes on a class supply of hat cutouts. Give each child one of the hats and instruct her to glue it to a paper circle (head). Next, have her draw eyes and a mouth on the head. Then, on separate paper circles, guide her to write words that end with her rime. Have her glue the resulting word family to the head to form a caterpillar's body. Encourage her to add caterpillar details before displaying the completed craft. When time permits, lead youngsters to read each of the cool caterpillars!

Trudy Tilton
Olathe Head Start
Olathe, KS

READING
tips & tools

Body Language
Spelling high-frequency words

Weave creative thinking into reading practice with this active idea. Give a different high-frequency word card to each of several groups of students. Instruct students in each group to form the letters with their bodies to spell their word. When a group has formed its word, have classmates read it. **For a center activity**, take a photograph of each word formed, outline each letter on the photo, and put the photos in an album. A child reads the album, writes each word on a sheet of paper, and then uses one or more words in a sentence.

Kate Wonders
Carlisle Elementary
Carlisle, IA

tip For a concrete demonstration, have students use objects to spell the words.

Sounds Like Fun!
Segmenting and blending words

How can a twist on the traditional game Mother, May I? foster phonological awareness practice? Read this! Have a small group of students line up in a row. Then say a word and invite a child to slowly say each sound in the word. For example, if you say *fish*, he says, "/f/, /i/, /sh/." Have the remaining youngsters count the total number of sounds in the word to determine how many steps the child will take toward the teacher. As he takes the steps, lead the group to repeat the individual sounds and then say the word. Continue with different students and words until one child reaches the teacher.

Amy Lawrence
Neason Hill Elementary
Meadville, PA

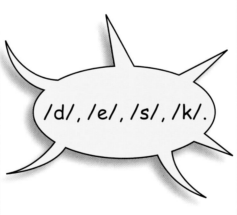

/d/, /e/, /s/, /k/.

What's Missing?
Literature response, comprehension

Several skills are tucked into this step-by-step activity. After reading a story aloud, instruct each student to draw and write about his favorite part of the tale. Next, display *beginning*, *middle*, and *end* word cards. Invite each child to briefly share his work, identify where in the story his favorite part took place, and post his paper next to the corresponding label. When each child has had a turn, ask if there are any important story events missing. If so, lead the group to name the missing parts and write each one on a sheet of paper. Then guide youngsters to put the papers in order for each section and use the papers to retell the story.

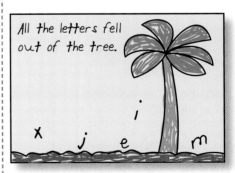

Sorting Activity

Each child cuts out a copy of the first card set below and sorts the cards on a copy of page 141. **For a more challenging sort,** he cuts out and sorts a copy of the second card set.

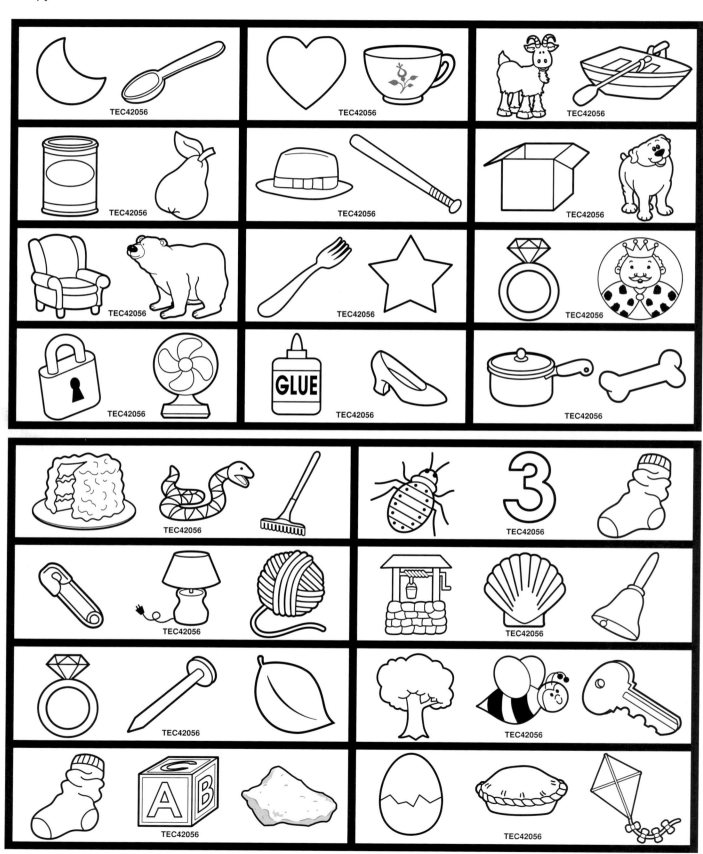

Name _____

Pick a Pond

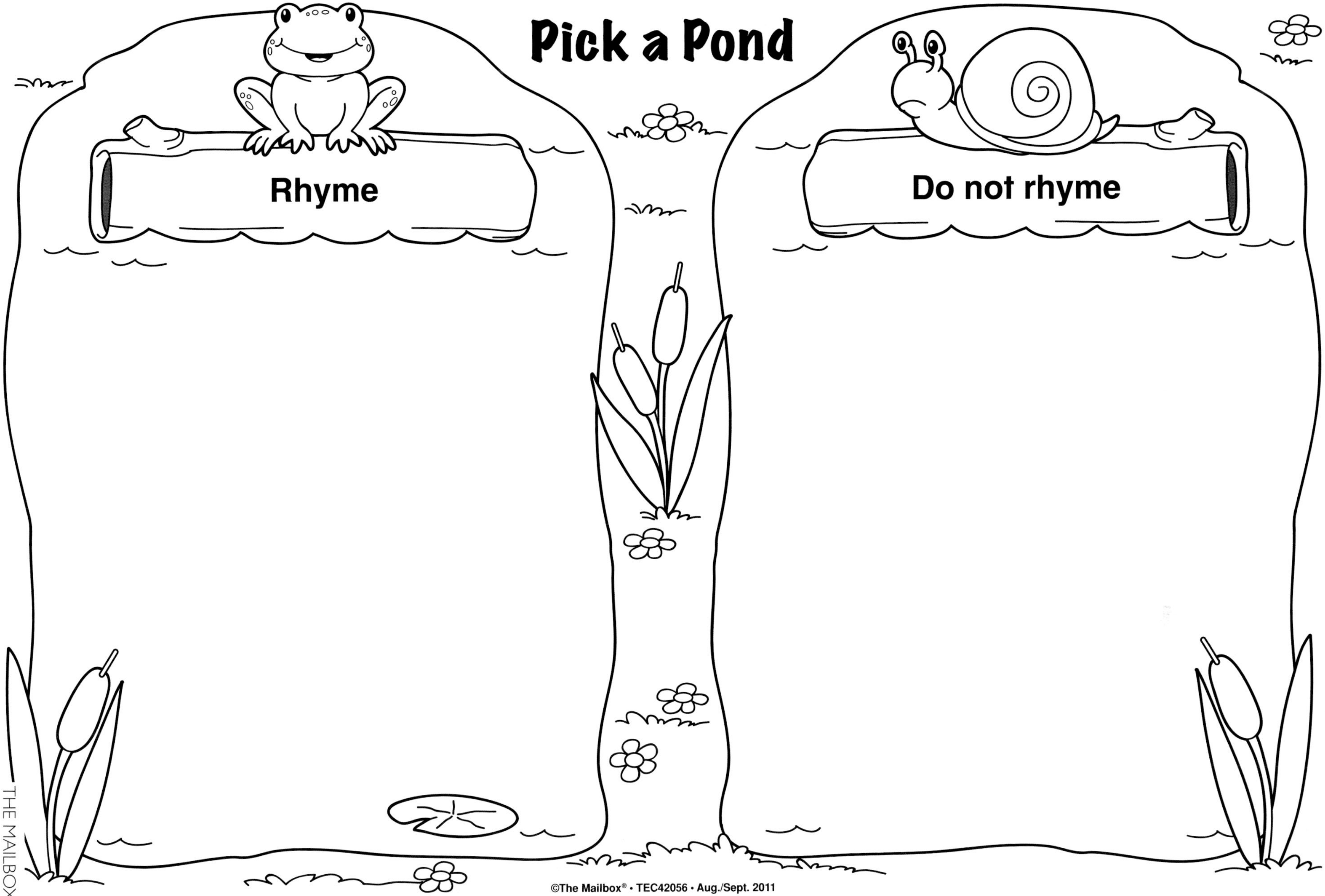

Rhyme

Do not rhyme

©The Mailbox® · TEC42056 · Aug./Sept. 2011

Note to the teacher: Use with the sorting activity on page 140.

Each child cuts out a copy of the first card set below and sorts the cards on a copy of page 143. Then he matches each picture card to its word card. **For a more challenging sort**, he writes *an* or *ap* to complete each word on the second card set; then he cuts out and sorts the cards.

TEC42058	TEC42058	TEC42058
TEC42058	TEC42058	TEC42058
map TEC42058	**cap** TEC42058	**pan** TEC42058
van TEC42058	**fan** TEC42058	**nap** TEC42058

m___ ___ TEC42058	f___ ___ TEC42058
p___ ___ TEC42058	cl___ ___ TEC42058
m___ ___ TEC42058	n___ ___ TEC42058
l___ ___ TEC42058	v___ ___ TEC42058

Name _____

Word Family Roundup

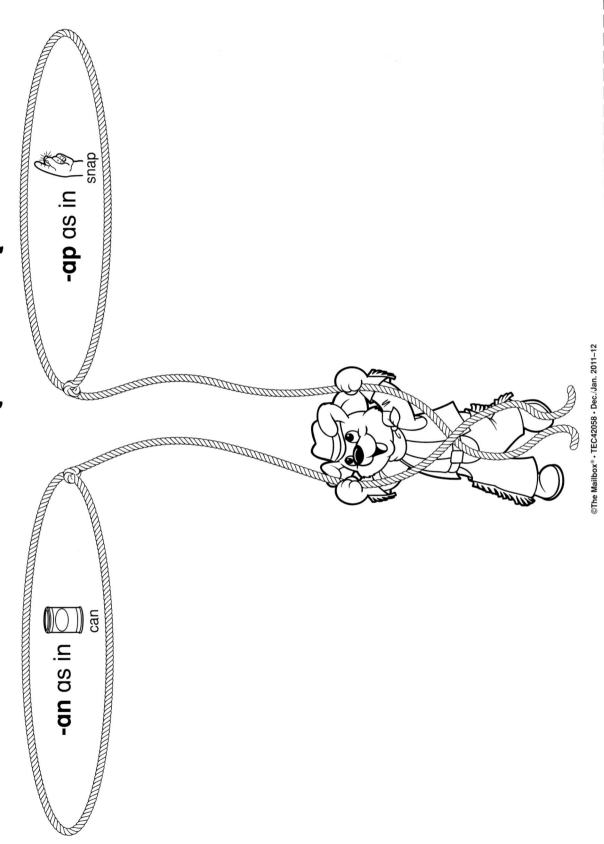

-ap as in

snap

-an as in

can

Note to the teacher: Use with the sorting activity on page 142.

Each child cuts out a copy of the first card set below and sorts the cards on a copy of page 145. (He sets aside any cards that do not match the sort.) He uses the second card set for additional practice.

red	two	black
come	eight	six
five	green	here
pink	ten	white

orange	blue	four
three	have	brown
yellow	one	nine
little	seven	purple

TEC42060 (appears on each card)

Two Cute Koalas
Sorting Mat

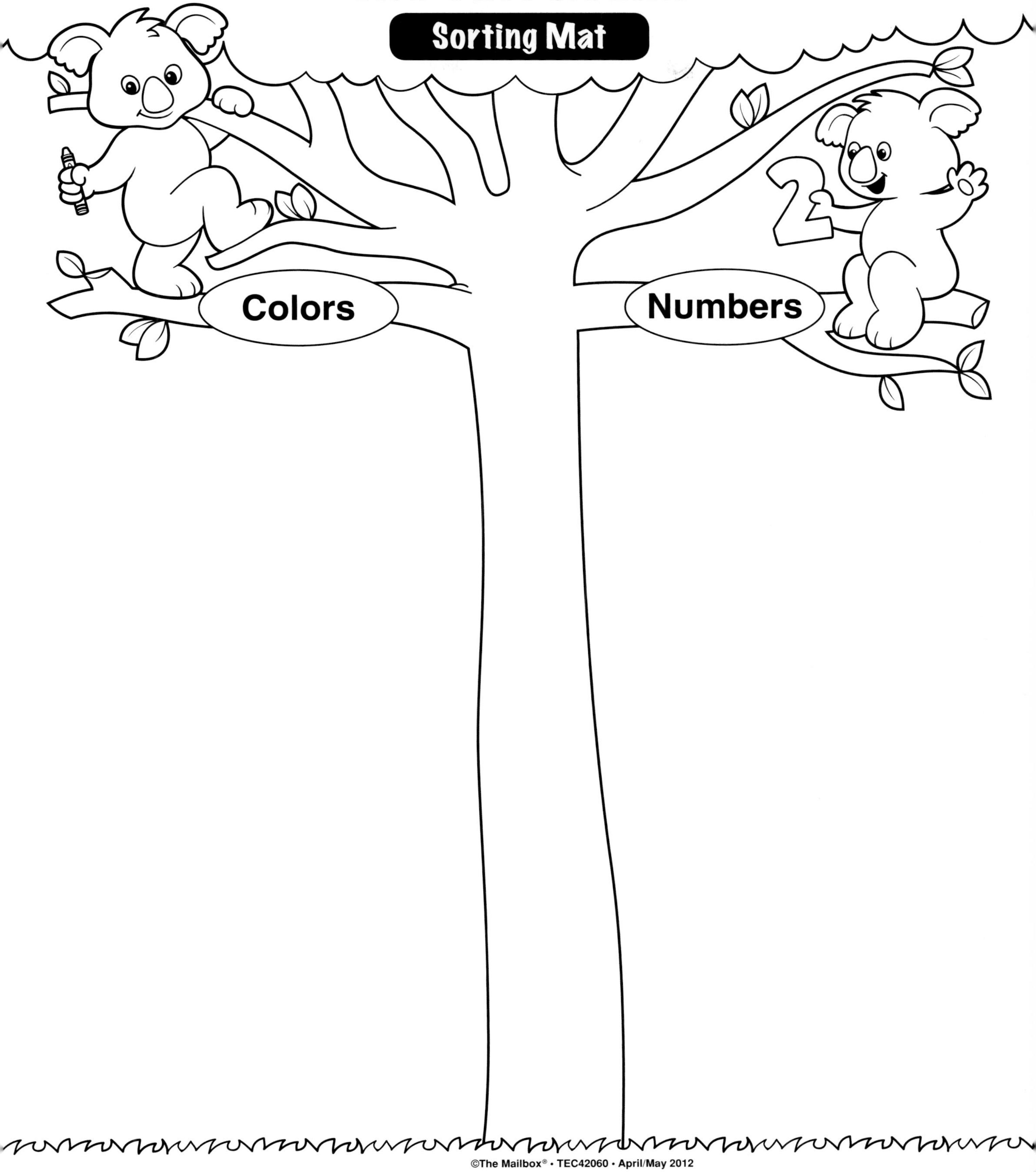

Colors

Numbers

Each child cuts out a copy of the first card set below and sorts the picture cards on a copy of page 147. **For more sorting practice,** she cuts out and sorts a copy of the second card set.

picture cards for CVC words

picture cards for words with blends and digraphs

Yee-haw!

Sorting Mat

short a as in

not short a

Pizza and Pepperoni Patterns

Use with "*P* Is for *Pizza*" on page 129.

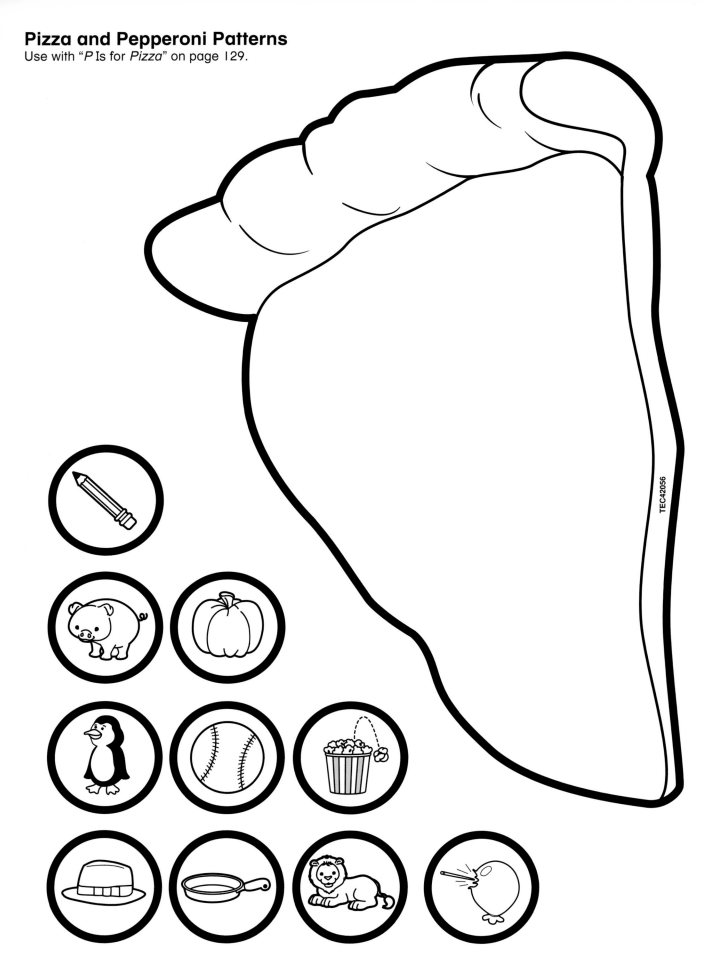

TEC42056

Name _____

Letters and Lunches

✏ Write uppercase letters to match.

Bonus: Write your name. Then write the matching uppercase or lowercase letters.

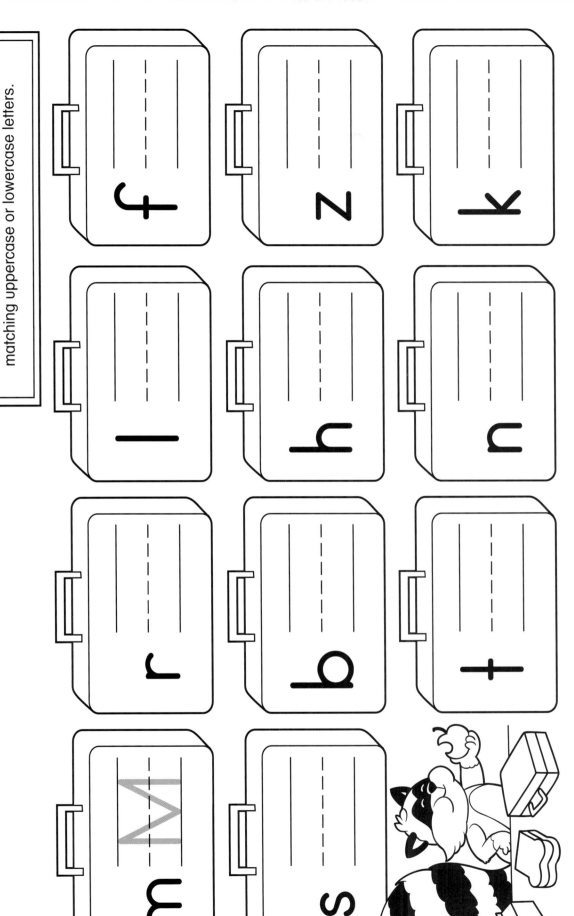

Name _____

Piggy's Picnic

✂ Cut. ✋ Count the syllables. Sort.

🔵 Glue to match.

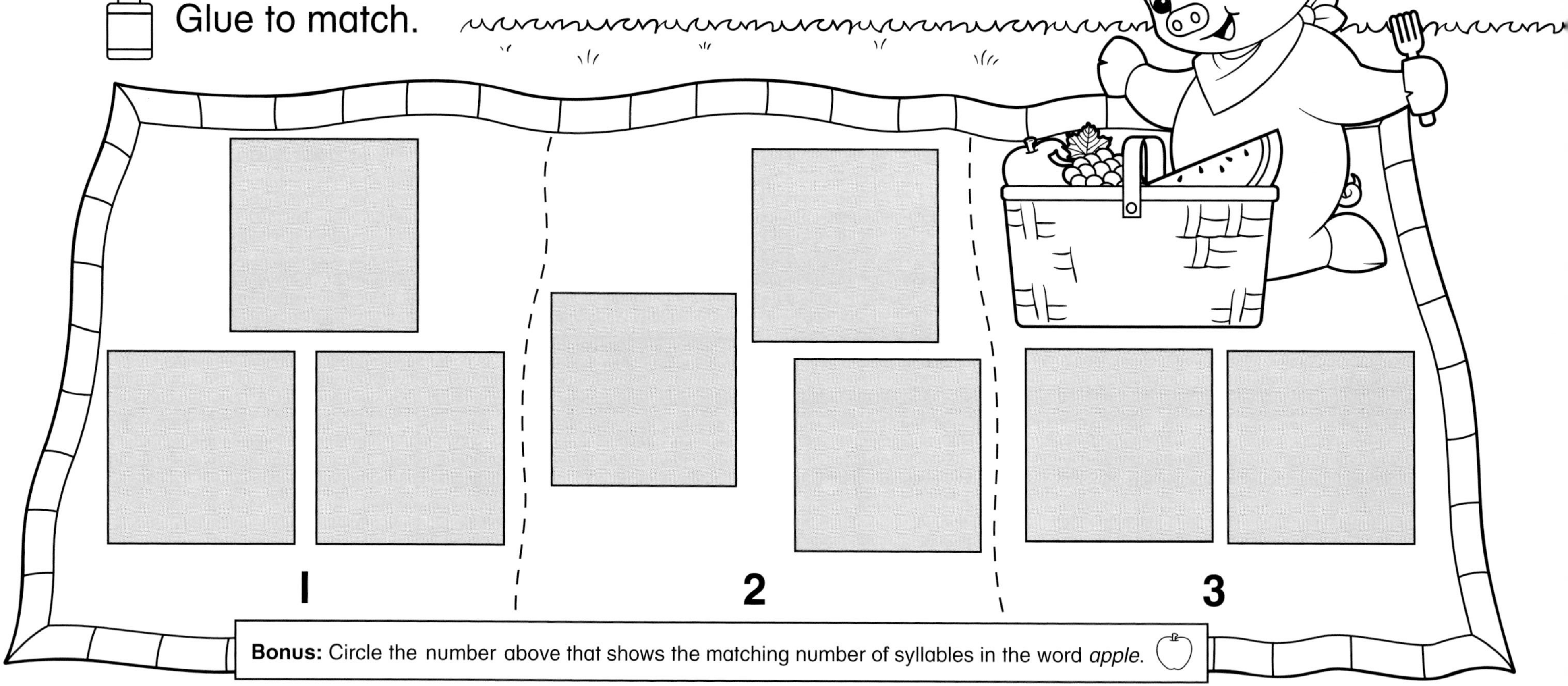

1   2   3

Bonus: Circle the number above that shows the matching number of syllables in the word *apple*.

©The Mailbox® • TEC42057 • Oct./Nov. 2011

TEC42058

TEC42058

TEC42058

TEC42058

TEC42058

TEC42058

TEC42058

TEC42058

TEC42058

TEC42058

TEC42058

TEC42058

TEC42058

TEC42058

TEC42058

FuN at the Park!

Read.
Write **yes** or **no**.

1. The has a big .

_____

2. The has a little .

_____

3. The has a little .

_____

4. Is the by the ?

_____

5. Is the by the ?

_____

6. Can the see the ?

_____

Bonus: Write to tell the number of  you see.

Engine Patterns
Use with "Toot, Toot!" on page 137.

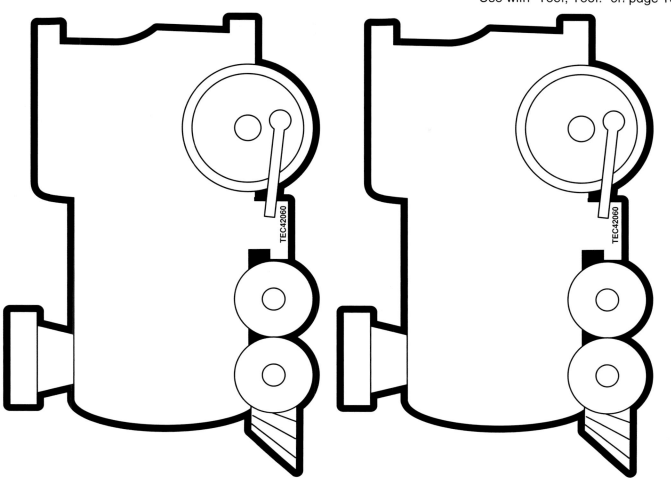

TEC42060

Car Pattern
Use with "A Reading Highway" on page 137.

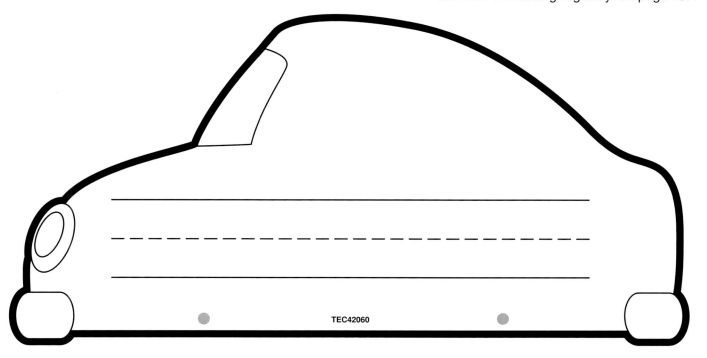

TEC42060

Whee!

🖍️ Color by the code.

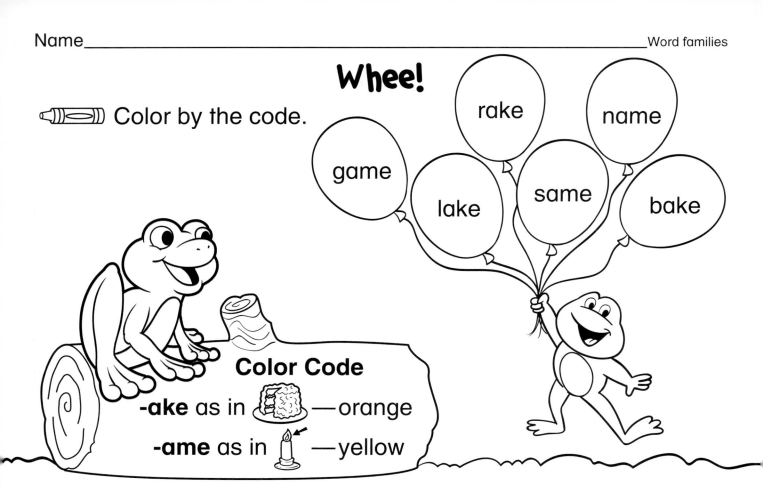

balloons: game, rake, name, lake, same, bake

Color Code

-ake as in 🍰 —orange

-ame as in 🕯️ —yellow

✏️ Write the **ake** and **ame** words to match.

-ake	-ame
_____	_____
_____	_____
_____	_____

Bonus: Use the letters **m**, **n**, **s**, and **t** to make words with **ail**. Write the **-ail** word family.

Read and Do!

The Best Pet

Bubba is a green frog.

He is our class pet.

We will not let him out to play.

He must stay very wet!

1. 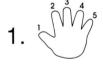 Count the words. ✏️ Write how many. _____

2. ✏️ Write the pet's name. _____

3. 🖊️ Circle the words that end with **t**.

4. ✏️ Write the word that ends with **g**. _____

5. 🖊️ Circle the color word.

| frog | wet | green | play |

Bonus: Do you think Bubba would be a good pet? Why or why not?

Picture Cards

Use with "Pickup Sticks" on page 138.

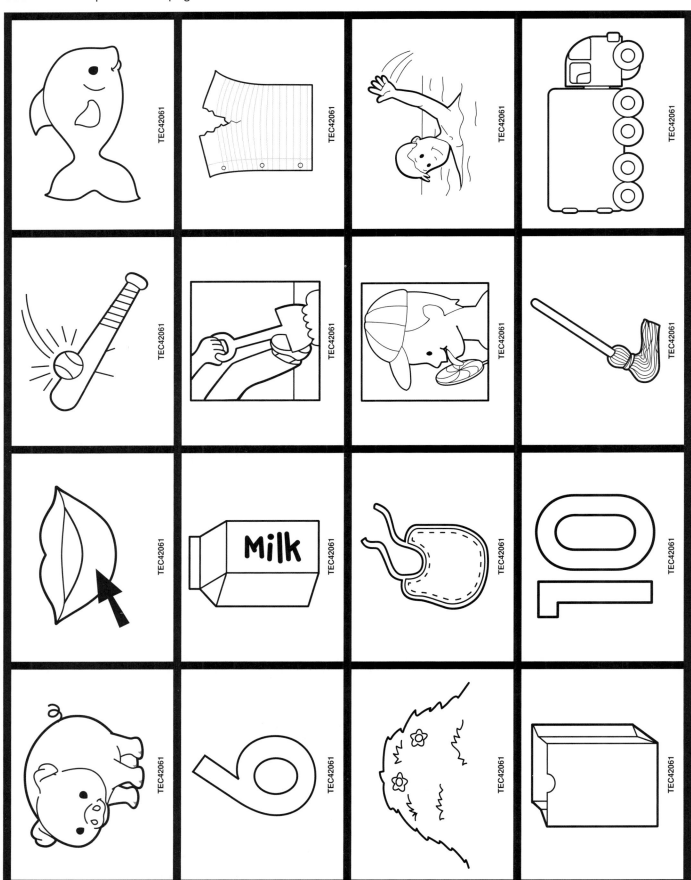

SIMPLE SCIENCE

simple SCIENCE

Match It!
Investigating smell, sound, and sight

getting ready
- Put in each of several lunch bags a different type of object that has a distinct odor, such as an orange, cinnamon sticks, or coffee grounds. Make small holes in each bag; close the bags. Obtain a picture card to match each object.

- Put in each of several paper lunch bags a different type of object that has a distinct sound, such as rice, coins, and paper clips. Close the bags. Obtain a picture card to match each object.

- Trace several different objects on black construction paper. Cut out the tracings so they resemble shadows of each object.

activity

Ask a small group of students how each of their senses can help them identify objects. Show youngsters the picture cards and shadows. Guide youngsters to use their senses to match each bag and object that was traced to the corresponding picture card or shadow.

Debbie Patrick, State College, PA

It smells like an orange.

Color Creations
Mixing primary colors to make secondary colors

getting ready
- Partially fill three transparent cups with water.

- Set out red, yellow, and blue tubes of food coloring.

- Put a stirrer by the cups.

activity

Drip drops of yellow food coloring into a cup of water. Invite youngsters to share what they think happens when two different colors are mixed together. Next, slowly add drops of red food coloring to the yellow-tinted water and stir until students see the color orange emerge. Then lead youngsters in singing the song shown. To continue, tint the water in a different cup yellow. This time, slowly add drops of blue food coloring to the water to see the color green revealed. For the final round, tint the water in the last cup blue and slowly add drops of red food coloring to change its color to purple. **To review**, have youngsters draw to show the two mixed colors for each of the resulting secondary colors.

Jeanne-Marie Peterson
Early Childhood Development Center
Charlottesville, VA

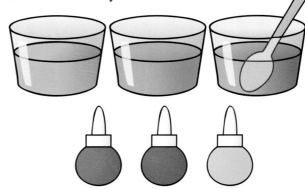

(sung to the tune of "Head and Shoulders")

[Red] and [yellow] make [orange], make [orange].
[Red] and [yellow] make [orange], make [orange].
Mix two colors and see a new color!
[Red] and [yellow] make [orange], make [orange].

simple SCIENCE

A Bubbling Eruption
Investigating changing matter

getting ready
- Have each student paint a volcano on a sheet of construction paper. *(Allow time to dry.)*
- Gather baking soda, vinegar (tinted red), a medicine dropper, a teaspoon, and a drip pan.

activity

 Gather a small group of students. Sprinkle a teaspoon of baking soda at the top of a child's volcano. Then have him use a medicine dropper to gently squirt the baking powder with vinegar until it is covered. As the baking powder and vinegar mixture (lava) is bubbling (erupting), help him lift up his paper over the drip pan so the lava trickles down the volcano. Then invite a different child to take a turn. Lead the group to comment on the same bubbly reaction and similar lava tracks. After each child has had a turn, have youngsters compare their volcanic art and describe their observations. **For further exploration**, encourage each child to take another turn on the same paper to discover how the lava will tend to trickle down the same tracks made in the first eruption.

Sonya McTeague, Hollis Academy for Children, Hollis, NH

COOL!
When the volcanoes dry, the baking soda residue mimics ash, revealing the location of the eruption as well as the lava tracks.

Where's the Worm?
Animal disguises and defenses

getting ready
- Cut out a class supply of brown paper ovals (worms).
- Set out a class supply of paper, crayons, and glue.

activity

 Discuss with youngsters how some animals blend into their surroundings to sneak up on prey or hide from predators. For example, a white rabbit blends in with snow and a green snake blends in with a leafy tree. Then give each student a paper worm and a sheet of paper. Instruct her to draw a scene in which the worm can "hide" and then glue the worm to her paper. Post students' drawings on a display with the title "Where's the Worm?" Then encourage youngsters to search and find each camouflaged critter.

simple SCIENCE

Block That Light
Understanding how shadows are created

getting ready
- Display a sheet of green bulletin board paper, decorated as shown.
- Have each child draw an animal's head, cut it out, and glue it to a craft stick to make a puppet.
- Place a flashlight near the paper and dim the lights.

activity
Invite a few students at a time to explore how to cast shadows on the green paper with their puppets and the flashlight. Guide youngsters to realize that shadows can be made by blocking sunlight or artificial light. Then encourage students to answer questions such as "How can you make a shadow larger?" and "What happens to the shadow when you turn the puppet?"

Around and Around
Investigating the water cycle

getting ready
- Tape one end of a length of yarn to each child's desk.
- Give each child four clear beads, four white beads, and four blue beads.
- Display a simple water cycle chart.

activity
Use the chart to review the water cycle with students. Then tell youngsters that the clear beads represent evaporation, the white beads represent condensation, and the blue beads represent precipitation. Have students use the beads to make water cycle patterned bracelets. When each child is finished with her bracelet, help her tie it around her wrist. Then lead youngsters in singing the song and performing the actions shown. Guide students to realize that, like the beads on their bracelets, the water cycle is continuous.

The Water Cycle
(sung to the tune of "If You're Happy and You Know It")

Water travels in a cycle; yes, it does!
Water travels in a cycle; yes, it does!
It goes up—evaporation,   *(Wiggle fingers up.)*
Makes a cloud, that's condensation,   *(Use arms to form a cloud.)*
It comes down—precipitation.   *(Wiggle fingers down.)*
Yes, it does!

Cathy Caudill
Eastside Elementary
Cynthiana, KY

simple SCIENCE

See the Seedling!
Observing plant growth

getting ready

- Cut out a flowerpot frame, similar to the one shown, for each student.
- Gather a class supply of resealable plastic bags, lima beans, damp paper towels, and tape.
- Fill a spray bottle with water.

activity

Here's a clever way to add a bit of pizzazz to a bean plant activity. Direct each child to personalize a frame and decorate it as desired. Next, have him put a lima bean on a damp towel and gently fold the towel over the bean. Then guide him to put the wrapped bean in a bag. Help him seal the bag, tape it to the undecorated side of the frame, and tape the craft to a window so the bag side faces the sun. Explain how the water from the towel coupled with sunlight will help the bean grow. Then, as days pass, encourage each child to use the water bottle to gently spray his young plant, keeping the towel moist. During the extended observation, have him examine his plant and record his observations. Lead him to make a connection with the hidden growth that takes place in a real flowerpot as he sees how the lima bean (the seed) grows roots and how a stem grows up from the seed to form leaves and flowers.

Colby Mason, Butler Elementary, Butler, IN

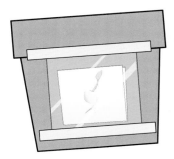

Animals and Their Babies
Living things change as they grow

When my baby is born, it walks on four legs and likes to hear me purr. Draw a blue line under the picture of my baby.

getting ready

- Write on separate cards each adult animal name: *bear, cow, hen, dog, cat, goat, frog, owl, duck, horse, deer,* and *butterfly.*
- Make a class supply plus one more of the recording sheet on page 165.

activity

To activate prior knowledge, lead students to brainstorm a list of different adult animal names and the corresponding baby names. Then give each child a copy of the recording sheet. Tell youngsters you are going to pretend to be an adult animal describing its baby and they each need to find the matching animal on the paper. Next, choose a card and give clues about the corresponding baby animal. For example, to have a hen describe its chick, say, "My little baby hatches out of an egg, it walks on two feet, and it has feathers." Then give a direction such as "Draw a red circle around my baby." To create an answer key, complete the desired task on the extra copy of the recording sheet. Then continue with each remaining adult animal card.

Beth Parry, Zane North Elementary, Collingswood, NJ

Drip, Drop!
Exploring rain

getting ready
- Tape a coffee filter over the opening of a clear jar.
- Set out an eyedropper and a small container of water.

activity

Drip drops of water on the coffee filter. Invite youngsters to share what they think will happen. Continue to drip drops of water on the filter while explaining how the filter acts like a cloud as it collects water. When the filter is saturated, drops of water begin to fall into the jar. Lead youngsters to conclude that, just as the water drops into the jar, rain falls from a cloud when the droplets are too heavy for the air to hold.

Marie E. Cecchini
West Dundee, IL

A Closer Look
Understanding the growth and changes of living things

getting ready
- Make a class supply of the patterns on page 166. On each magnifying glass, cut out a window where indicated.
- Gather a clear plastic cup, pebbles, soil, grass seeds, and a brad for each student.

activity

Have each child cut out a copy of the magnifying glass and blank wheel patterns. Help her use the brad to attach the wheel behind the magnifying glass. Next, guide her to put a handful of small pebbles and some soil in a cup. Have her use a real magnifying glass to examine her grass seeds and then have her draw what she sees on a wheel section. To continue, encourage her to sprinkle several seeds in her cup and cover the seeds with a half-inch of soil. Instruct her to put the cup near a sunny window and observe it daily, adding water as needed. Over time, direct her to draw changes—such as the growth of roots, the first sprout, and a full cup of grass—on the three remaining sections of her wheel. When her project is complete, invite her to turn the wheel to revisit the growth of grass seeds.

Jennifer Reidy
Halifax Elementary
Halifax, MA

tip➔ Use the bonus wheel pattern on page 166 as a reference or for added support.

Centered on Senses

Spotlight the five senses with these science center options!

ideas contributed by Linda Edwards, Brinson Elementary, New Bern, NC

That's Touching

Cut a hole in the side of a large lidded box and place a large variety of textured collage items in the box. Secure the lid. Provide construction paper and glue. A student puts his hand into the hole and feels an item. He names whether the item is soft, bumpy, or smooth. Then he pulls it out and glues it to his paper. He repeats the process until he has made a unique textured collage.

Good Taste

Make a class supply of page 164 and put the copies at a center along with salty, sweet, and sour foods for youngsters to taste. For example, you might provide a potato chip, a chocolate kiss, and a lemon wedge for each child. A child tastes a food and then decides whether it is salty, sweet, or sour. Next, he draws a picture of it in the appropriate section of his sheet. To show his opinion of the food's taste, he colors the appropriate face. Then he continues with each remaining food.

The 5 Senses

Hearing Match

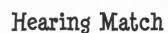

Gather several items that make noise, such as a bell, a triangle instrument, rhythm sticks, and a maraca. Make an audio recording of each item. Then place the recording and items at a center. A child explores the noise made by each item. Then he plays the recording, identifying each item after hearing its sound.

I See It!

Partially fill a plastic jar with rice. Bury a variety of small items in the rice and secure the lid. Set out I Spy books and hidden-picture books with the jar. A youngster manipulates the jar to look for the items. He also peruses the books, searching for hidden objects and noticing the details in the pictures.

Splendid Smells

Gather several scented candles and, for each one, make a simple card that has a picture or word to represent the scent. Place the candles and cards at a center. A child smells each candle and then matches it to the appropriate card.

Name _____

Do You Like It?

Listen for directions.

Sour	Sweet	Salty
:) :(	:) :(	:) :(

Note to the teacher: Use with "Good Taste" on page 163.

Baby Animals

cub 	calf 	chick 
puppy 	kitten 	kid 
tadpole 	owlet 	duckling 
foal 	fawn 	caterpillar 

©The Mailbox® • TEC42060 • April/May 2012

Note to the teacher: Use with "Animals and Their Babies" on page 161.

THE MAILBOX **165**

Magnifying Glass and Wheel Patterns
Use with "A Closer Look" on page 162.

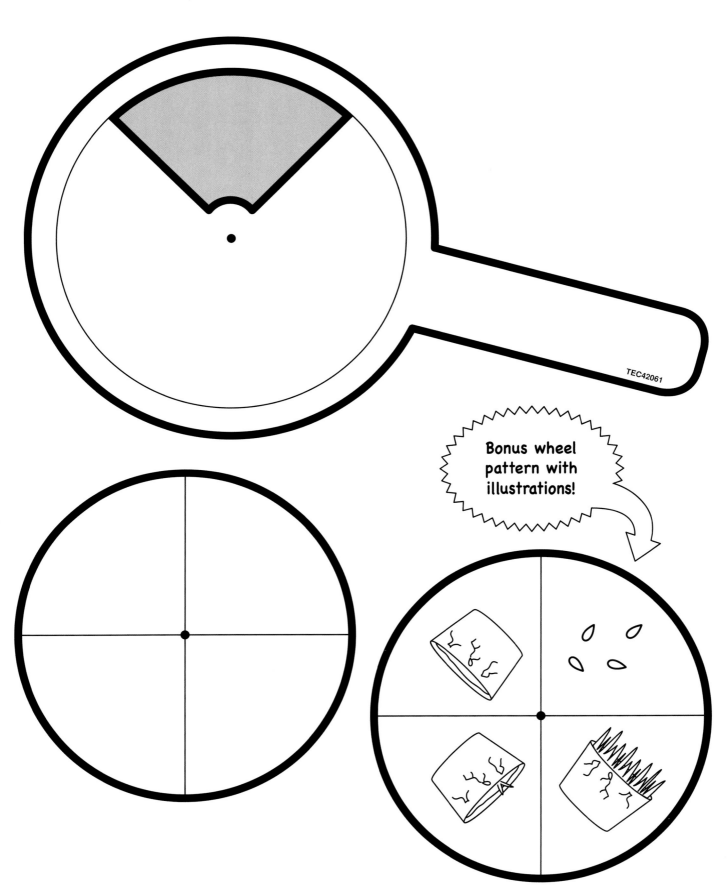

Bonus wheel pattern with illustrations!

TEC42061

'TIS THE SEASON

'Tis the Season

On the Bus

Use this partner game to reinforce making and comparing sets. Write a different number from 1 to 10 on each of ten bus cards (patterns on page 169). Set out 20 Unifix cubes (passengers). To set up the game, the partners stack the bus cards facedown and each player takes ten passengers. To play, each child takes a card, reads the number, and places a matching number of passengers on her bus. Then the partners compare the passengers on their buses to determine whose bus has more. After removing the passengers from the buses, players take another turn.

Jennifer Reidy, Halifax Elementary, Halifax, MA

(sung to the tune of "Clementine")

We love apples, juicy apples.
They are red and very sweet.
Let's go pick them from the big trees.
They are such a tasty treat.

Oh My, Apples!

This apple-themed tune is perfect for a variety of skills! Display the song on chart paper. After singing it several times, choose from the ideas below.

Rhyming: Guide students to identify the rhyming words.

High-frequency words: Instruct students to point out words such as *we*, *they*, *are*, *go*, *from*, and *a*.

Concepts of print: Ask students to point out where the song begins and ends, capitalization, and punctuation.

Comprehension: Invite youngsters to brainstorm titles for the song.

Deborah Garmon, Groton, CT

Find That Apple!

Review high-frequency words with this small-group activity. On each of several upside-down disposable cups, write a different high-frequency word. Place the cups in a line and set a large red pom-pom (apple) nearby. Review the words with the group. Then have youngsters close their eyes while you secretly hide the apple under one of the cups. Invite a volunteer to name a word and lift the cup to check whether the apple is hidden there. Continue until the location of the apple is revealed. Then invite a student to secretly hide the apple to play another round.

Marie E. Cecchini
West Dundee, IL

Don't miss the patterning **skill sheet** on page 170!

TEC42056

TEC42056

Tools for School

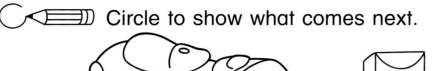

 Circle to show what comes next.

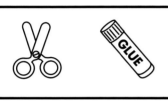 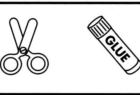     

Bonus: Draw a pattern with .
apples

Name

Oops!

Lotto game: letter identification or plane shapes Cut out a copy of one set of cards from page 172 to make caller's cards. (Color as needed.) Give each child a copy of this page and a copy of the appropriate game cards. (For the math cards, each child colors the shapes.) Students cut out the game cards and glue each card to a blank board space. Then they play the game like traditional lotto. (To call a space for the math game, say a color and a shape.)

Game Cards
Use with "Oops!" on page 171.

shape cards

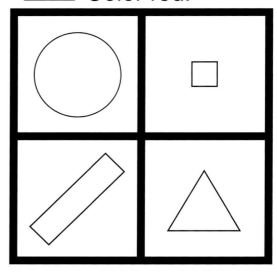

Color red.

letter cards

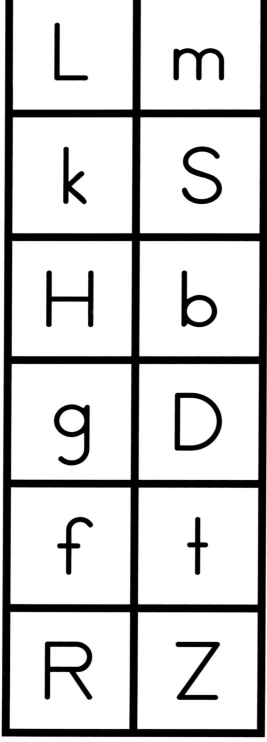

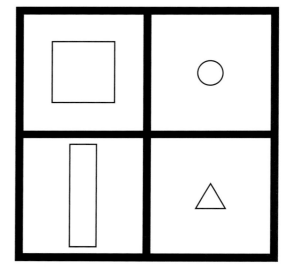

Color blue.

Color green.

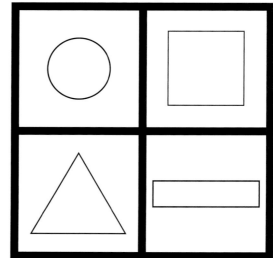

Have each child cut out a copy of the booklet backing below and page 174. Then help her stack the pages in order behind the cover and staple the stack atop the backing. After reading booklet pages 1–5, guide her to follow the directions on booklet page 6. **For additional skill reinforcement**, ask students to name the pictures on booklet pages 1–5 and highlight the corresponding words.

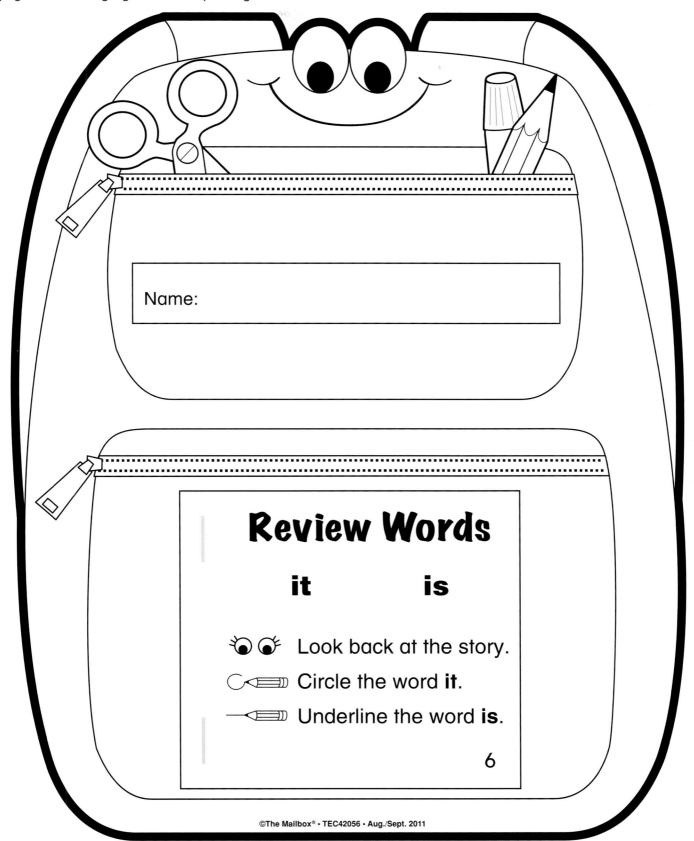

Name:

Review Words

it   is

👀 Look back at the story.

✏ Circle the word **it**.

✏ Underline the word **is**.

6

School Time

It is time for crayons.

1

It is time for books.

2

It is time for pencils.

3

It is time for friends.

4

Later, it is time to go home.

5

Note to the teacher: Use with the directions on page 173.

'Tis the Season

Spooky Houses

Scare up some **number word** fun with this partner game. To make two gameboards, trim two black paper rectangles so they resemble houses and glue 15 yellow squares (windows) to each house. Label each of ten craft sticks with a number word from *one* to *five*, writing each word two times. Put the craft sticks word-side down in a cup. Set out the gameboards and cup with a supply of small seasonal erasers. To play, each child takes a stick from the cup, in turn, and reads the number word. Then he places that number of erasers on the windows of his gameboard and sets the stick aside. Play continues until one player covers all the windows on his gameboard.

Tina Bellotti, George A. Jackson Elementary, Jericho, NY

Putting on Patches

Review **high-frequency words** with the help of a scarecrow. On a copy of the scarecrow pattern on page 176, write several high-frequency words. Give each child a copy of the prepared page and a supply of trimmed sticky notes. Then name a word and have him find the word on the scarecrow and cover it with a sticky note (patch). Continue until students cover each word with a patch. **For a whole-group variation,** laminate an enlarged scarecrow cutout, use wipe-off markers to write words for the week, and invite different students to cover each word with a large sticky note.

Nancy Siewers
Amvet Boulevard School
North Attleboro, MA

tip → To make a large scarecrow, trace a student on a sheet of bulletin board paper. Then draw facial features and overalls.

Roll and Write

Small-group members practice **counting and number formation** with this seasonal die. Cover a large foam die with paper. Then draw or stamp small pumpkins (instead of dots) on each side of the die. To begin, give each child a whiteboard and a marker. Have a youngster roll the die. Then direct each child to count the pumpkins and write the matching number on her board. After checking for accuracy, have students wipe off their boards to be ready for another roll of the die.

Tina Bellotti

Putting on Patches

©The Mailbox® • TEC42057 • Oct./Nov. 2011

176 THE MAILBOX **Note to the teacher:** Use with "Putting on Patches" on page 175.

Name_____ Fall

Frame Game

Number recognition to 20

- -

Lotto frame game: Cut out a copy of the game cards from page 178 to make caller's cards. Give each child a copy of this page and a copy of the game cards. Students cut out the cards and glue each one to an empty board space. Then they play the game like traditional lotto.

10	14	20	15
18	11	13	16
12	17	9	19

MORE Ways to Use the Cards

Math Center: For practice *modeling numbers*, cut out two or three copies of the game cards. Place the cards, blank paper, glue, and crayons at the center. A student glues a card to his paper and then uses the crayons to draw that many turkeys, pies, or leaves.

Group Game: All you need to play this *counting game* is a set of game cards. Put the cards in a container and have students sit in a circle. To play, one child takes a game card and reads its number aloud. Then he struts around the outside of the circle as he and his classmates orally count each student he passes. When the class says the number he drew, he gently taps the shoulder of the corresponding classmate and says, "Gobble, gobble." The two youngsters trade places, a new number card is drawn, and play resumes. Play until each game card is used or time runs out.

Have each child cut apart a copy of pages 179 and 180. Then help him staple the booklet pages in order behind the front cover. For each booklet page, have students draw additional illustrations to match the plural word in the sentence. **For additional skill reinforcement,** ask students to complete text-related tasks, such as underlining *here* and *pumpkin* on each page, circling the capital letter at the beginning of each sentence, or tracing the vocabulary words.

Ready for Pumpkins

Pumpkins

by _____

Seeds

Here are pumpkin seeds.   1

Here are pumpkin sprouts.   2

Here are pumpkin plants.

3

Here are pumpkin flowers.

4

Look! Here are pumpkins!

5

Note to the teacher: Use with the directions on page 179.

Pass the Cookies!

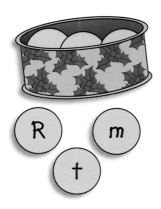

Students take a short break from **identifying letters** when a star cookie is revealed! Write the letters of the alphabet on separate paper circles (cookies). Draw a star on each of several additional cookies. Place all the cookies in a holiday tin. To play, have youngsters take turns removing cookies from the tin and naming each letter shown. When a child removes a star cookie, have her say a holiday phrase, such as "Ho, ho, ho!" signaling her classmates to rub their tummies and repeat the phrase. Continue until the tin is emptied or as time permits. **To review other skills,** label the cookies with numbers for number identification or high-frequency words for reading.

Beth Haynes, Bluff Park Elementary, Hoover, AL

A Penguin Poem

This adorable rhyme is perfect for reviewing a variety of literacy and math skills. Simply choose one or more of the options below.

Five Little Penguins

Five little penguins, waddling on the ice.
The first one said, "This is really nice."
The second one said, "I am having fun."
The third one said, "Please, don't run."
The fourth one said, "I have fallen twice."
The fifth one said, "Look out—thin ice!"
Then *crack* went the ice. Did you hear that sound?
Now five little penguins, swimming all around!

Concepts of print: Post a copy of the poem. Invite youngsters to take turns using a pointer to point to the title, track print while chanting the poem, and point to the beginning and end of the poem.

Word work: Post a laminated copy of the poem in a student-accessible location. Place dry-erase markers nearby. Invite youngsters to do text-related tasks, such as highlighting two-letter words, underlining the first word in a sentence, and circling rhyming words. **To extend rhyming practice,** ask students to name additional words for each pair of rhyming words.

Ordinal numbers: Label each of five penguin cutouts with a different ordinal number from "first" to "fifth." Give each penguin to a child. Lead students in reciting the poem. As each ordinal number is named, direct the child with the corresponding penguin to stand in front of the group.

Doria Owen
William Paca/Old Post Road Elementary
Abingdon, MD

How Many Snowballs?

Review **number words, number identification,** and **counting** with these snazzy snowpals. For a small group, label the bottom of a large sheet of paper with the numbers 1 to 10. Place a set of matching number word cards in a bag and set out a few bingo daubers. To begin, invite a child to take a card and read the word. Have her find the matching number on the paper and use a bingo dauber to make a snowpal's body with the corresponding number of dots (snowballs). Then ask a different child to take a turn. After all ten snowpal bodies are made and the ink is dry, have group members draw details to complete the snowpals.

Emily Wright, Selinsgrove Elementary, Selinsgrove, PA

Reach High!

Change the **first** letter.

✏️ Write to match the picture.

✏️ Cross out the matching first letter.

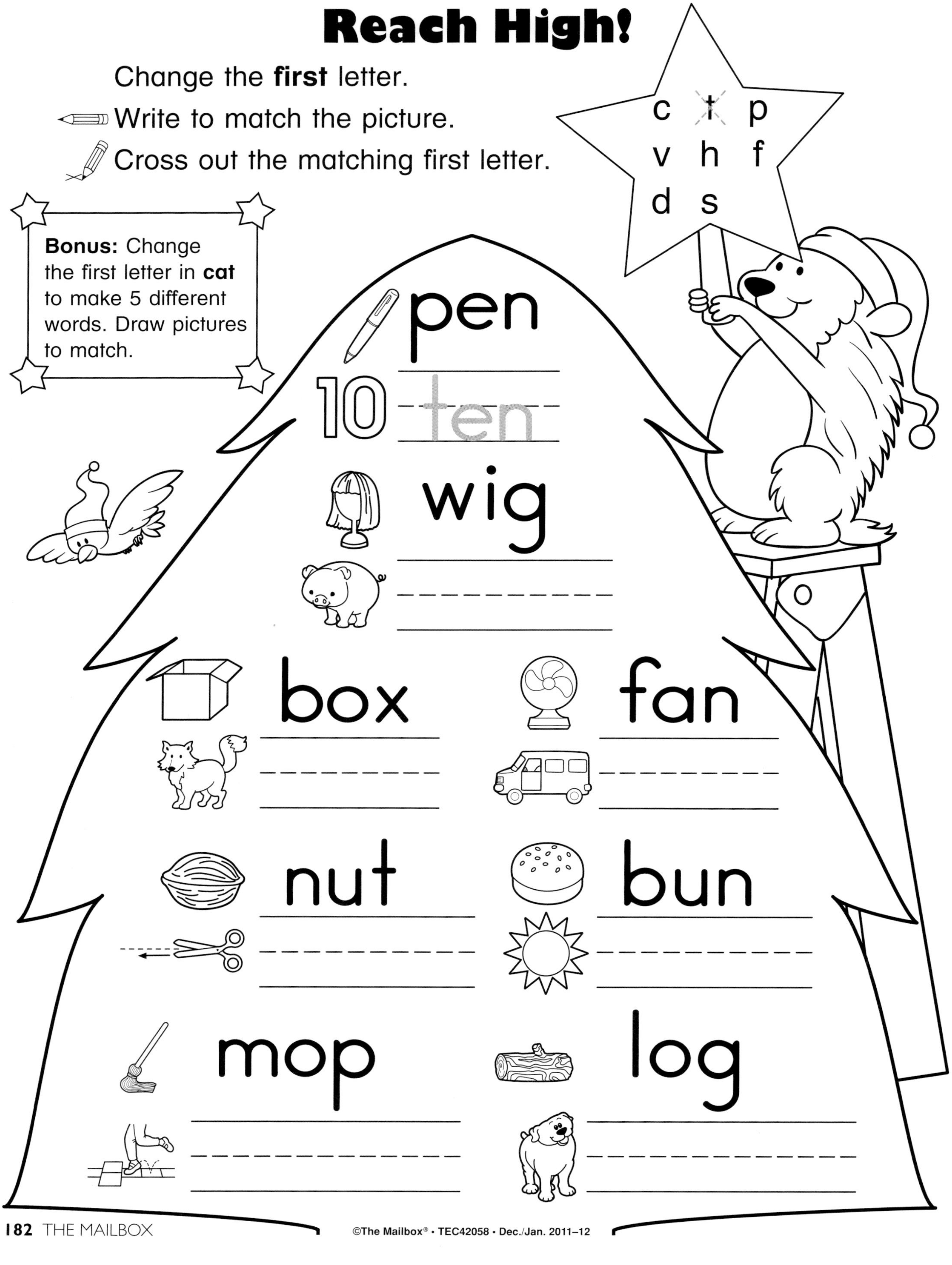

Star letters: c ~~t~~ p / v h f / d s

Bonus: Change the first letter in **cat** to make 5 different words. Draw pictures to match.

pen

10 ~~ten~~

wig

box

fan

nut

bun

mop

log

Toss and Tell

Word families

1	2	3	4	5	6
bat	can	rip	mop	bug	sun
cat	ran	zip	hop	mug	fun
hat	pan	lip	pop	hug	run

Small-group game: Give each child a copy of this page and game markers. Provide a die for the group. When it is a player's turn, she tosses the die, reads a word in that column of her gameboard, and marks the space. Play until one player marks three spaces in a column or six spaces in a row.

©The Mailbox® • TEC42058 • Dec./Jan. 2011–12

Have each child cut apart a copy of pages 184 and 185. Then help him staple the booklet pages in order behind the front cover. **For additional skill reinforcement,** ask students to complete text-related tasks, such as underlining high-frequency words or circling question marks with a red crayon and periods with a blue crayon.

1

Do penguins lay eggs?
Yes, they do.

3

Do penguins slide?
Yes, they do.

What Do Penguins Do?

Name _____

©The Mailbox® • TEC42058 • Dec./Jan. 2011–12

2

Do penguins hop?
Yes, they do.

Note to the teacher: Use with the directions on page 184.

THE MAILBOX **185**

’Tis the Season

Where’s My Burrow?

Youngsters match groundhogs to burrows for these center activities. To make a burrow, fold down the top of a small brown paper bag and crumple the top. Next, cut away the center of a paper plate, glue shreds of green paper (grass) to the rim, and then staple the plate to the top of the bag to complete the burrow. Then choose one or more of the options below.

Word families: Label a burrow for each rime you would like to feature. Write words with the corresponding rimes on copies of the groundhog cards on page 187 and then cut out the cards. A child drops each groundhog into its matching burrow. To record his sort, he writes the words that form each word family on a sheet of paper.

Number words: Label a burrow for each number word you would like to review. For each number word, set out the same number of groundhog cards (cards on page 187). A child reads each number word and drops a matching number of groundhogs in the burrow. To make the activity self-checking, label the bottom of each burrow with the corresponding numeral.

Addition: Label each of several burrows with different addition problems. Cut out a supply of groundhog cards (page 187) to match the greatest sum. For each problem, a child puts the matching number of groundhog cards for each addend in the burrow. Then she uses the cards to solve the problem and writes the corresponding number sentence on a sheet of paper.

Andrea Singleton, Waynesville Elementary, Waynesville, OH

Wild and Woolly Writing

Foster kindergartners’ use of figurative language with this imaginative activity. For each child, fold a sheet of construction paper in half and cut the top layer to form flaps, as shown. Discuss with youngsters what it means to feel lionlike and lamblike. Next, have each child cut apart a copy of the lion and lamb cards on page 187. Instruct him to glue a card on each flap of the prepared paper. When the glue dries, have him fold back the paper to focus on one animal at a time. Then guide him to write and complete the sentence starters shown behind the corresponding critters and have him draw pictures to match his writing. Lead youngsters to share their projects when time permits.

Ada Goren, Winston-Salem, NC

I am as gentle as a lamb when I…
I am as wild as a lion when I…

I am as gentle as a lamb when I read books.

A Green Treat

Do all leprechauns have to have a reputation for being mischievous? Not with this tasty idea! While students are out of the room, hang colorful crepe paper streamers from the top of your door frame so they look like a rainbow. Place a festive snack—such as shamrock cookies, green-tinted pudding, and punch—at each child’s seat. Then write a note on the board from a leprechaun inviting the class to enjoy the St. Patrick’s Day surprise.

Alyson Lewis, Meigs Primary, Middleport, OH

Groundhog Cards
Use with "Where's My Burrow?" on page 186.

TEC42059

TEC42059

TEC42059

TEC42059

TEC42059

TEC42059

Lion and Lamb Cards
Use with "Wild and Woolly Writing" on page 186.

TEC42059

TEC42059

Buggy Love

Group game: initial consonants or numbers to 30 Cut out a copy of one set of cards from page 189 to make caller's cards. Give each child a copy of this page and a copy of the appropriate game cards. (For the literacy cards, each child draws a heart around the initial consonant for each picture shown.) Students cut out the game cards and glue each card to a blank board space. Then they play the game like traditional lotto.

initial consonant cards

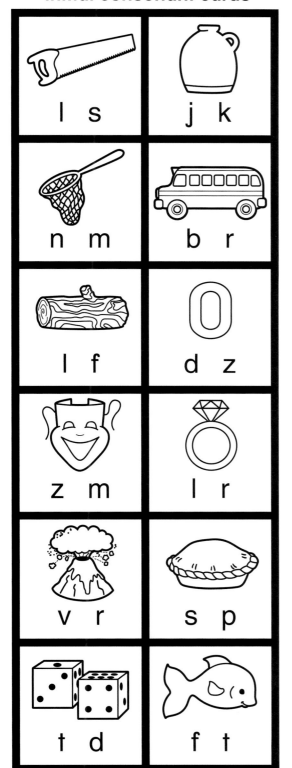

number cards

24	16	30
17	27	11
20	18	22
29	13	25

Math Skill Variation

For **number order** practice, have youngsters mark the space for the number that comes before or after a given number. For example, say, "Mark the space for the number that comes after 16," for youngsters to put a marker on the number 17. To keep track of the numbers called, make a T chart and put each caller's card in the corresponding column.

 tip For added fun, have each child color a heart (free space) on her gameboard before she glues her cards in place. Her extra game card can be thrown away.

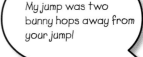

My jump was two bunny hops away from your jump!

'Tis the Season

Happy Hoppers!

How many bunny hops can a child cover in one jump? How about two jumps? Find out with this **nonstandard measurement** activity. Cut apart several copies of the bunny cards on page 191. Tape the cards to the floor to form a nonstandard line of measurement. Put a strip of tape across one end of the line to make a starting line. To begin, invite a child to stand behind the starting line and then jump forward one or two times. Lead the group in counting aloud the number of bunny hops covered in the jump. For added fun, have classmates hop one time in place for each number named. Continue until each child has had a turn to jump. For a **graphing connection**, have each youngster put a sticky note on a numbered grid to show her total number of bunny hops covered in a jump.

Jennifer Frankle
M. C. Riley Early Childhood Center
Bluffton, SC

"Egg-ceptional" Ideas

rain

My dog does not like rain.

Use these vocabulary eggs to jumpstart students' **springtime writing**! For this center, cut apart the word strips on page 191 and put them in separate plastic eggs. Put the eggs in a basket with writing paper. A child takes an egg, opens it, and reads the word. She uses the word in a sentence and then writes the sentence on a sheet of paper. She continues with different eggs as time permits. **For an added challenge**, have each child take two or three eggs and have her incorporate each of the words in a story.

Jennifer Brent
Vance Elementary
Raleigh, NC

Pond Play

Hop, hover, and waddle—oh my! Use this cute song to discuss **vocabulary** related to action at the pond.

SIGH!

(sung to the tune of "Hickory, Dickory, Dock")

The pond is a great place to play.
Which critters are out today?
[There are some frogs]
[Hopping on logs.]
The pond is a great place to play!

Continue with the following: *Raccoons wash their paws and stretch out their claws; Fireflies are bright, lighting the night; Dragonflies hover, looking for cover; Some flies buzz by—the frog does sigh; There is a duck waddling in muck.*

Beth Marquardt, St. Paul's School of Early Learning, Muskego, WI

Bunny Cards
Use with "Happy Hoppers!" on page 190.

TEC42060

TEC42060

TEC42060

TEC42060

Word Strips
Use with "'Egg-ceptional' Ideas" on page 190.

sun	wind
rain	umbrella
bunny	eggs
flower	basket

TEC42060

Toss and Tell

High-frequency words

	1	2	3	4	5	6
	look	this	here	see	up	out
	will	are	am	like	have	little
	is	said	get	my	do	we

©The Mailbox® • TEC42060 • April/May 2012

Small-group game: Give each child a copy of this page and game markers. Provide a die for the group. When it is a player's turn, he tosses the die, reads a word in that column of his gameboard, and marks the space. Play until one player marks three spaces in a column or six spaces in a row.

Ending punctuation

A Rainy Day

Color the  by the code.

Write a **.** or **?** at the end of each sentence.

Color Code
telling sentence (.) — red
asking sentence (?) — blue

1. I see five ducks

2. Is the big duck wet

3. Ducks like rain

4. The duck is yellow

5. Do you like rain

6. The duck has a hat

7. Do you have a hat

8. I like to play

9. Is the grass wet

10. Do you see me

Bonus: Write a sentence to answer the question. Do you have a red hat?

©The Mailbox® • TEC42060 • April/May 2012

Reproducible Booklet

Have each child cut apart a copy of this page. Then help him staple booklet pages 1–4 in order between construction paper covers. Direct him to glue the song card to the front cover. For booklet page 1, have him draw a picture of himself planting the seed. For booklet pages 1–4, guide him to match the words in the song text to the words in the art. Then lead youngsters in singing the song while pointing to the words on each booklet page.

song card

Grow a Flower
(sung to the tune of "Row, Row, Row Your Boat")

I will plant a seed.
The flower will be mine.
It needs some water, soil, and air.
It also needs sunshine!

booklet pages 1–4

I will plant a seed.

1

The flower will be mine.

2

It needs some water, soil, and air.

3

It also needs sunshine!

4

Beach Ball Bounce

This summer-style activity is perfect for a variety of skills. Use one of the options below to label a pair of beach ball cutouts for each twosome in your class, making sure each pair of beach balls makes a unique match. To begin, give each child a cutout and name the skill. Then bounce a real beach ball as a signal for students to "bounce" around the room and make their matches.

Equivalent forms of a number: Write or draw a representation of a number on one beach ball and write a different way to represent the same number on the other ball.

High-frequency words: Write the same word for each matching pair of beach balls.

Final consonants: Write a consonant on one ball and, on the other ball, draw a picture (or glue a clip art image) of an object whose name ends with the consonant.

Liz Mooney, Central Rayne Kindergarten, Rayne, LA

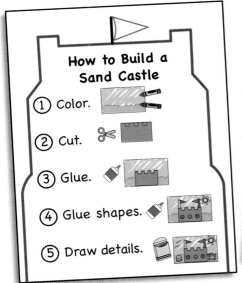

Super Sand Castles

Students **follow written directions** to build these unique sand castles. Prepare a direction sheet similar to the one shown. Display the directions and set the following materials nearby: sheets of white paper, half sheets of brown paper, paper shapes, crayons, scissors, and glue. Each child in a small group follows the directions to build a sand castle. Then lead youngsters to compare and contrast the completed castle structures.

Cindy Barber, Fredonia, WI

Sunny Day

Addition skills are sure to shine with this quick-to-prepare center. Write a different number on each of several large paper circles (suns). Set out the suns, a supply of yellow and orange paper strips (rays), and blank paper. A child chooses a sun and writes its number at the top of a sheet of paper. Next, he takes a combination of yellow and orange rays to equal the sun's number and arranges them around the sun. Then he writes a corresponding addition sentence on his paper. He continues to write number sentences using different combinations of yellow and orange rays as time permits.

Choose and Do!

① Write the matching lowercase letters.

(Aa)

B S H G
M V D N
R F Y E

② Write by **10s** to 100.

10, 20, 30,...

Write by **5s** to 50.

5, 10, 15,...

③ Write the words to match.

④ ✏ Draw.

🖍 Color the dog brown.

Color the cat orange.

Color the frog green.

⑤ Draw 3 🐜.

How many antennae?

How many eyes?

How many legs?

⑥ Solve. Draw a picture to match.

5 pigs are in the mud.

4 more pigs get in the mud.

How many pigs are in the mud in all?

Note to the teacher: Give each child a copy of this page. Have him write on a separate sheet of paper to complete one or more of the activities.

Frame Game

Place value

Lotto!

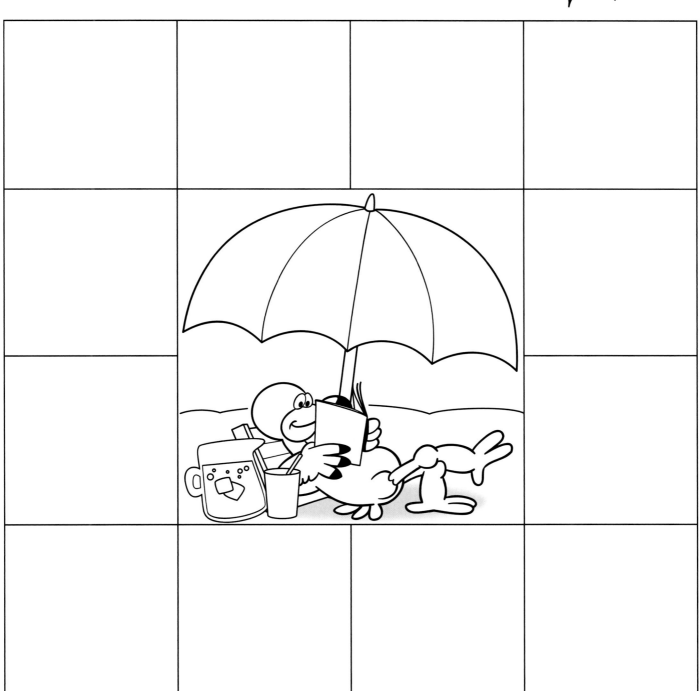

Lotto frame game Cut out a copy of the game cards from page 198 to make caller's cards. Give each child a copy of this page and a copy of the game cards. Students cut out the cards and glue each one to an empty board space. Then they play the game like traditional lotto.

Game Cards

Use with "Frame Game" on page 197.

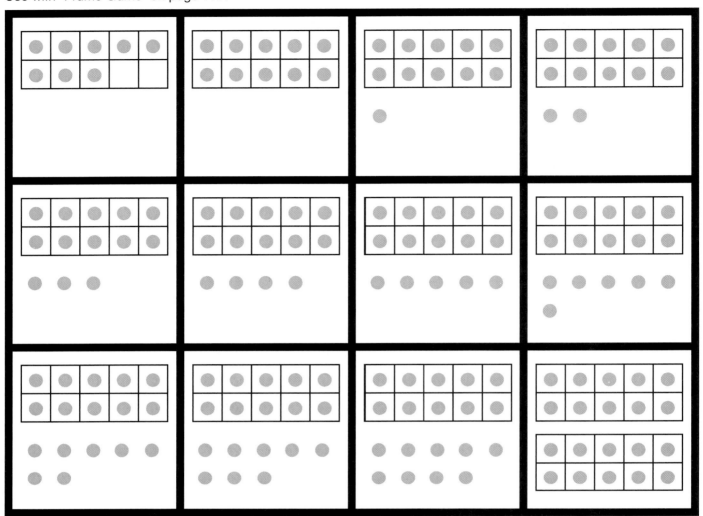

MORE Ways to Use the Cards

Math and Writing Center: For practice with *counting* and *writing sentences*, set out two or three copies of the game cards, story paper, glue, and crayons. A student glues a card to his paper and writes to complete the sentence "I see [matching numeral] [noun] at the beach." Then he draws a picture to match.

Whole-Group Activity: All you need to demonstrate *forming groups of ten* is a set of game cards and your students. Show a game card. For each group of ten shown on the card, invite a child to stand; for each of the ones shown on the card, invite a youngster to squat next to the ten(s). Repeat this step with a different game card. Then lead students to count the ones to see if together they form a group of ten. If they do, have one of the youngsters stand with fanfare while the remaining nine return to a designated area.

I see 12 fish at the beach.

Have each child cut apart a copy of pages 199 and 200. Then help him staple the booklet pages in order behind the front cover. After reading the booklet, lead a discussion about what happens on booklet page 7. **For additional skill reinforcement,** ask students to complete text-related tasks, such as highlighting the animal names, telling what Octopus sees, or underlining the color words with matching-color crayons.

1

Octopus sees a sea star

3

Octopus sees a sea horse

Octopus in the Ocean

Name _____

2

and a green sea turtle too.

Note to the teacher: Use with the directions on page 199.

WRITING

Draw and Write!

A Really Good Book

Note to the teacher: Have each child think of a book he really likes. Then ask him to draw a picture of his favorite part of the book and write about it. If desired, save the students' papers and have youngsters complete a similar activity each month to show his writing progress.

Draw and Write!

My Weekend

©The Mailbox® • TEC42056 • Aug./Sept. 2011

Note to the teacher: Ask each child to draw a picture of something she did during her weekend and then write about it. Repeat the activity throughout the year, as desired.

Name _____

Fall Is Here!

Think: What are your favorite fall activities?

Draw.

Write.

Name _____

Treats for Two

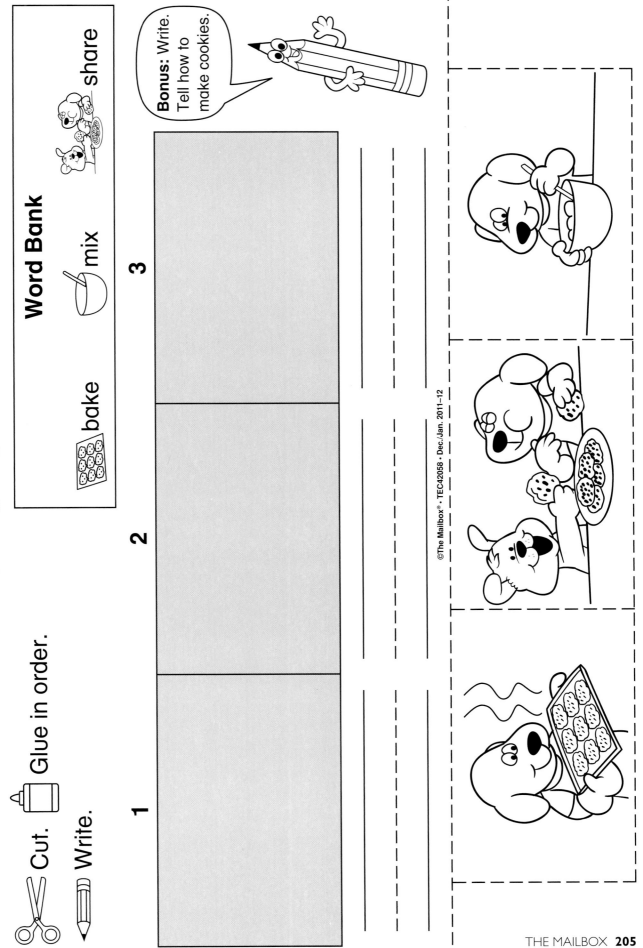

Cut. Glue in order. Write.

Word Bank

bake   mix   share

1   2   3

Bonus: Write. Tell how to make cookies.

©The Mailbox® • TEC42058 • Dec./Jan. 2011–12

Name _____

A "Bear-y" Happy Holiday

There are many ways to celebrate this time of year.

read stories

light candles

sing songs

open gifts

make cards

eat food

What do you do?

_____

_____

_____

_____

Whoosh!

Think: A big gust of wind blows away your favorite toy!

Draw.

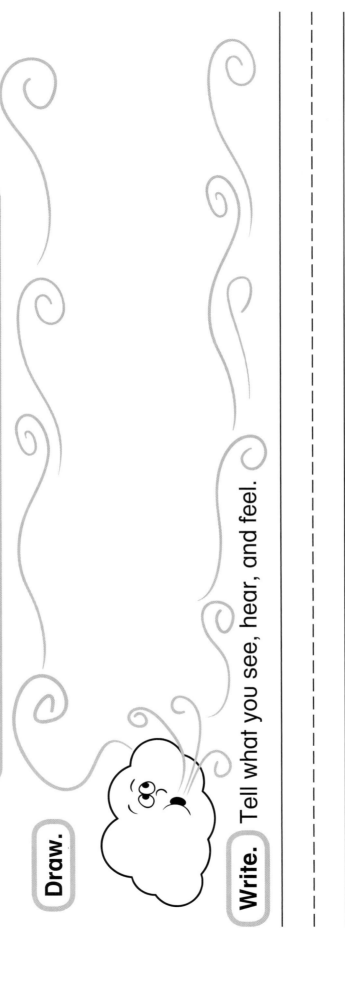

Write. Tell what you see, hear, and feel.

- - - - - - - - - - - -

Three Baby Birds

✂️ Cut. 🧴 Glue in order.

✏️ Write about each picture.

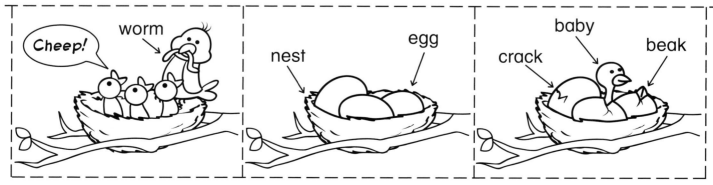

Plan a Story

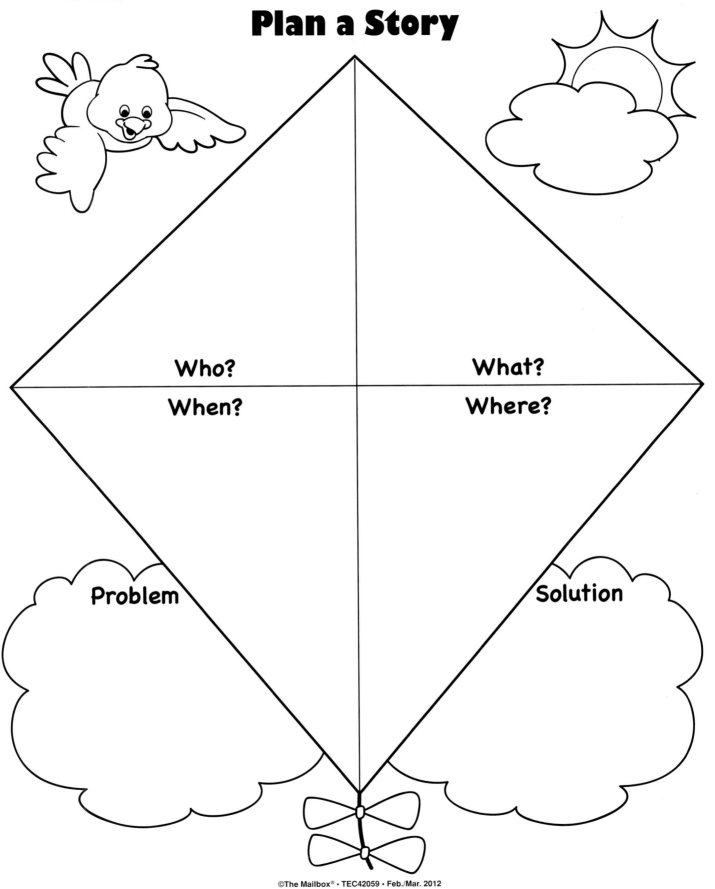

Who?

What?

When?

Where?

Problem

Solution

Note to the teacher: Have each child use a copy of this page to plan a seasonal story.

Name _____

Pick a Prompt

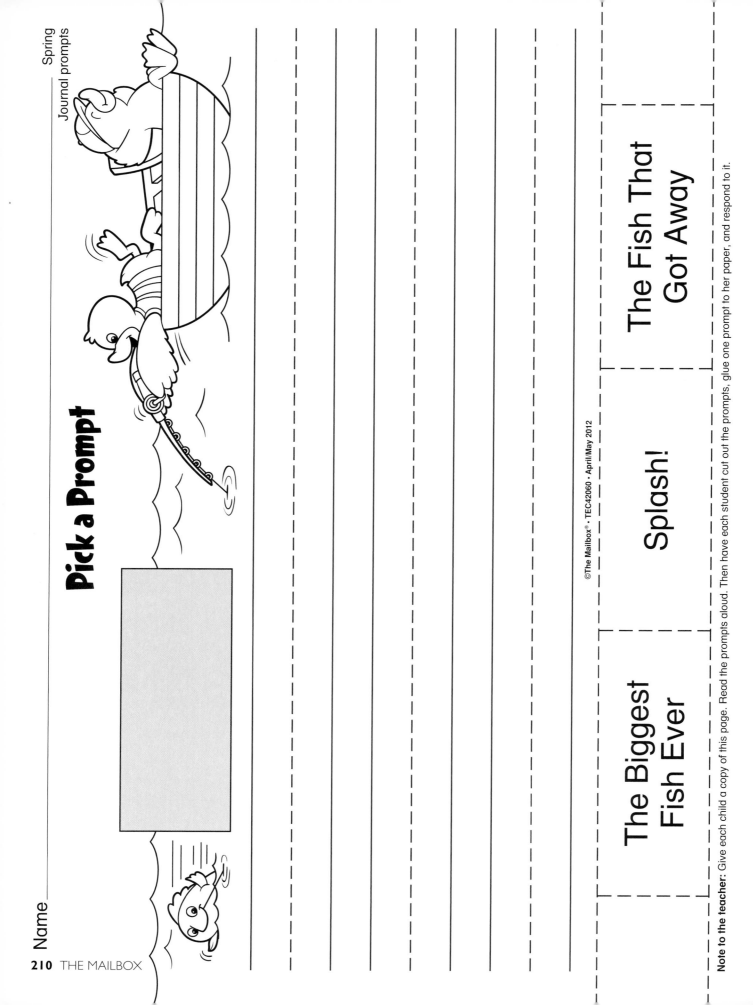

©The Mailbox® • TEC42060 • April/May 2012

| The Biggest Fish Ever | Splash! | The Fish That Got Away |

Note to the teacher: Give each child a copy of this page. Read the prompts aloud. Then have each student cut out the prompts, glue one prompt to her paper, and respond to it.

Name _____

A Fun Beach Day

Think: Pretend you are at the beach with your family.

Draw.

Write.

_____

- -

_____

- -

_____

_____

- -

_____

Game Day

Circle 2 mistakes in each sentence.

Write each sentence correctly.

sam cannot go

_____

- - - - - - - - - - - - - - - - - - -

_____

what can Sam do.

_____

- - - - - - - - - - - - - - - - - - -

_____

sam can fix it?

_____

- - - - - - - - - - - - - - - - - - -

_____

look at Sam go

_____

- - - - - - - - - - - - - - - - - - -

_____

Bonus: Write a sentence that tells where you think Sam is going.

LITERACY UNITS

Start the Day

Add these skill-based ideas to your morning routine to give your students something to crow about.

With Language and Literacy

Extra, Extra!

Asking and responding to appropriate questions

This simple idea requires no supplies and is sure to improve youngsters' social skills. Each morning, ask a student to share something that happened at home the night before or another tidbit of news. Remind the rest of the class to practice good listening skills. When the youngster is finished speaking, invite a volunteer to ask him a question about what he shared. Then help the child appropriately answer the question. Now that's a great way to start the day!

Goldy Hirsch, Beacon School, Brooklyn, NY

Toss and Say

Producing rhyming words

For this small-group activity, tape a picture card in each section of a large grid to make a rhyming mat. Then select a child to toss a beanbag onto the mat. After she tosses it, invite group members to name words that rhyme with the picture on which the beanbag landed. Continue until each child has had a turn to toss. For added fun, encourage youngsters to name nonsense words too!

Jennifer Reidy, Halifax Elementary, Halifax, MA

Search and Find

Letter identification

Tune up youngsters' letter skills with this interactive song activity. Copy the song on chart paper; below the song, write each student's first name. Then look at the first letter in each student's name and write each different letter on a separate card; put the cards in a bag. To start the day, sing the first verse of the song. Next, invite a volunteer to remove a card from the bag and name the letter. Write the letter on each of two sticky notes to fill in the blanks in the second verse. Then lead youngsters in singing the verse. Finally, invite volunteers to use Wikki Stix manipulatives to circle the names that begin with the corresponding letter.

Jennifer Reidy

(sung to the tune of "Row, Row, Row Your Boat")

Welcome, welcome friends.

Welcome back, I say.

Choose a letter from the bag

For our name game today!

We chose the letter A .

Now look at our class list.

Find the names that start with A .

Check that none are missed!

Monika	Henry	Simone	Juan
Susan	Eva	Avery	Hunter
Rachel	Marcus	Tamika	Ayden
Alice	Brock	Liam	Carmen

David	David
Elise	Elise
Tommy	
Addison	
Ryan	Ryan
Micah	
Katie	
Seth	

Daily Sign-In

Writing one's name

What does students' writing have in common with attendance taking? Find out with this idea! Copy your class list on chart paper and laminate it. When a child arrives in the morning, he uses a wipe-off marker to write his name on the corresponding line. At the end of the day, simply wipe the chart clean for the next morning. Not only will you know who is at school, but you'll also have a quick way to observe students' name-writing progress.

Brook Baglini
Main Elementary
Athens, PA

A Ready-to-Use Reference

Feature students' names and photos in alphabetical order to make a chart similar to the one shown. Then choose one or more of the activities below to use with the chart.

- Practice **initial consonants** by naming a letter and inviting volunteers to count how many students' names begin with that letter.

- Have students use the chart as a reference to **spell classmates' names**.

- Encourage youngsters to refer to the chart as they put a set of name cards in **alphabetical order**.

Jennifer Reidy
Halifax Elementary
Halifax, MA

Adam	
Claire	
Collin	
Haleigh	
Jesus	

Scarecrow, Scarecrow

How silly can you be?

You made Grace laugh.

But you didn't make me!

A Poem for All Seasons

Recognizing classmates' names, tracking print

By simply changing the character, this rhyme is perfect for year-round use! Write the poem on sentence strips and put them in a pocket chart. Glue a copy of the appropriate character card from page 216 to a craft stick to make a pointer. Place a class set of name cards and the pointer near the pocket chart. To begin, invite a volunteer to slide her name card in the appropriate space to complete the poem. Then have her use the pointer to track the print as you lead students in reading the poem aloud. Repeat the activity throughout the season until each child has had a turn.

Vanessa Rivera, La Luz Elementary, La Luz, NM

TEC42056

TEC42056

TEC42056

TEC42056

Alphabet Express

From writing letters to making chugging sounds, students are sure to be on board with these train-related ideas!

Letter Locomotive

Letter knowledge

Students write letters in alphabetical order at this center activity. Write several uppercase and lowercase letter pairs on a long length of paper, leaving spaces for the missing letters. If desired, use a different color to write the vowels. Then color and cut out copies of the train engine and caboose patterns on page 219 and glue each cutout on the appropriate end of the paper. Laminate the resulting locomotive to make it reusable. A child uses a wipe-off marker to write the missing letters. Then she points to each letter as she quietly sings an ABC song. After confirming accuracy, she wipes it clean for the next engineer to take a turn. **For an easier version**, write half of each letter pair for youngsters to write matching letters on the lines.

Jennifer Frankle
M. C. Riley Early Childhood Center
Bluffton, SC

Ready to Roll!

Letter matching, writing

The first train to have a full load of lettered cars is the winner of this partner game! To prepare a gameboard, make a copy of page 220 and write a different letter on each engine. Label five sides of a cube to show each of the chosen letters. On the remaining side, write "All aboard!" To play, a child rolls the cube and writes the letter rolled on its corresponding train car. If "All aboard!" is rolled, players pretend a train has stopped to pick up passengers and say, "All aboard!" No letters are written, and the same player rolls again. Partners continue to take turns until a winning train is ready to roll with each of its cars labeled. **For a more advanced version**, have youngsters write the partner letter for each featured letter.

adapted from an idea by Jennifer Frankle

Get Aboard!

Letter identification

All your kindergartners are welcome to be part of this class train! Write different letters on individual sticky dots. Give each child a dot. Have him identify the letter and then attach the dot to his clothing. As the train's engineer, say the first two lines of the chant shown to welcome a student aboard. Lead youngsters in saying the next two lines while the child with the matching letter pretends to be a train car and gets in line behind you. When each of your students is part of the train, conclude the activity by chanting the last two lines. **For a shorter version**, provide uppercase and lowercase letter dots for two youngsters to get aboard at a time.

Jennifer Frankle, M. C. Riley Early Childhood Center, Bluffton, SC

Teacher:
Chugga, chugga, choo, choo,
Letter [S], there's room for you.

Students:
[S, S], we see you.
Chugga, chugga, choo, choo!

Final verse:
Chugga, chugga, oh yes,
We're the ABC Express!

Line 'em Up

ABC order

Your little engineers assemble a letter train for this small-group activity. Write letters on separate paper squares. Then glue two circles (wheels) on each square to form train cars. On an additional train car, glue a triangle as shown to form a train engine. To begin, set out the train engine and one train car. A group member then takes a different car and slides it in front of or behind the existing car to put it in alphabetical order. Continue as time permits. **For a center activity**, set out the prepared materials for a youngster to assemble the ABC train independently.

Jennifer Frankle

Name That Letter!

Letter-sound associations

Youngsters chug letter sounds in response to this whole-group song activity. Invite several students to stand in a line, ready to act as a train. Secretly share a letter sound with the train members. Next, lead the class in singing the song shown. At the song's end, have train members repeat the designated sound in rhythm with the tune as they chug like a train across the room. Then invite seated youngsters to name the letter associated with the sound. Continue until each child has had a turn to be a part of a train.

(sung to the tune of
"When the Saints Go Marching In")

Oh, when the train starts comin' round,
Oh, when the train starts comin' round.
We will hear the sound of a letter
When the train starts comin' round.

 See page 221 for a practice page on initial consonants.

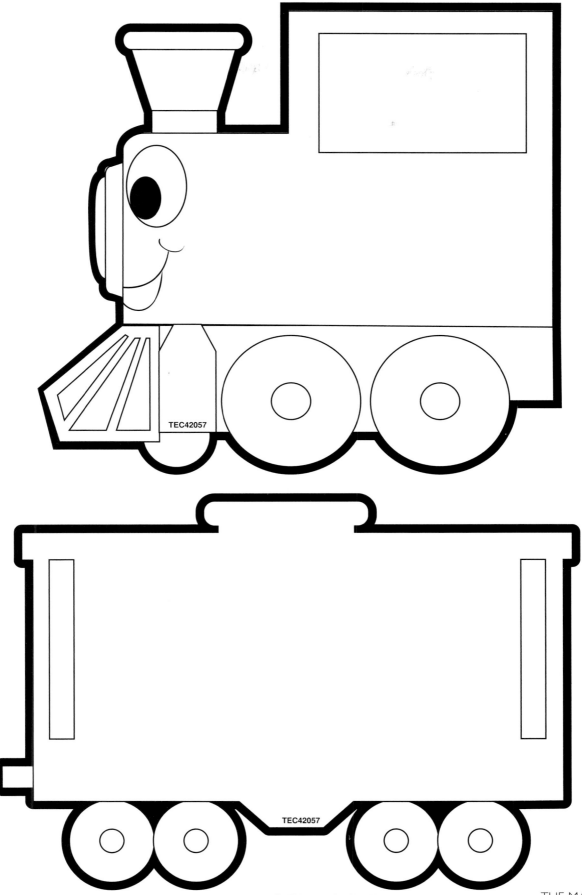

TEC42057

TEC42057

Ready to Roll!

Partner Game Use with "Ready to Roll!" on page 217.

Going Places

 Write each missing letter.

Cross out the matching letter.

p	m	v	s	r	n
d	l	g	f	t	h

___ap

___ing

___at

___en

___esk

___amp

___ig

___est

___an

___un

___ish

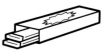

___um

"Purr-fect" for High-Frequency Words

Choose one or more of these ideas to use with just about any word list.

Hear It?
Making connections to print

Motivate youngsters to listen for specific words during this reading activity. On the board write two or three words that appear frequently in a set of sentences or a selected story. Have each child choose a word and write it on a blank card. Then gather youngsters for the reading activity. When a child hears his word, have him hold up his card. To acknowledge students' correct recognition, invite a child to point to the word in the text. **For a variation**, showcase one word each day and have youngsters snap, stomp, or clap each time they hear or read the word of the day.

Kate Wonders, Carlisle Elementary, Carlisle, IA

T-H-E Spells The
Song

Be prepared for students to eagerly recognize, read, and write the word *the* just about anywhere after singing this little ditty! **For different word practice**, simply replace *the* with a three-letter word of your choice.

> *(sung to the tune of "Three Blind Mice")*
>
> *T-H-E, T-H-E,*
> That spells *the*.
> That spells *the*.
> *The* is a word we are learning to know.
> We can read it or write it wherever we go.
> We can say it fast or say it slow.
> *T-H-E, the, the, the*!

Ms. Moster, Saint Antoninus, Cincinnati, OH

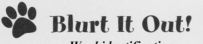

Blurt It Out!
Word identification

When students are granted permission to blurt out words, enthusiasm for a word search is the result! To begin, review the spelling of a word. Then encourage each youngster to search for the word in a book of her choice. Each time she sees the word, have her blurt it out with a sing-song, squeaky, or gruff voice. If desired, have each youngster put a small sticky note by each blurted word for you to check when time permits.

Kate Wonders

 tip → Make a math connection! Draw a tally mark each time the word is identified; then repeat the activity with different words. Later, compare tally marks in a chart to determine the popularity of each word.

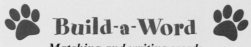

Build-a-Word
Matching and writing words

Here's a simple setup that's perfect for center practice. Set out a list of words, letter tiles to spell each word, and paper. A child uses the tiles to form the word and then writes it on a sheet of paper. **For an added challenge**, have him write a sentence using each word.

Kate Wonders
Carlisle Elementary
Carlisle, IA

Mark
see
can
like

Under Cover
Words in context

Your supersleuths name the hidden words for this big-book activity. In advance, use sticky notes to cover high-frequency words in a big book. Then gather youngsters for a read-aloud. For each sticky note, guide youngsters to use context clues to name the hidden word. **For a spelling connection**, invite youngsters to tell you how to spell each word on the sticky note before showing the hidden word.

Kate Wonders

I see two feet.

Two ☐ in boots.

Read the Room
Kate Wonders likes to post high-frequency words around the room for regular reading practice throughout the day!

Personalized Placemats
Home-school connection, review

These mighty mats make practicing high-frequency words at home extra fun! Give each child a large sheet of construction paper labeled with her name and a copy of a grid featuring high-frequency words. Have her cut out the words and glue them to her paper as desired. When the mat is dry, laminate it for durability. Then send each mat home with a note encouraging family members to use the placemat during mealtime and asking their kindergartner to read the words. **For different skills**, program grids with seasonal vocabulary, shapes, math facts, or sentences for youngsters to practice.

Amy Percoskie
Fox Hill School
Burlington, MA

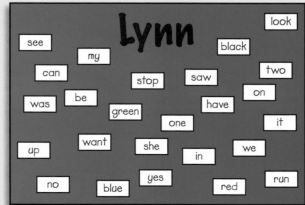

 Don't miss the **skill sheet** on page 224!

Name _____

Here, Fishy, Fishy!

Listen for directions.

are

is

and

my

in

can

see

it

was

the

you

like

Bonus: Pick a fish. Write a sentence using the word.

©The Mailbox® • TEC42058 • Dec./Jan. 2011–12

Note to the teacher: Direct youngsters to circle, color, and underline words as desired. For example, say, "Use a red crayon. Color the fish that shows the word *you*."

Fabulous Fairy Tale

Follow-Ups

These kid-pleasing ideas can be used with any fairy tale!

⭐ Wave the Wand ⭐

Story details

Students' sparkly wands add magical flair to identifying fairy tale–related facts. To make a wand, have each child tape a craft stick to a tagboard star cutout. Then have her brush a thin layer of diluted glue on the star and sprinkle glitter over the glue. To use the wands, make true-and-false statements about a featured fairy tale. If the statement is true, have students wave their wands in the air. If the statement is false, have youngsters hold their wands in their laps.

Janice Burch, Tri-Valley Elementary, Downs, IL

⭐ Creative Castles ⭐

Identifying story elements

After sharing a favorite fairy tale with youngsters, lead them to make this shapely story map. Have each child trim the top of a sheet of construction paper so that it looks like the top of a castle. Then have him fold the castle and label each section on the front and back as shown. Guide him to write and draw story element details in the corresponding sections to complete the map. **For a home-school connection,** encourage youngsters to use their castles as they share the fairy tale with a family member.

adapted from an idea by Janice Burch

Wear It and Read It!

Beginning, middle, and end

These crafty crowns double as tools to help youngsters retell a story. For each student, trim a paper headband so that when it is rolled it resembles a crown. (Leave extra space on one end to staple it later.) Label each of three sections on the headbands as shown. To make a crown, guide each child to draw or write the beginning, middle, and end of an assigned fairy tale in the appropriate sections. When she is satisfied with her work, staple the crown to fit her head. Encourage youngsters to wear their crowns and share their stories as time permits.

Fairy Tale Theater

Retelling a story

A puppet theater center is sure to inspire repeated retellings of a favorite fairy tale! To make an open theater, cut away one side of a large box. Then cut an opening on the opposing side that is large enough for students' hands to fit through. Decorate the outside of the box with fairy tale–related scenes as desired. Place the box at a center along with paper, craft sticks, and other art supplies. Students use the supplies to make fairy tale puppet characters related to a chosen tale. Then they use the props to dramatize a retelling of a favorite fairy tale.

Janice Burch
Tri-Valley Elementary
Downs, IL

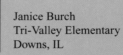

Same or Different?

Comparing and contrasting

This Venn diagram is a perfect follow-up after sharing two different fairy tale selections or two different versions of the same tale. Draw two overlapping objects related to the tales, such as forest trees or castles. Write the featured fairy tale selections to label the resulting diagram. Then invite youngsters to share similarities and differences and record their responses in the corresponding sections.

adapted from an idea by Janice Burch

Focused on Writing

Youngsters' writing skills get to the point with these supersimple ideas.

Captain Capitalization

Capitalizing the first word in sentences

Unleash your students' superhero smarts with this no-prep activity! Model writing a short story, purposefully beginning each sentence with a lowercase letter. When a child notices a mistake, encourage her to be Captain Capitalization; invite her to "fly" to the chart and "save" the story by correcting the capitalization error. Then lead the group in giving three cheers for Captain Capitalization. Continue until the story is complete and each error has been corrected.

Kate Wonders
Carlisle Elementary
Carlisle, IA

A Big, Brown Bear

One day, I went for a walk in the woods. I saw a big, brown bear! It was eating berries. The hungry bear did not see me. I quickly ran away and never went back to that part of the woods again!

Do you have a pet?

I see cats on the rug.

Can you see the frog

The End?

Determining ending punctuation

This small-group activity gives students plenty of practice with periods and question marks. Write sentences on sentence strips, omitting the ending punctuation, and then laminate the strips. Place the strips in a pocket chart. With a small group of students, remove a strip and read the sentence. Guide youngsters to determine the correct end mark. Then have a child use a wipe-off marker to write the correct punctuation mark at the end of the sentence. Return the strip to the chart and continue with each remaining strip. **For independent practice,** label the back of each strip with the appropriate punctuation mark to make the activity self-checking. Place the sentence strips and wipe-off markers at a center.

Kate Wonders

High-Five Writing

Generating ideas about a topic

Use this handy approach during prewriting conferences. After a child shares his writing topic, have him hold up one hand. Then direct him to count off five details he will include in his writing. After he shares his ideas, give him a high-five and encourage him to get "write" to work!

Kate Wonders

For a practice page on **how-to writing**, see page 229.

What Do You Say?
Writing to answer a question

Get your kindergartners writing as soon as they arrive each day! Personalize a class supply of cards with students' names and their corresponding photos. Then tape a laminated speech bubble to each card. Put the cards and wipe-off markers at a table. Each morning, have youngsters write on their speech bubbles to respond to a featured question, such as "Do you like pizza?" or "How did you get to school today?" **For an alternative**, have students write messages to each other from time to time.

Suzanne Ward
Caledonia Centennial School
Caledonia, OH

All About Me
Writing using high-frequency words

What hot topic do young children like to write about? Themselves, of course! Lead each child to write a sentence about herself on a sheet of paper. Help her use high-frequency words—such as *I*, *am*, *have*, and *like*—in her writing. Next, encourage her to write more sentences on other sheets to make booklet pages. Bind the pages between construction paper covers. Then instruct her to illustrate each booklet page and embellish the front cover as desired. When the autobiographies are complete, arrange for youngsters to each have some time to share their books.

Jenna Barton, Forks Elementary, Easton, PA

Guess Who?
Writing a letter

Your young supersleuths are sure to enjoy solving these class mysteries. Help each child secretly write a letter, sharing personal details such as gender, eye color, hair color, and a favorite activity. To sign the letter, he merely makes a question mark. Next, collect the letters and use a code of your choice to know who wrote each letter. When time permits, read a letter aloud and then say, "Who can solve the case of the unsigned letter?" Guide youngsters to use the clues to solve the case! Continue until each author has been revealed.

Kate Wonders
Carlisle Elementary
Carlisle, IA

Step-by-Step

How to

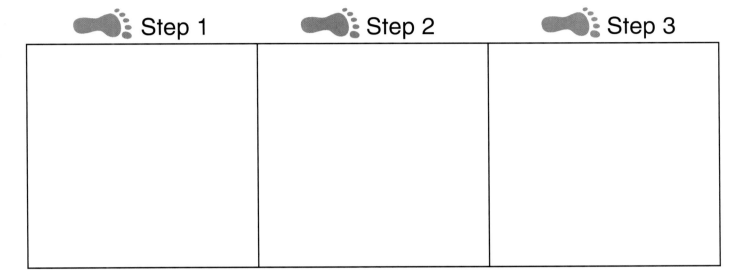

✏️ Draw.

👣 Step 1   👣 Step 2   👣 Step 3

✏️ Write.

First, _____

_____

Next, _____

_____

Lastly, _____

_____

©The Mailbox® • TEC42060 • April/May 2012

Note to the teacher: Give each child in a small group a copy of this page. Help him complete the how-to blank for a chosen topic. Then guide him to name three steps associated with the topic. For each step, direct him to draw a picture and write a sentence in the designated areas.

THE MAILBOX **229**

"Scoop-er"
Letter and Word Games

Dish up learning and fun with this sweet collection of games for whole and small groups.

ideas contributed by Kate Wonders
Carlisle Elementary, Carlisle, IA

Which Bowl?

Initial consonants

Scoop up some phonics practice with this whole-group game. Label each of three plastic bowls with a different consonant. Place in a paper bag small objects or pictures of objects whose names begin with the letters on the bowls. Set the bag and bowls in an open area along with a clean ice cream tub containing large pom-poms (ice cream scoops) and an ice cream scooper. To begin, arrange the class into two teams. Direct a player from Team 1 to remove an object from the bag and have his team say its name and the first letter in the word. The player then uses the scooper to put an ice cream scoop in the matching bowl. If he is correct, the team earns a point. If he is not correct, no points are earned and Team 2 takes a turn. The first team to earn ten points wins.

 tip ⟶ This game is easy to adapt to review a variety of skills.

Ice Cream Social

Matching uppercase and lowercase letters

Students are on the move to match ice cream scoops and cones with this idea. Give half the class scoop cutouts programmed with different uppercase letters. Give the remaining students cone cutouts programmed with the matching lowercase letters. To begin the game, record the time and say, "Ice cream social!" signaling youngsters to move around the room to match ice cream cones and scoops. After everyone has found their partner, check the clock to record the game time. Then collect the cutouts and shuffle and redistribute them to play again. For each round, encourage students to develop strategies to work faster and beat their best time.

Scoop Relay

Word families

For each of several teams, write a word-family ending on a large cone cutout. For each cone, label ice cream scoop cutouts with consonants, most of which will make real words in the word family. Put each team's scoops in a clean ice cream container. At your signal, have the first player on each team race to find a scoop that makes a real word and put it above the cone. Team members take turns until the cone has a predetermined number of scoops. Then players sit and say, "Yummy!" to announce their completion of the race.

Mix and Move!

High-frequency words

Making words is the object of this letter manipulative game. For each small group, write letters to form words of your choice on separate ice cream scoop cutouts. Give each group a set of scoops and an ice cream bowl cutout. On your signal, encourage players to move the scoops to make as many real words as possible. Instruct each team to record their words as they play. After three to five minutes, stop the game and compare the word lists to see which team spelled the most words accurately. **For an easier version**, provide a word list for youngsters to use as a reference.

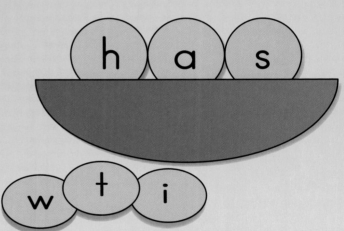

Shake It Up

Alphabetical order

Letters get into ABC order quickly with this small-group game. Place a set of letter tiles in a plastic cup for each player. To play, each student empties his cup and quickly arranges his letters in alphabetical order. The first player to put all his letters in order wins!

Name _____

Supersweet Treats

✏ Write the word for each picture.

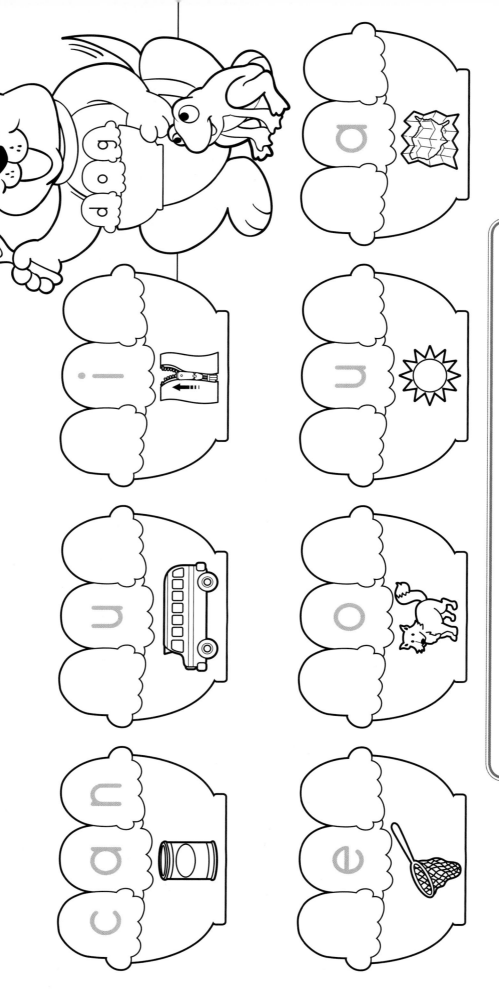

d o g

b a g

c a n

b u s

z i p

s u n

f o x

n e t

Bonus: Change the middle letter to write two different words. bag

LITERATURE UNITS

Leo the Late Bloomer

Written by Robert Kraus
Illustrated by Jose Aruego

*Leo can't read, write, draw, or eat neatly. He's a late bloomer!
Every day his father watches him for signs of blooming. Then,
suddenly, in his own good time, Leo blooms!*

*ideas contributed by Jennifer Reidy, Halifax Elementary
Halifax, MA*

What Does It Mean?

Building prior knowledge, making predictions

Help students understand what it means to bloom with this flower-related idea! Display a large flower cutout. Ask students what it means when a flower blooms. Then ask, "Does watching a flower make it bloom faster?" After students share their thoughts, prompt them to share how they think a person could bloom. Next, show students the cover of the book and read the title aloud. Have youngsters predict what the book might be about and write their predictions on the flower cutout. After reading the story, help students evaluate their predictions.

Flower Flaps

Identifying the beginning, middle, and end

Students make connections to the growth of a flower and Leo's maturation with this idea. Give each child a sheet of paper folded in half vertically. With the fold to the left, have him draw a flower on the paper. Next, help him cut the top layer of paper to divide the flower into thirds and label the resulting flaps as shown. Discuss with youngsters how a flower begins underground, grows upward, and ends as a flower. Then prompt him to draw an event from the beginning of the story behind the bottom flap, from the middle of the story behind the middle flap, and from the end of the story behind the top flap. Encourage students to use this visual guide to retell the story!

We're Blooming!

Making text-to-self connections

Your kindergartners are blooming just like Leo! Have each child make a simple flower stick puppet as shown. Then reread the book with youngsters, stopping after page two. Say, "Leo is still learning to read. If you're learning to read, raise your flower." Comment on how everyone learns at different speeds. Then continue reading, stopping to discuss each new skill Leo is working on and encouraging students to raise their flowers if they are working on this skill as well.

OLIVIA

Written and illustrated by Ian Falconer

Olivia the pig is good at many things—such as wearing people out, trying on clothing, and building magnificent sand castles. It's certainly easy to love this splendid swine!

● See a **writing activity** on page 240.

Move the Cat

Answering questions about a story

After a read-aloud of the story, revisit the page that shows Olivia moving the cat. Then place a stuffed toy cat in your room. Ask a student a question about the book. Then encourage the child to randomly move the cat to a different location just like Olivia does! Continue with other questions.

How does Olivia feel about naptime?
Why do you think Olivia moves the cat?
Why do you think the ballet picture is Olivia's favorite?
When at the beach, how does Olivia's mother know she's had enough?
Why do you think Ian likes to copy Olivia?
How is Olivia different from a real pig?
Why do you think the illustrator only chose to use the colors red and black?
If you were the illustrator, what colors would you choose?

Barbara Mason Worobey, Deposit Elementary, Deposit, NY

Splat!

Dictating information

Olivia tells her mom that she could make a painting just like the one in the museum. No doubt your youngsters will feel the same way! Place a piece of white bulletin board paper on a table. Then encourage each child to load a paintbrush with red or black paint and then gently tap the handle against her opposite hand, flicking the paint onto the paper. Prompt youngsters to dictate information about the art process and the connection to the story. Then display students' paintings and the information in the hallway for all to see!

I'm Good at That!

Making text-to-self connections

Get a red clothing item or accessory, such as a scarf, sunglasses, or a bracelet. To begin, encourage youngsters to name things Olivia is good at. Next, give the red item to a child and invite her to wear it. (She's sure to feel just like Olivia!) Have the child share something she is good at. Continue with each remaining child.

Barbara Mason Worobey

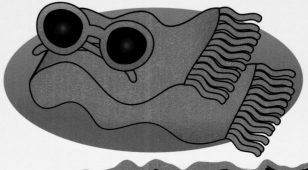

Snowmen at Night

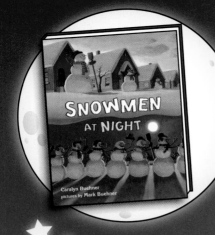

Written by Caralyn Buehner
Illustrated by Mark Buehner

A little boy ponders why the snowman he made the day before looks droopy. He concludes that snowmen must be having a wild time at night, going sledding, ice skating, having enthusiastic snowball fights, and more!

ideas contributed by Beth Parry, Zane North Elementary, Collingswood, NJ

Nighttime Activities
Recalling story details

There's sure to be a flurry of excitement about this engaging recall activity! Gather youngsters in a circle and lead them in singing the song shown as they pass a snowman cutout around. At the end of the song, encourage the child with the snowman to recall a story event to answer the question. Then sing again for another round!

(sung to the tune of Did You Ever See a Lassie?")

Have you ever seen a snowman,
A snowman, a snowman?
Have you ever seen a snowman
Look droopy and sad?
Well, he's been up all night.
He played until daylight!
Have you ever seen a snowman
Look droopy and sad?

The Disappearing Snowpal
Making predictions, observing changes in matter

Stack two ice cubes in each of two clear plastic cups. On the outside of each cup, draw an outline around the cubes and then add snowpal details to the shape. Place one of the cups in a freezer (or outside if the temperature is much colder than your classroom). Next, have youngsters share their predictions about what will happen to the snowpals as time passes. When you notice the classroom snowpal has melted a bit, gather your students to take a look, compare the height of the snowpal to the drawn outline, and reevaluate their predictions. Then compare the classroom snowpal to the one in the freezer. Guide youngsters to understand how the warmth in the room contributed to the ice melting.

Kindergartners at Night
Writing

What would your youngsters like to do if they could stay up at night like the snowmen in the story? Make this class book to find out! Encourage each child to think about an imagined nighttime adventure. To make a book page, help her write to complete the sentence "If [student's name] stayed up at night, _____." Then have her draw a picture to match. Bind the completed pages between construction paper covers with the title "Kindergartners at Night." During a reading of the finished class book, encourage youngsters to join you in reading the repetitive text.

If Amber stayed up at night she would play on the swings at the playground.

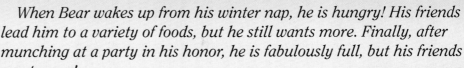

Bear Wants More

Written by Karma Wilson
Illustrated by Jane Chapman

When Bear wakes up from his winter nap, he is hungry! His friends lead him to a variety of foods, but he still wants more. Finally, after munching at a party in his honor, he is fabulously full, but his friends want more!

Beth Parry, Zane North Elementary, Collingswood, NJ

On the Move

Developing new vocabulary

Scamper, *hop*, *shuffle*, and *romp*—acting out the unique verbs in the story is sure to foster students' understanding of unfamiliar terms! During a rereading, pause after the sentence "He waddles outside and roots all around." Guide youngsters to demonstrate what the bear might look like as he waddles and roots. Then continue reading, pausing after other unfamiliar movement-related words for youngsters to act out.

What Happened?

Retelling the story

Your young artists develop cooperation skills as they create the scenery for this dramatic retelling! Organize youngsters into four small groups and give each group a piece of bulletin board paper. Have the members of one group work together to draw a bear's den on their paper. Have other groups draw a strawberry patch, a field of clover, and a pond with fish. Place the finished scenery on the floor in an open area. Then guide youngsters in role-playing the bear and his friends as they go from his den to each food source and back to his den again!

Sentences and MORE!

Word order, reading with expression

To prepare for this pocket chart activity, write simple story-related sentences on paper strips and then cut apart the words. Place one sentence in your pocket chart with the words scrambled. Encourage students to help you place the words in order. Then guide youngsters in reading the sentence aloud. While students watch, write one of the words on a card using all uppercase letters. Next, show youngsters a page in the story that contains a word with all uppercase letters. As you read the corresponding sentence, lead students to notice how you emphasize the word. Then place the card in the pocket chart over the matching word. Have students reread the sentence, emphasizing the word appropriately.

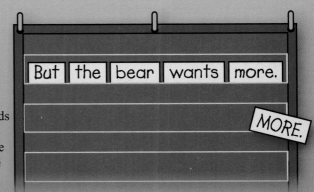

 See page 241 for a **practice page** on recalling story details.

Move Over, Rover!

Written by Karen Beaumont
Illustrated by Jane Dyer

Rover

There is a terrible rainstorm, but Rover is nice and dry in his doghouse. Soon Cat, Raccoon, Squirrel, and a host of other animals join Rover in his snug little house. But when Skunk tries to get in, all the animals abandon their shelter!

ideas contributed by Jennifer Reidy, Halifax Elementary, Halifax, MA

🐾 Rover's Treats 🐾

Answering questions about a story

Students pretend to give Rover's ball a little action during this circletime activity. Cut apart a copy of the bone cards on page 242 and place them in a clean dog dish (or disposable bowl). Gather youngsters around the dish. Then roll a blue ball, just like Rover's, to a child. Have her take a bone and help her read the question on it. When the question is answered, have her roll the ball to the child who answered the question. **For a writing activity,** instruct each child to glue a bone card to a sheet of paper. Help her read the question and then have her write or draw her response.

🐾 Act It Out! 🐾

Dramatizing a story

This engaging story lends itself to an expressive dramatization! Assign each character from the story to a different youngster and designate an area beneath a table as the doghouse. Begin reading the story, prompting the student playing Rover to pantomime the dog's actions and then pretend to fall asleep in the doghouse. Continue reading, directing each character to join the dog in his house and prompting youngsters to flee when the skunk arrives!

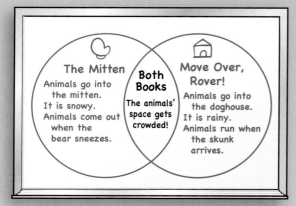

The Mitten
Animals go into the mitten.
It is snowy.
Animals come out when the bear sneezes.

Both Books
The animals' space gets crowded!

Move Over, Rover!
Animals go into the doghouse.
It is rainy.
Animals run when the skunk arrives.

🐾 That Sounds Familiar! 🐾

Making text-to-text connections

Move Over, Rover! has a similar story structure to Jan Brett's *The Mitten*. Draw a Venn diagram on your board. After reading *Move Over, Rover!*, read aloud *The Mitten*. Ask students to discuss how the texts are alike and different, having them point out where the information should be placed on the diagram. Finish the activity by having students name which book is their favorite!

tip → Move Over, Rover! can also be compared to Audrey Wood's *The Napping House*!

Rattletrap Car

Written by Phyllis Root
Illustrated by Jill Barton

It is really hot and Poppa, Junie, Jakie, and the baby want to go to the lake. Will their rattletrap car make the trip? It will with the help of some random objects and a bucket of chocolate marshmallow fudge delight!

ideas contributed by Janice Burch, Tri-Valley Elementary, Downs, IL

Wonderful Word Play!

Rhyming

Use the engaging nonsense rhymes in the story for this engaging activity! Recite the couplet shown and then encourage students to name words that rhyme with *drum*. Continue with the options given.

[Flippita fluppita brum brum brum],
Tell me a word that rhymes with [drum].

Continue with the following: *Fizzelly sizzelly thunketa thunk, trunk; Lumpety bumpety spitter spitter sput, cut; Clinkety clankety bing bang pop, top*

Family in Story	Car Mechanic
used beach ball to fix tire	would put on a new tire
used surf board to fix floor	would use tools to put in a new floor

Successful Car Maintenance

Distinguishing between fact and fiction

Draw a two-column chart on your board and label it as shown. Have youngsters recall how the family fixed the flat tire. Write a description in the first column. Then have students name how a mechanic might fix the problem and write a description in the second column. Continue with other car problems the family faced, leading students to conclude that the family's method of car maintenance is imaginary and would not work in the real world. To conclude, have each student draw a picture of a broken-down car and, using his imagination, write how he would fix it!

What a Car!

Retelling story events

Students are sure to remember several story details with this fun prop! Give each child a sentence strip divided into six sections. Instruct her to number each section from 1 to 6, in order, from left to right. In the first section, have her draw a hot sun for the beginning of the story. In sections 2 through 5, lead her to draw the items used to repair the car: a beach ball, surf board, thermos, and boat. Next, have her draw a lake in section 6 to show that the car made it to the lake. To make the tire prop, have each child color a paper plate so it resembles a tire. Then cut two slits in the plate, large enough to display one section of the strip at a time. Help each child thread her sentence strip through the slits and tape the ends together to form a circle. Encourage her to use the completed prop to retell the story. **For a writing connection**, have her write on a sheet of paper a sentence that corresponds with each of her drawings.

Olivia Gets Dressed

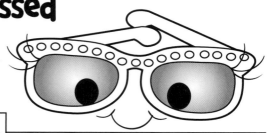

✏️ Draw Olivia wearing clothes.

✏️ Label your picture.

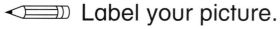

○ Word Bank ○			
hat	pants	shoes	bathing suit
shirt	dress	sunglasses	earmuffs
cap	purse	backpack	mittens

Bonus: Draw a picture of yourself wearing your favorite clothes. Label your picture.

More Munchies!

✂ Cut. 🧴 Glue to show what Bear ate.

Bonus: Draw a bear eating your favorite food.

©The Mailbox® • TEC42059 • Feb./Mar. 2012

grass	ice cream	berries	clover
bugs	fish	honey cakes	apple

Bone Cards

Use with "Rover's Treats" on page 238.

How do you think Rover feels when the animals squeeze into his home?

TEC42060

What do you think the animals will do the next time it rains?

TEC42060

Why did the animals run out of the doghouse?

TEC42060

What do you think Rover will do the next time it rains?

TEC42060

Why did the skunk leave the doghouse?

TEC42060

How does Rover feel at the end of the story? Why?

TEC42060

Why do you think Rover and Cat didn't fight like cats and dogs sometimes do?

TEC42060

What other animals might live in the area and want to join Rover?

TEC42060

What do you think wild animals normally do when it rains?

TEC42060

If you were caught in the rain, what would you do?

TEC42060

©The Mailbox® • TEC42060 • April/May 2012

MATH UNITS

Just "Ripe"!

Apple-themed ideas that reinforce early kindergarten math skills

ideas by Kate Wonders, Carlisle, IA

Apple Seed Actions

Counting sets

Here's an activity that couples math with movement! Cut out a super-size apple and ten large seeds that fit inside the apple. To begin, attach some seeds to the apple and lead students in counting them. Then name an action, such as jumping jacks or hopping, and have youngsters perform the action as they count the seeds again. Then remove the seeds and continue as time permits. **For an ordering numbers activity,** number the seeds from 1 to 10 and invite volunteers to "plant" them, in order, on a chart.

One, two, three, four.

Bountiful Bushels

Making sets

There will be apples aplenty at this hands-on center! Number ten bushel basket cutouts (pattern on page 246) from 1 to 10 and program the backs with matching dot sets for self-checking. Place the bushel baskets at a center along with a supply of red, yellow, and green pom-poms (apples). A child takes a bushel basket and puts the corresponding number of apples above it. He continues with each bushel. Then he flips over the bushels to check his work.

See the **skill sheet** on page 247.

Name

An Orderly Orchard

Bonus: Color the apples on the tree. Write how many in all.

✂ Cut.

🧴 Glue to match.

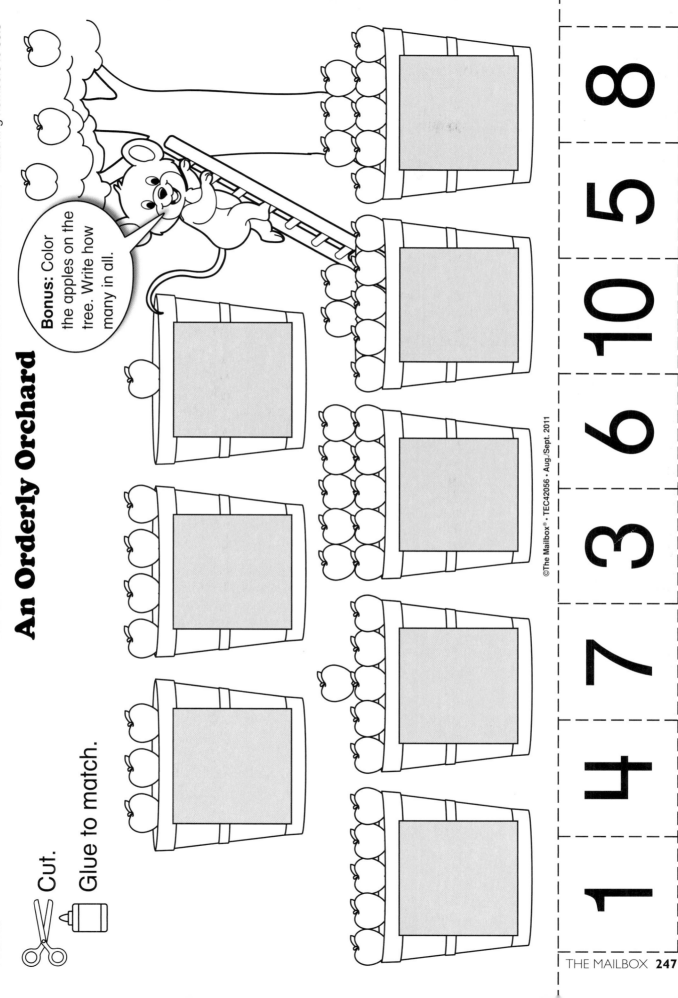

©The Mailbox® • TEC42056 • Aug./Sept. 2011

8

5

10

6

3

7

4

1

Harvesting Number Sense

Count on this crop of farm-related activities to help your kindergartners harvest an abundance of math skills.

ideas contributed by Kate Wonders
Carlisle Elementary, Carlisle, IA

Pass the Potato
Counting

For this whole-group game, have students stand in a circle, and hand one child a clean potato (or a potato cutout). To begin, say a number. Have youngsters pass the potato around the circle while counting aloud to that number. When the featured number is reached, the child holding the potato says, "Time to harvest the potatoes!" signaling youngsters to pretend to use a shovel to dig up a potato. Continue with more rounds as time permits.

Moo! Quack! Neigh!
Counting up one and back one

Farm animals can be a noisy bunch! Make a farm animal's sound a desired number of times and have students silently count up to the number. Then have each child write the number on a wipe-off board. After checking for accuracy, invite a student to say *count up one* or *count down one*, and instruct youngsters to write the corresponding number. Check the numbers and explain any corrections before starting a new round. For added fun, invite students to make the animal sounds.

tip → Display a number line to help youngsters count up or down.

Sheep Shearing
Comparing sets

Youngsters pretend to trim a fluffy sheep when they participate in this harvest-time partner game. Give each twosome a sheep cutout (pattern on page 250), a pair of dice, and 24 cotton balls. The partners put the cotton balls on the sheep. Then each child takes a turn rolling the dice and removing that many cotton balls from the sheep. Players determine who has more cotton balls and that child says, "Baa!" If partners have an equal number of cotton balls, they remain silent. To play again, the duo simply puts the cotton balls back on the sheep.

Baa!

The Mystery Egg
Matching sets to numbers

Your little farmers crack eggs at this center to find out what belongs in the empty egg! Draw a question mark on a plastic egg and put a different number of small objects, such as mini erasers, in each of eleven plastic eggs. Write a corresponding number for each stuffed egg on the inside of a clean and sanitized egg carton. For the last space that corresponds with the empty egg, write a different number. To solve the mystery, a child counts the objects to match each stuffed egg to its number in the carton. Then he finds the empty space, writes the number on a strip of paper, and draws a matching number of objects to show what should have been hidden in the empty egg.

Count-a-Doodle-Doo!
Ordering numbers

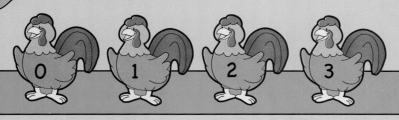

Students at this center are sure to enjoy putting these roosters in a row! On each of several rooster cutouts (pattern on page 250), write a different number for youngsters to put in sequential order. Put the roosters and a long strip of green paper (grass) at a center. A child lines up the roosters in order on the grass. Then she quietly counts up from the least to the greatest number and says, "Count-a-doodle-doo!" If desired, have her copy the numbers onto a sheet of paper.

Go to page 251 for a **practice page** on ordering numbers.

Carrot Construction
Identifying and writing numbers

Eleven.

Students use carrot cutouts to form numbers during this small-group activity. Cut out several orange copies of the carrot pattern on page 250. To begin, show five different numbers cards. Invite a child to secretly select a number and use the carrots to form the number. While she works, encourage group members to guess which number was selected. When finished, instruct youngsters to name the number. Then have each child write the number on a sheet of paper. After checking students' work, ask a different child to take a turn forming a number.

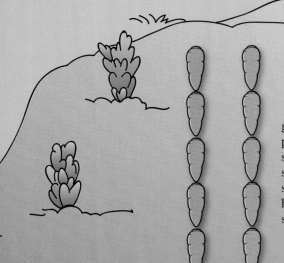

Sheep Pattern
Use with "Sheep Shearing" on page 248.

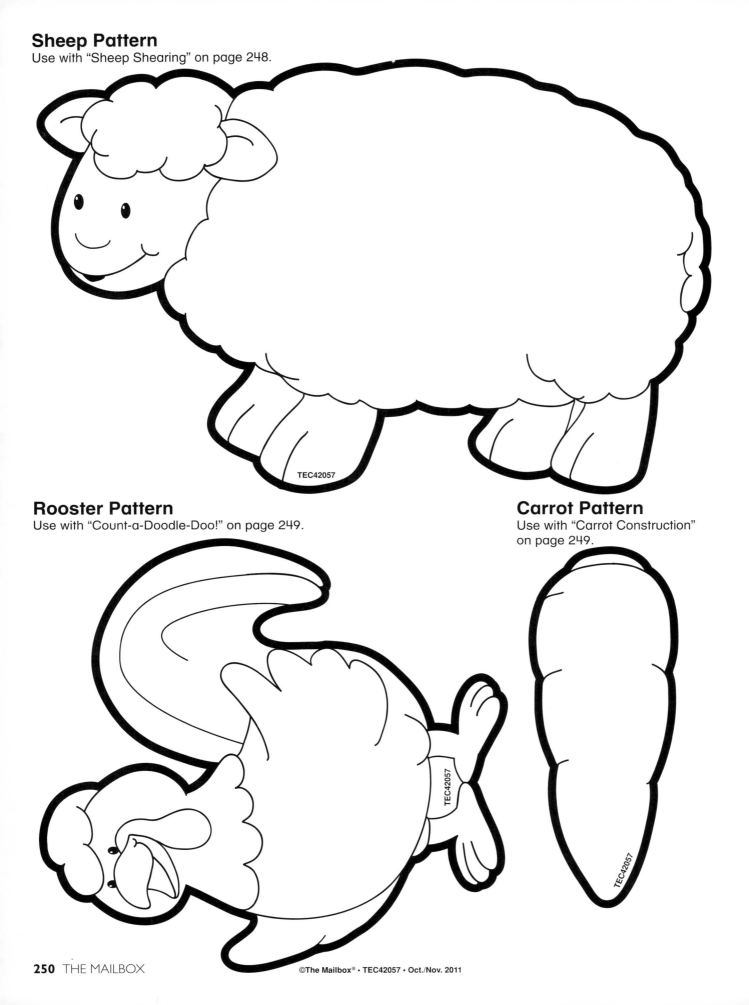

TEC42057

Rooster Pattern
Use with "Count-a-Doodle-Doo!" on page 249.

Carrot Pattern
Use with "Carrot Construction" on page 249.

TEC42057

TEC42057

©The Mailbox® • TEC42057 • Oct./Nov. 2011

Tending the Crops

 Write the missing numbers.

 Cross out each matching number.

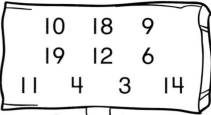

10   18   9
19   12   6
11   4   3   14

2, ___, 4   7, 8, ___

16, 17, ___   ___, 12, 13

4, 5, ___   9, ___, 11

___, 13, 14

___, 15, 16

Bonus: Write the numbers from **1** to **20** in order.

3, ___, 5

18, ___, 20

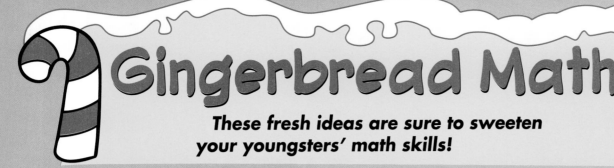

Gingerbread Math

These fresh ideas are sure to sweeten your youngsters' math skills!

Shapely Cookies

Shape recognition

Make these delightful gingerbread pals as a fun way to practice shape recognition! Set out a class supply of plain gingerbread cookie cutouts and different paper shapes. Invite each child to use the shapes to add desired details to his gingerbread cookie. When he is satisfied with his work, have him record the number of each shape he used on a blank card. Then invite each child to share his project with the class and tell how many of each shape he used.

Jennifer Frankle
M. C. Riley Early Childhood Center
Bluffton, SC

▬	–4
●	–2
▲	–6
■	–2

1st 2nd 3rd 4th 5th 6th 7th 8th 9th 10th

A Sweet Lineup

Ordinal numbers

To prepare this partner center, cut out a copy of the small gingerbread cookie cards on page 254. Color the buttons on each card a different color. Then put the cards at a center along with a paper strip labeled with the ordinal numbers 1st through 10th. To begin, one child gives a direction for her partner to put a card above a specific ordinal number on the strip. For example, she might say, "The gingerbread cookie with the green buttons is fourth." After placing the appropriate card on the strip, Partner 2 gives her partner a direction in the same manner. Children continue until all ten cards are on the strip.

Ada Goren, Winston-Salem, NC

How Many?
Nonstandard measurement

Your kindergartners are sure to enjoy measuring themselves in units of gingerbread cookies! In advance, mount on a wall cutout copies of the small and large gingerbread cookie cards from page 254 as shown. To measure, have a child stand next to the smaller cards and lead the group in counting the number of cards equal to his height. Next, direct students' attention to the other set of cards. Discuss with students how they think the difference in the size of cards will affect the measurement. Then have the child stand next to the larger cards to get measured. Lead students to compare their predictions with the actual measurement. **For further exploration during center time**, encourage each child to record her measurement for each set of cards.

Ada Goren, Winston-Salem, NC

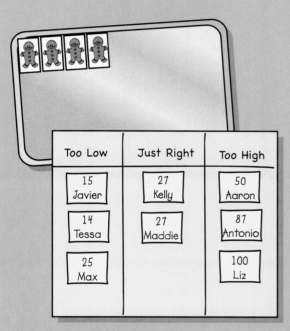

Too Low	Just Right	Too High
15 Javier	27 Kelly	50 Aaron
14 Tessa	27 Maddie	87 Antonio
25 Max		100 Liz

Fill the Cookie Sheet
Estimation

How many cookies will fit on a cookie sheet? Students will find out at this mouthwatering center. Place a large cookie sheet at a center along with a supply of small gingerbread cookie cards (cards on page 254), sticky notes, and a chart labeled as shown. A child estimates how many cookies will fit on the cookie sheet without overlapping and writes the number on a personalized sticky note. Then she places cookies on the sheet and counts how many fit. After comparing the actual number to her estimate, she attaches her sticky note to the appropriate column on the chart.

Ada Goren

tip Do not display the chart until each child has made a prediction.

Heads and Tails
Matching coins

Invite your youngsters to take a pretend trip to the bakery when they play this partner game! Give each twosome a copy of page 255, a paper clip, a pencil, and a crayon. To begin, Player 1 uses the pencil and paper clip to spin and names the coin. Then she colors a cookie with that coin. (If there are no matching coins left, her turn is over.) Then Player 2 takes a turn. Alternate play continues until all the cookies are colored.

Jennifer Frankle
M. C. Riley Early Childhood Center
Bluffton, SC

Small Gingerbread Cookie Cards

Use with "A Sweet Lineup" on page 252 and "How Many?" and "Fill the Cookie Sheet" on page 253.

Large Gingerbread Cookie Card

Use with "How Many?" on page 253.

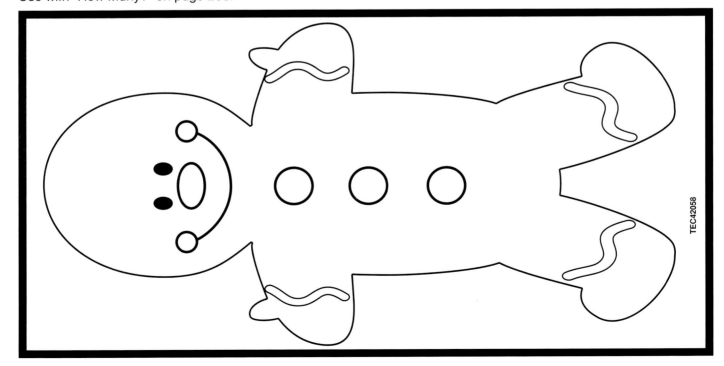

Names _____ and _____

Fresh From the Oven

nickel

penny

quarter

dime

©The Mailbox® · TEC42058 · Dec./Jan. 2011–12

Partner Game Use with "Heads and Tails" on page 253.

Made-to-Order for
Money Skills

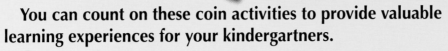

You can count on these coin activities to provide valuable learning experiences for your kindergartners.

ideas contributed by Kate Wonders, Carlisle Elementary, Carlisle, IA

Who Is That?

Naming coins and their values

Coin characters are sure to help your youngsters improve their money skills. Have each child cut apart a copy of the coin character cards on page 258. Introduce each character by sharing its name and its value. Guide youngsters to color and add desired details to each card to help them remember each character. To use the cards, slowly name details about one coin without naming it. Have youngsters hold up the coin character that matches his prediction of the mystery coin. After checking for accuracy, continue with a different coin description.

Penelope Penny

Nina Nickel

Devin Dime

Quincy Quarter

Cha-ching!

Identifying coins and their values

For this small-group game, place one card labeled for each coin—penny, nickel, dime, quarter—and a card labeled "Cha-ching!" in a small bag. At one side of a large open space, invite a child to hold the bag and be Mr. (or Ms.) Money. Have remaining youngsters stand in a long line at the opposite side. To play, the children in line say, "How much is it, Mr. Money?" Then Mr. Money removes a card without looking and holds it up. Players respond by naming the coin and its value and taking the matching number of small steps forward. When youngsters reach Mr. Money's side, they sit and snap, instead of step, to match each coin's value. When Mr. Money removes the "Cha-ching!" card from the bag, seated and standing students rush back to the start and a different child is asked to lead a new round.

Count the Kids
Adding pennies and nickels

In this whole-group activity, your students are the coins! Tell each student that he represents a penny. Then ask one child to stand in front of the group. Continue inviting youngsters to the front until five students are standing. Then give a predetermined signal to alert the five children to link arms. Guide youngsters to understand that five pennies equal one nickel. Then ask additional students to join the nickel until there are five more, and they link arms to make another nickel. Continue in this manner until each student is standing. Then find your class's value by leading youngsters in counting the nickels and pennies.

How Many Pennies?
Comparing coin values

For this center activity, set out a coin card for each coin value you would like to review. Place the cards and a supply of imitation pennies at a center. A child places on each card the number of pennies equal to the coin's value. Then she compares the number of pennies on each card and orders the coins from the smallest to the largest value.

Bonus song!

Ten Cents
(sung to the tune of "Ten Little Indians")

One little, two little, three little pennies,
Four little, five little, six little pennies,
Seven little, eight little, nine little pennies,
Ten pennies equal one dime!

In the Bank
Counting coins

This "cent-sational" idea doubles as a classroom management plan. Laminate a piggy bank cutout and secure ten loop sides of self-adhesive Velcro fasteners to the bank. Attach the hook side of a Velcro fastener to each of the following plastic coins: five pennies, two nickels, and five dimes. Display the cutout and tell students that their goal is to accumulate 50 cents in the bank. When your kindergartners exhibit exceptional behavior, attach a penny to the bank. Each day, lead students in counting the money in the bank. Guide a volunteer to trade in coins so that the fewest coins possible are displayed. When 50 cents (five dimes) is displayed, reward students with extra playtime or a different special treat.

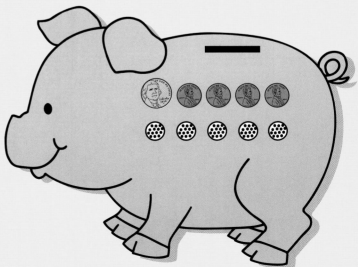

Coin Character Cards

Use with "Who Is That?" on page 256.

Penelope Penny

TEC42059

Nina Nickel

TEC42059

Devin Dime

TEC42059

Quincy Quarter

TEC42059

Addition and Subtraction Barnyard

With the help of some fun barnyard friends, your students are sure to enjoy plenty of math skills practice.

ideas contributed by Janice Burch, Tri-Valley Elementary, Downs, IL

Pigs in Puddles
Addition number sentences

Roll it! A child finds out how many pigs go into the mud with every roll of a die! To prepare this center, draw pig faces on 12 sticky dots and attach them to a set of counters, such as two-sided counters, buttons, or Unifix cubes. Place the pigs and a brown foam shape (mud puddle) at a center along with a die. A youngster rolls the die, puts the corresponding number of pigs in the puddle, and writes the number on a sheet of paper. Next, he rolls the die again to put more pigs in the puddle and writes that number on his paper. Then he writes the corresponding addition sentence, using the pigs in the puddle to help him solve the problem. **For an added challenge,** set out six more pigs and have him roll the die three times to write number sentences with three addends.

3   2
3 + 2 = 5

A Stand-Up Barn
Solving story problems

Animals go in and out of a barn during this small-group activity. To make a barn, trim a sheet of construction paper so it resembles a barn and cut a T shape into the front to make barn doors. Draw barn details as desired and then glue the barn to the open end of a tissue box to make it three-dimensional. Cut a flap on the back of the barn to serve as an exit. Then lead students to solve story problems using animal counters and the barn. For example, say, "Three cows and two horses go into the barn. How many animals are in the barn in all?" or "Seven hens go into the barn. One hen comes out. How many hens are left in the barn?" Invite volunteers to use the counters to act out and solve each story problem. **For a learning mat alternative**, have youngsters manipulate counters on a barn cutout.

Three cows go into the barn.

 tip → Color cubes can represent animals—red cubes can be roosters, white cubes can be cows, and yellow cubes can be ducks!

Where Are the Eggs?
Addition or subtraction

For this whole-group activity, your young farmers search for missing eggs! Write addition or subtraction problems on paper strips to have at least one per student. Put the problems in separate plastic eggs and secretly hide them around the classroom. Also, set out a large basket with a note from Mr. Farmer similar to the one shown. Invite students to hunt for the farmer's eggs. When a child finds an egg, he sits near the basket, opens the egg, and clucks like a hen. When all youngsters are seated, lead each child to take a turn reading her problem and telling the answer. Cluck, cluck!

Please help!
I've lost my eggs!

Mr. Farmer

Shoes for a Horse
Addition and subtraction

Students are sure to want to help a barnyard horse by playing this whole-group game! Give each of four teams a U cutout (horseshoe). Tell students that the barnyard horse has lost its shoes, and it is up to your class to replace them. Then give each group eight math problems. Players take turns writing number sentences on a sheet of paper until each problem is solved. Next, group members check the completed page for accuracy. When group members are in agreement, they each give a thumbs-up, alerting you to check the paper. For each correct answer, players take turns drawing a black dot (horseshoe detail) on the horseshoe. When the horseshoe has eight black dots, encourage players to serve as helpers for other teams. When you have all four horseshoes, congratulate students for successfully providing a new set of shoes for the horse!

Feeding Time
Addition, subtraction, or mixed practice

Which animal will arrive at the feeding trough first? Youngsters find out by playing this partner game! For each twosome, set out a copy of the gameboard from page 261, two animal counters (game markers), a set of math flash cards, and a die. Each player puts a marker on START. Player 1 takes a card and solves the problem. If he is correct, he rolls the die and moves his marker the appropriate number of spaces. If he is incorrect, his turn is over. Then Player 2 takes a turn. Alternate play continues until an animal reaches the feeding trough!

Feeding Time

START

FINISH

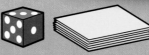

See the **addition practice page** on page 262.

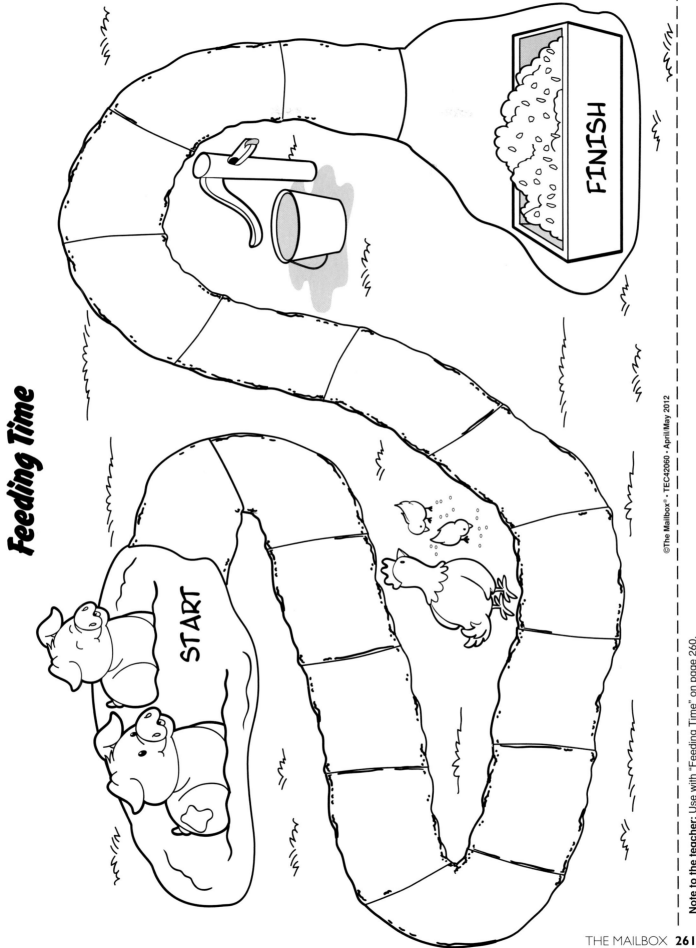

Feeding Time

START

FINISH

©The Mailbox® • TEC42060 • April/May 2012

Note to the teacher: Use with "Feeding Time" on page 260.

Nice Neighbors

Write. Cut. Glue to match.

Bonus: Draw 4 pigs in the mud. Then draw 2 more pigs. Write the matching number sentence.

+2

+1

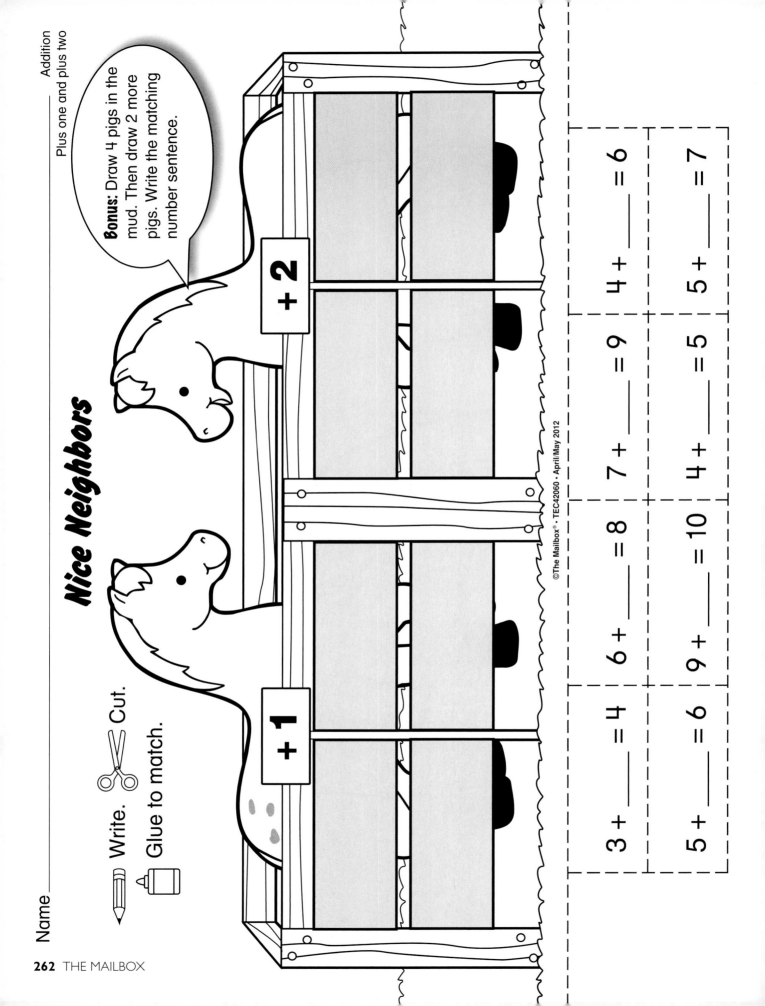

3 + ___ = 4

5 + ___ = 6

6 + ___ = 8

9 + ___ = 10

7 + ___ = 9

4 + ___ = 5

4 + ___ = 6

5 + ___ = 7

Lemonade 25¢

Lemonade Math

This big batch of math activities is sure to be refreshingly fun!

ideas contributed by Karin Bulkow
Washington School for Comprehensive Literacy
Sheboygan, WI

Straw by Straw

Demonstrating nonstandard measurement

Drinking straws are the perfect tools for this hands-on measurement center. Set out a supply of two-inch plastic drinking straw pieces along with lemonade-making supplies, such as a lemon, a measuring cup, a plastic pitcher, a bag of sugar, and a mixing spoon. A child chooses one of the objects and draws it on a sheet of paper. Next, she estimates the object's length in straw pieces and records it on her paper. Then she lines up straw pieces beside the object to measure its length. She counts the pieces and records the actual length beside her estimate. After she compares the two numbers, she repeats the process with the remaining objects.

Likeable Lemons

Making a tally chart

Find out if more students like or dislike lemons with this taste-test activity. Draw a yes/no chart on the board and title it with the question shown. Then give each child a small piece of lemon and encourage him to taste it. Have him make a tally mark in the appropriate section of the chart to declare his preference for lemons. After each child has had a turn, lead youngsters to draw conclusions about the data display. For more tally mark practice, erase the information on the chart and follow up with a different question, such as "Do you like lemonade?"

Do you like lemons?

yes	no
|||	₩

tip ➔ To make a floor graph, use yarn lengths to make grid lines and flat coffee stirrers or craft sticks to make tally marks.

Picking Lemon Pairs

Matching addition problems and sums

Students use problem-solving strategies to play this partner game. Cut out a copy of the lemon cards on page 265. Set out the cards, a large tree cutout, and a plastic pitcher in your game area. Players randomly arrange the problem cards facedown on the tree. Then they shuffle and deal the number cards. Each player puts her number cards faceup in her game space. To take a turn, a player picks a card from the tree and solves the problem. If she has the lemon card with the matching sum, she puts both cards in the pitcher. If she does not have the matching sum, she returns the problem card to the tree. The first child to put all her cards in the pitcher is named the lemonade maker and then she helps her partner make the remaining matches.

How Heavy?

Comparing weight

Are books heavier than lemons? Some are, and some are not! Challenge your students to compare the weight of classroom objects to that of a lemon with this interactive idea. Pass a real lemon around so each child can feel its weight. Next, place the lemon on one side of a balance scale; have students describe what happens and explain why. Then invite a child to hold up a classroom object and encourage students to predict which is heavier: the lemon or the object. Have classmates who think the lemon is heavier than the object squat down low and have students who think the lemon is lighter stretch their arms up high. As the child puts the object on the balance scale, help youngsters make connections to compare the two weights. Your youngsters are sure to have a good time as they continue to explore with different objects of varying weights!

Lots of Lemonade

Exploring capacity

Students size up portions of lemonade during this small-group activity. Set out several clear plastic containers in different sizes. Also provide a measuring cup and a large container of yellow-tinted water (lemonade). Have students compare the sizes of the containers, discussing their thoughts about which of the containers hold the most or the least liquid. Next, have students use the measuring cup to find out how many cups of lemonade each container holds. Guide students to order the containers from the one that holds the least liquid to the one that holds the most liquid. Then invite each student to draw and label his observations on a sheet of paper.

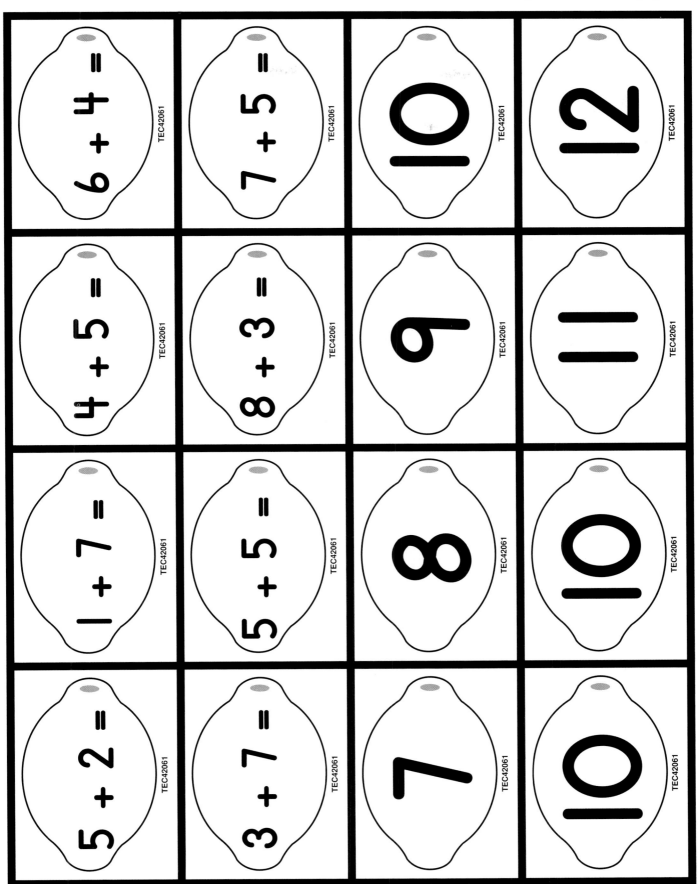

Cool Cups

Subtract.

 Cross out ☐ to show your work.

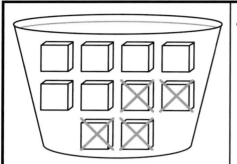

$10 - 4 =$ ____

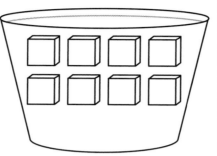

$8 - 1 =$ ____

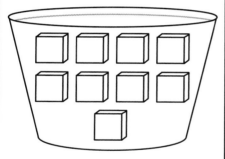

$9 - 5 =$ ____

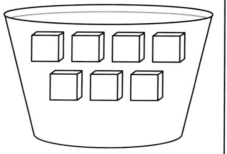

$7 - 2 =$ ____

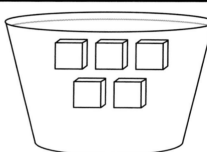

$5 - 5 =$ ____

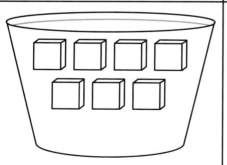

$7 - 6 =$ ____

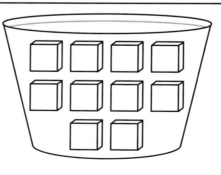

$10 - 8 =$ ____

$6 - 3 =$ ____

Bonus: Draw 10 ice cubes. Cross out cubes to equal your age.
Write a subtraction problem to match your drawing.

SEASONAL UNITS

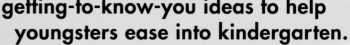

Nice to Meet You!

6 getting-to-know-you ideas to help youngsters ease into kindergarten.

1 Meet Your Classmates
Student introductions

Each of your youngsters gets a warm welcome with this pocket chart activity. Tape individual student photographs to separate cards and then write students' first names on a different set of cards. In a pocket chart, place the photo cards facedown and the name cards faceup. To begin, flip a photo card and guide the corresponding student to find his name card. Have him show his cards to the group and say his name, thereby signaling seated youngsters to say, "Hi, [child's name]." Then have him set the cards aside. Continue until each child has had a kindergarten welcome.

Dorinda Katz, Study Elementary, Fort Wayne, IN

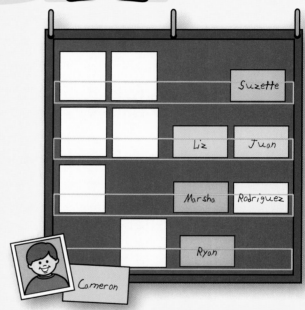

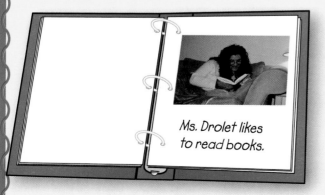

Ms. Drolet likes to read books.

2 Teacher at Night
Teacher introduction

Looking for an amusing way to help students get to know you? Make this photo book! On each of several sheets of paper, secure a photograph or draw a picture that highlights an evening activity you enjoy. Then write a simple caption on each page, modeling your text after the book *Snowmen at Night* by Caralyn Buehner. Slide the pages into separate sheet protectors, put them in a three-ring binder, and add the title "[Your name] at Night." Read the book to students on the first day of school, elaborating as desired, and then place it in your classroom library for youngsters to read on their own. **To extend the activity**, have each youngster make a page for a book titled "Students at Night."

Amy Hart, St. Sylvester School, Pittsburgh, PA

3 Super Sleuths!

Listening for directions

Students solve mysteries during this active listening game. To play, have youngsters sit in a circle and rest both hands on the floor in front of them. Then secretly select a mystery person and give a clue about the child, such as "The mystery person has brown hair." To respond, each child who has brown hair keeps her hands on the floor and each child who does not have brown hair moves her hands to her lap. Continue with different clues until the mystery person is the only one with her hands on the floor. Encourage her to stand up and take a bow before you start a new round.

Karen Guess, St. Richard's School, Indianapolis, IN

4 Who's Who?

Name recognition

This photographic matching book is bound to help students learn their classmates' first and last names. To make a page, glue a student photo to a sheet of paper; below it, write the child's first name on the left side of the page and his last name on the right side. Make a page for each student and laminate the pages for durability. Then stack the pages between construction paper covers, bind the resulting booklet across the top, and cut each page in half vertically. To use the book, encourage youngsters to flip through the pages, mixing and matching their classmates' names and faces.

Sarah Guell, Cambria-Friesland School District, Cambria, WI

5 Perfect Pairs

Visual discrimination

This partner activity is perfect for students to meet and greet each other. Gather a different picture or shape cutout for every two students and puzzle-cut each one into two pieces. To begin, randomly distribute the pieces and direct youngsters by saying, "Make a match!" When the pairs are made, give each twosome a few minutes to get acquainted before collecting and redistributing the pieces for another chance to make a new friend.

Amy Rodriguez, Public School 212, Brooklyn, NY

6 Very Special Vests

Speaking in a group

Individual preferences are on display when students put on these vests. Give each child a paper grocery bag vest similar to the one shown. Have her use magazine cutouts or art supplies to decorate her vest with pictures and objects that describe her or things she likes. When she is finished, invite her to wear her vest as she tells the class about herself.

Kim Lockley, Longfellow Elementary, Houston, TX

Kindergarten Kickoff

Welcome your team of students to school with these winning activities! Go, team!

ideas contributed by Laurie Gibbons, Huntsville, Alabama

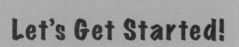

Let's Get Started!

Team cheer, morning activities

This catchy cheer is perfect for welcoming students! To prepare, label each of six megaphone cutouts with a different grade from kindergarten through fifth grade. Invite six students (cheerleaders) to stand in front of the class, each with a different megaphone. Then lead youngsters in chanting the cheer, having each cheerleader hold up her megaphone during the appropriate time. If desired, repeat the cheer throughout the year before introducing a new skill.

First grade's fabulous!	We'll learn to read.
Second grade's great!	We'll play math games.
Third grade's top-notch!	We'll form the letters.
Fourth grade's first-rate!	We'll write our names.
By fifth grade, we know more than all the rest,	It's fun to learn at school each day.
But kindergarten is the very best!	So, let's get started. Hip hip hooray!

Move That Ball!

Classroom management

Use this motivational display to foster good decision-making! Feature a large football field on a display. To begin, put a football cutout (pattern on page 272) on the 50-yard line and explain to students that the ball will move on the field in accordance with their behavior. When your class is recognized for exemplary conduct, such as walking quietly in the hall, move the ball toward the "HOME" end zone. If a troublesome comment is shared about the group, move the ball back five yards. When youngsters' good choices lead the ball into the "HOME" end zone, celebrate with a reward.

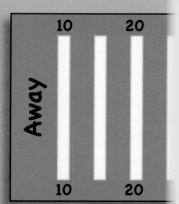

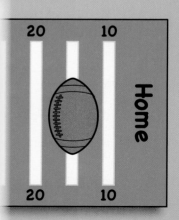

The Play Book

School rules

This class-made big book is perfect for a rule review. Along the bottom of separate large paper ovals (football-shaped pages), write different school rules. As you introduce each rule, show the corresponding page. Solicit students' help to illustrate the rule, or take pictures of students acting out the rule and glue the printed photos on the page. Then bind the completed pages between brown paper oval covers and add details as desired. Place the book in your classroom library for students to read.

The Play Book
Mrs. Cooley's
Kindergarten Team

A "Bear-y" Good Team

Skill review

There are lots of learning possibilities with this team of bears! To prepare, cut out ten copies of the bear pattern on page 272 and color each bear's shirt a different color. Then choose a skill below.

Comparing numbers: Post the bears on the board and draw a simple football field beside them. Announce a number from one to ten and have a volunteer move that many bears to the field. Guide students to determine whether there are more bears on or off the field.

Color words: On separate football cutouts, write color words to match the bears' shirts. Have students match each bear to its football.

Ordinal numbers: Display the bears in a line. To easily identify the first bear, put a paper football beside it. Then invite students to identify the first through the tenth bears by naming the bears' shirt colors.

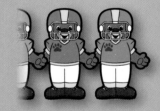

Go to page 273 for **more practice** with ordinal numbers.

Game-Bear Glyph

Following directions

Gather information about your new class with this glyph activity. Using the code shown as a guide, have each child listen for directions to color a copy of the bear pattern on page 272. Then showcase the bears on a football field display along with the code. Each day ask a glyph-related question that helps youngsters get to know their classmates. **For a graphing extension,** remove the bears and have each child respond to daily graph questions by placing his bear in the corresponding column or row.

Code

Bear Color
like football—brown
do not like football—grey (light black)

Helmet
boy—blue
girl—green

Uniform Trim
lost a tooth—yellow
never lost a tooth—orange

Uniform Shirt
have a brother or sister—red
do not have a brother or sister—blue

Uniform Pants
have a pet—red
do not have a pet—yellow

Cleats
ride the school bus—brown
do not ride the school bus—black

I have a sister, so my bear's shirt is red.

Bear Pattern
Use with "A 'Bear-y' Good Team" and "Game-Bear Glyph" on page 271.

TEC42056

Football Pattern
Use with "Move That Ball!" on page 270.

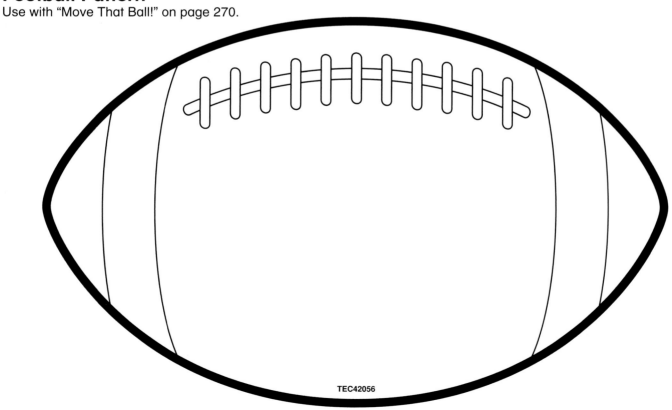

TEC42056

Name _____

Game Day!

Listen and do.

Bonus: Color the bear's uniform to match the team colors in the third locker.

Note to the teacher: Give each student a copy of the page and make one for your reference. On the reference copy, color-code the helmets, jerseys, and lockers. Use the reference to give students coloring directions that incorporate ordinal numbers. For example, say, "Color the second helmet green."

Make It! Display It!

Seasonal Work Toppers

These fun fall crafts are perfect for displaying your students' best work!

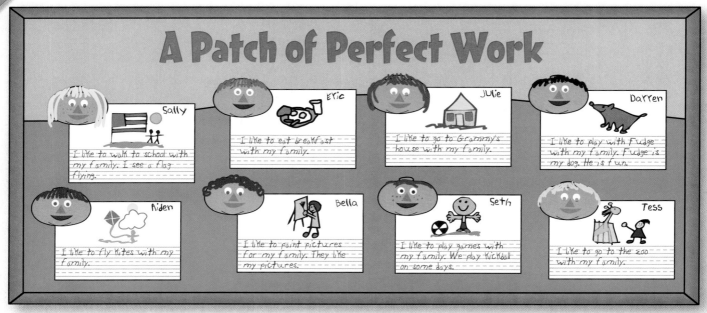

Have each child cut out an orange copy of the pumpkin pattern on page 276. On her pumpkin, encourage her to use craft supplies to add facial details that resemble her own. Post the pumpkins with student work samples and the title shown. *Marie E. Cecchini, West Dundee, IL*

Other Fall Work Toppers

Splendid Scarecrow: Have youngsters follow the directions on page 275 to make a scarecrow. Display the crafts with student work samples and the title "Harvesting Great Work!" *Sue Fleischmann, Sussex, WI*

3-D Gobbler: Have each child color, cut out, and glue a copy of the turkey head and feet patterns on page 276 to a brown paper circle (body). To make each feather, have her glue one end of a construction paper strip to the front of the body and the other end to the back to make a 3-D effect. Post the turkeys with work samples and the title "Gobbling Good Work!" *adapted from an idea by Dianne Young, Seymour Elementary, Ralston, NE*

Splendid Scarecrow

What You Need

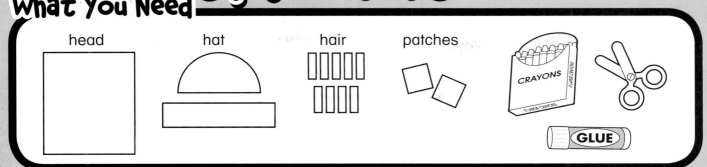

head   hat   hair   patches   CRAYONS   GLUE

What You Do

1 Fold. Unfold.

2 Cut.

3 Glue.

4 Glue.

5 Glue.

6 Draw.

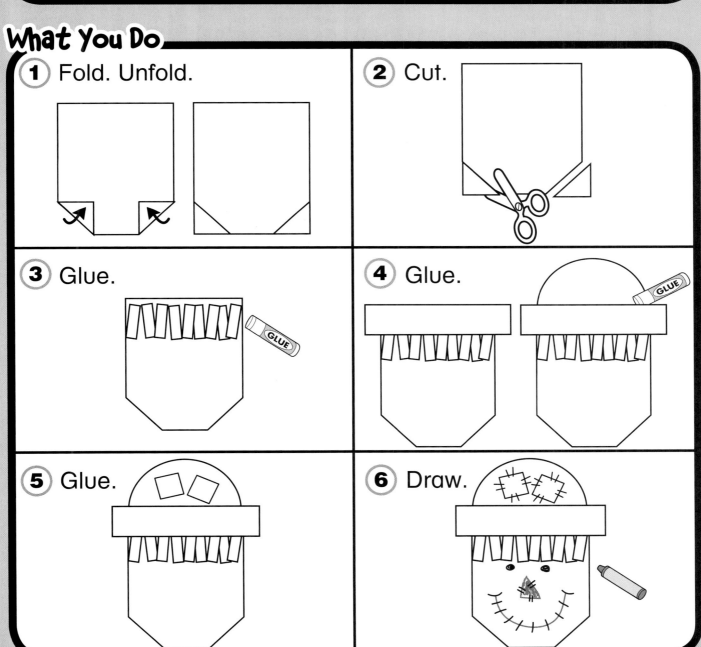

ON-YOUR-OWN art center: Put the activity card and the needed supplies at your art center.

Pumpkin Pattern
Use with "A Patch of Perfect Work" on page 274.

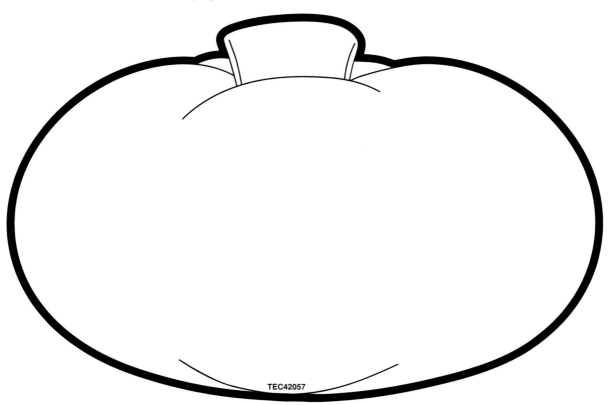

TEC42057

Turkey Head and Feet Patterns
Use with "3-D Gobbler" on page 274.

TEC42057

Seasonal Skill Practice

Thanksgiving

Here's a collection of social studies, math, and literacy ideas that your kindergartners are sure to gobble up!

SOCIAL STUDIES

Give and Get

Discuss with students how Native Americans helped the Pilgrims survive their first harsh winter. Then have youngsters mimic the generosity and thankfulness between Pilgrims and Native Americans with this sharing experience. Write each student's name on a pot cutout. Then give each child a pot that shows a name other than her own. Have her write and draw friendly messages and designs to decorate the pot. When the pots are complete, encourage each child, in turn, to announce the name on her pot and present it to her friend. *Understanding the meaning of Thanksgiving*

Janice Burch
Tri-Valley Elementary
Downs, IL

MATH

A Colonial Sort

Students identify pilgrim-related food, clothing, and tools at this center. To prepare, color and cut out a copy of the colonial cards on page 279. Put the cards, a paper plate, a small basket, and an empty toolbox (or a shoebox) at a center. A child sorts the cards by placing the food cards on the plate, the clothing cards in the basket, and the tool cards in the toolbox. **To extend the activity**, encourage youngsters to name modern items for each category. *Sorting*

Janice Burch

Tale or Truth?

Explore several stories with this book report activity. In advance, display a collection of fiction and nonfiction books about turkeys or Thanksgiving. Invite a child to choose one book. Read the title aloud, show some of the illustrations, and then ask students to predict whether the story is real or make-believe. After reading the story aloud, give each child a copy of the book report form on page 280. Help her write the book's title and then have her color a turkey to show whether the story is fiction or nonfiction. Next, direct her to draw an example to show how she knows that the story is make-believe or real. Repeat the activity with different books throughout the season. *Fiction and nonfiction*

Janice Burch, Tri-Valley Elementary, Downs, IL

LITERACY OR MATH

Two Terrific Turkeys

Turkey cutouts and paper feathers make for a versatile Thanksgiving-themed center! Cut out two copies of the turkey pattern from page 280. Also cut out a supply of construction paper feathers. Then choose one of the options below.

Uppercase and lowercase letters: Write *Uppercase* on one turkey and *Lowercase* on the other turkey. Then program the feathers with uppercase and lowercase letters. A child matches the feathers to the turkeys.

Letter-sound associations: Program each turkey with a different letter. On each of the feathers, glue (or draw) pictures whose names begin with the letters' sounds. A child matches the feathers to the turkeys.

Shape matching: Draw a different shape on each turkey. Then program feathers to match the shapes, varying the size and orientation of the shapes. A child matches the feathers to the turkeys.

Gerri Primak, Charlotte, NC

MATH

A Colorful Feast

Small-group members use Unifix cubes to prepare this balanced Thanksgiving meal! Gather Unifix cubes in the following colors: brown (turkey legs), yellow (corn on the cob), white (boiled potatoes), and red (cranberries). Place each set of cubes in a separate bowl and label each bowl with the food name.

To begin, give each child a paper plate. Pass around the bowls and have each group member serve himself a handful of each food. Next, instruct him to sort the cubes by color. Then name a food and have each child count to determine how many he has on his plate. In turn, ask each student to share the result. To conclude the lesson, direct each youngster to count the total number of cubes on his plate. **For a different skill**, encourage group members to compare the amounts of each food item. *Counting*

Gerri Primak

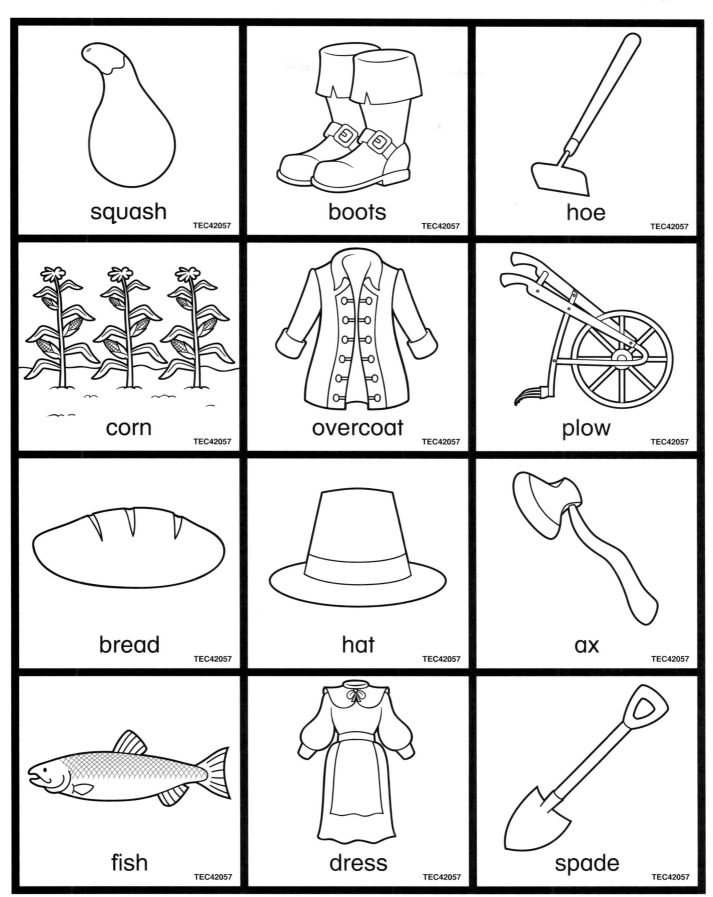

squash TEC42057

boots TEC42057

hoe TEC42057

corn TEC42057

overcoat TEC42057

plow TEC42057

bread TEC42057

hat TEC42057

ax TEC42057

fish TEC42057

dress TEC42057

spade TEC42057

Turkey Pattern
Use with "Two Terrific Turkeys" on page 278.

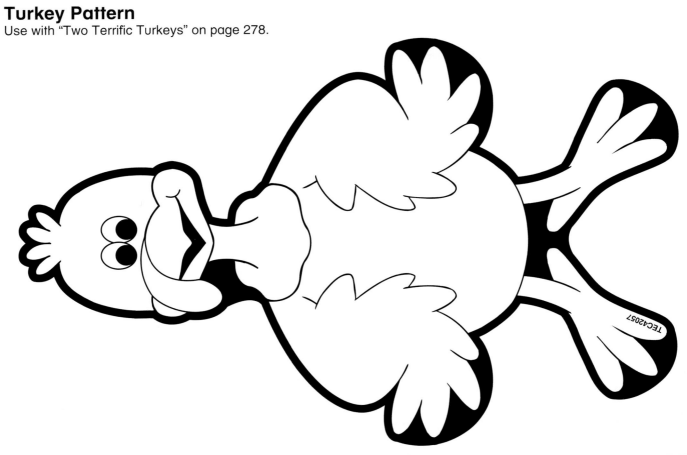

- -

Name _____

Tale or Truth?

Title: _____

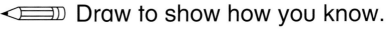 Color 1. ✏️ Draw to show how you know.

fiction

nonfiction

Note to the teacher: Use with "Tale or Truth?" on page 278.

Seasonal Skill Practice
Animals in Winter

Although some animals hibernate when winter weather arrives, your youngsters are sure to stay busy with these science, literacy, and math ideas.

ideas contributed by Jennifer Reidy
Halifax Elementary, Halifax, MA

SCIENCE
Sort It Out

Try this small-group activity to discuss how animals cope with the wintry weather. To prepare, write a different category—"migrates," "hibernates," "remains active"—on each of three sheets of construction paper. Then cut apart a copy of the animal cards on page 283. To begin, lead students to understand how migratory animals move to warmer temperatures, some animals may sleep through winter (hibernate), and other animals remain active and adapt to the colder temperatures. Then distribute the animal cards to group members. Invite youngsters, in turn, to show a card and tell whether the animal hibernates, migrates, or remains active in winter. Then have him place the card on the corresponding sheet of paper. ***Animal behaviors***

Migrates: butterfly, duck, robin
Hibernates: bat, frog, groundhog, chipmunk
Remains active: deer, fox, moose, rabbit, skunk

I really like to go skating.

A bear eats a lot before it sleeps in winter.

LITERACY
Wintry Habits

As youngsters think about how animals behave in winter, they may start to wonder if they do things differently too! Lead students in discussing things they do to get ready for winter as well as things they do differently because of winter weather. Then have each child fold a sheet of paper in half and unfold it. On one half, direct her to draw herself doing something she does during winter that is different from other times of the year. On the other half, have her draw an animal doing something differently because of winter. Then have her write or dictate a caption for each illustration. If desired, bind the completed pages into a class book titled "Wintry Ways." ***Drawing and writing about a familiar topic***

MATH
Cave Count

What do bears and snakes have in common? They both take winter naps! To prepare this center, set out paper, crayons, and a brown paper lunch bag (cave). Place in the cave ten brown Unifix cubes (bears) and ten green Unifix cubes (snakes). A child removes ten cubes from the cave and sorts them by bears and snakes. On a sheet of paper, she draws to show how many bears and snakes are in each set and writes the corresponding numbers. Then she circles the set that has more. She returns the bears and snakes to the cave and repeats the activity as time allows. ***Comparing sets***

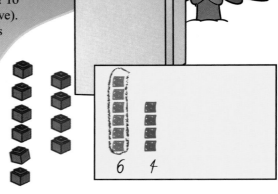

LITERACY
In the Snow

For this partner activity, give each twosome three white paper shapes (snow mounds) labeled as shown and a cutout copy of the animal cards on page 283. To begin, youngsters stack the cards facedown. A child takes a card and says the animal name aloud as he claps the matching number of syllables. Then he places the card on the snow mound labeled with the corresponding number. Alternate play continues until each card has been sorted. If desired, have students list the animals for each snow mound. ***Syllables***

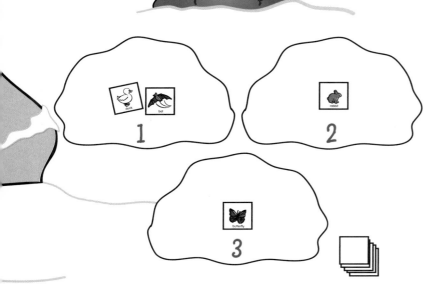

SCIENCE AND MATH
Bats on the Move

Your students will be on the lookout for these changes in temperature! In advance, display a wipe-off thermometer (or draw a thermometer on the board). Color the mercury to show a cold temperature. Then lead youngsters in the song shown and, at the appropriate time, color the thermometer to show a warm temperature. As a follow-up activity, have students pretend to be bats as you color a temperature on the thermometer. If you color a hot temperature, encourage your bats to flap their wings and "fly" around the room; if you color a cold temperature, have them freeze and pretend to be sleeping. ***Temperature***

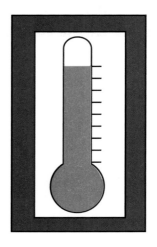

(sung to the tune of "Twinkle, Twinkle, Little Star")

Look at the thermometer.
Can you read the temperature?
When it's cold, bats are asleep.
Their eyes are closed in caves so deep.
When the temperature is high,
You might see them fly, fly, fly.

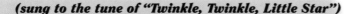

See page 284 for a **practice page** on graphing.

Use with "Sort It Out" on page 281 and "In the Snow" on page 282.

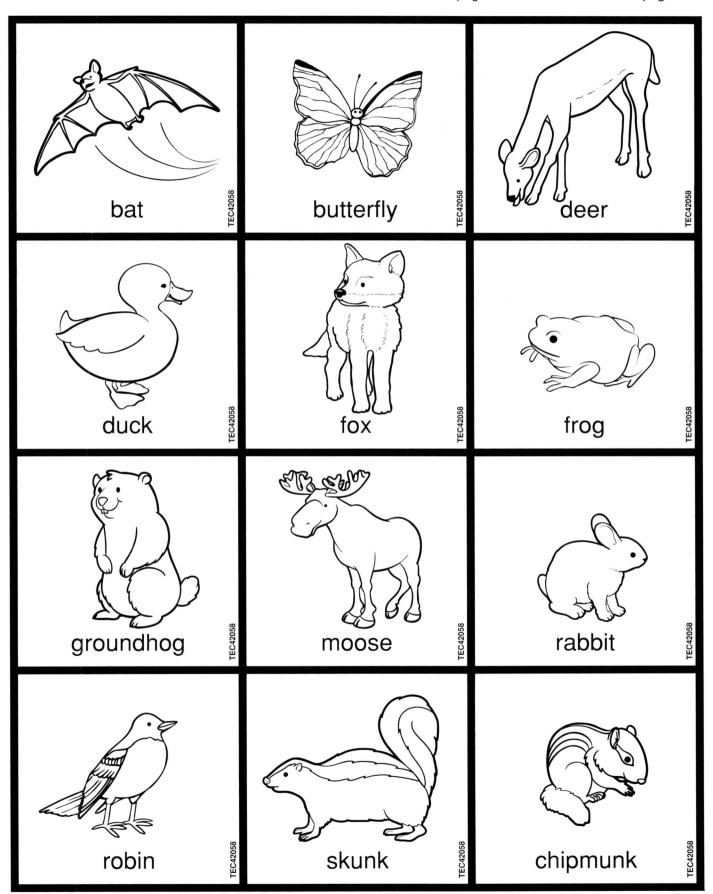

bat

butterfly

deer

duck

fox

frog

groundhog

moose

rabbit

robin

skunk

chipmunk

Name _____

Count.

Color to make a graph.

Snowy Fun

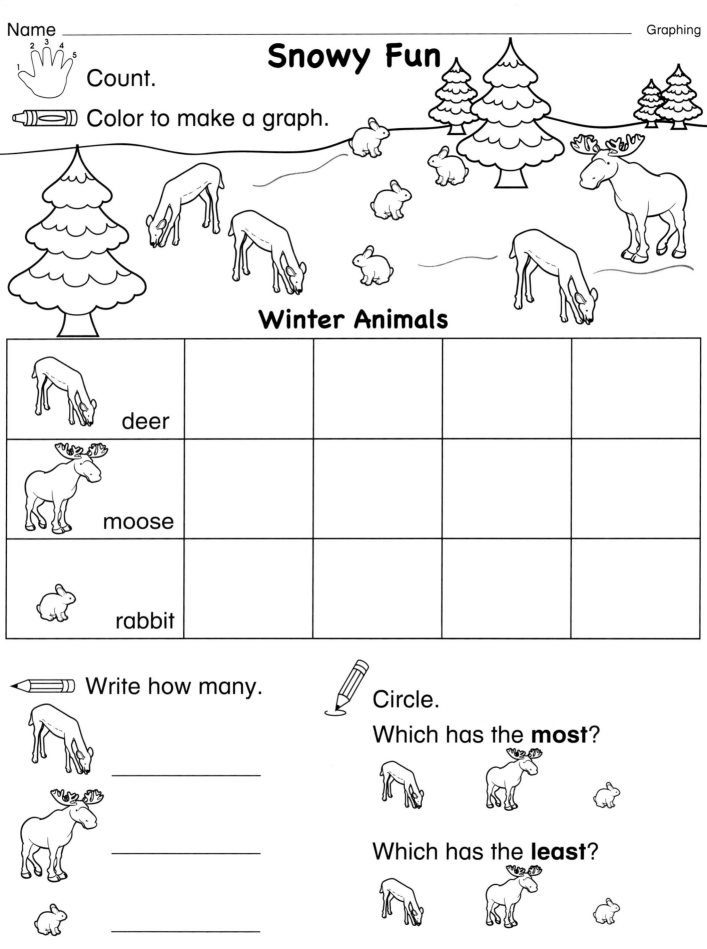

Winter Animals

deer				
moose				
rabbit				

Write how many.

_____

_____

_____

Circle.

Which has the **most**?

Which has the **least**?

Celebrate the 100th Day of School!

Mighty Mats

Get ready, get set, draw! To get ready, have each child write the number 100 in the center of a large sheet of paper. To get set, help her draw lines to make a total of ten sections around the number. To draw, direct each child to draw a set of ten matching objects in a section. Instruct her to make different sets in each of the remaining sections. Then encourage pairs of students to share their mats as they count by tens to 100 two times, using each mat as a guide. ***Counting by tens***

Vatesha Bouler, Sara Lindemuth Primary, Harrisburg, PA

Totally Tall

Students are sure to enjoy counting by fives with this giant giraffe. Give each child a yellow copy of the giraffe patterns on page 286. On each spot on the giraffe's neck, guide her to write each number as she counts by fives to 100. Then have her color, cut out, and glue the patterns to assemble the giraffe. Post the completed critters for a fantastic 100th Day display! ***Counting by fives***

Kimberly L. Fortner
Five Points Elementary
Lake City, FL

100th Day Ditty

Kindergartners will be counting by tens just about anywhere after they learn this little song. ***Counting by tens***

> *(sung to the tune of "The Farmer in the Dell")*
>
> 10, 20, 30,
> 40, 50, 60,
> 70, 80, 90,
> And 100 is the best!

Kiva English, Cato-Meridian Central School, Cato, NY

Say 100 Sentences!

Combine literacy and math with this 100th Day challenge. Announce a word of the day. Encourage youngsters to form a total of 100 sentences throughout the day that include the word. For each correct sentence shared, cross out a number, in sequence, on a hundred chart. ***Creating sentences, counting from one to 100***

Janice Burch, Tri-Valley Elementary, Downs, IL

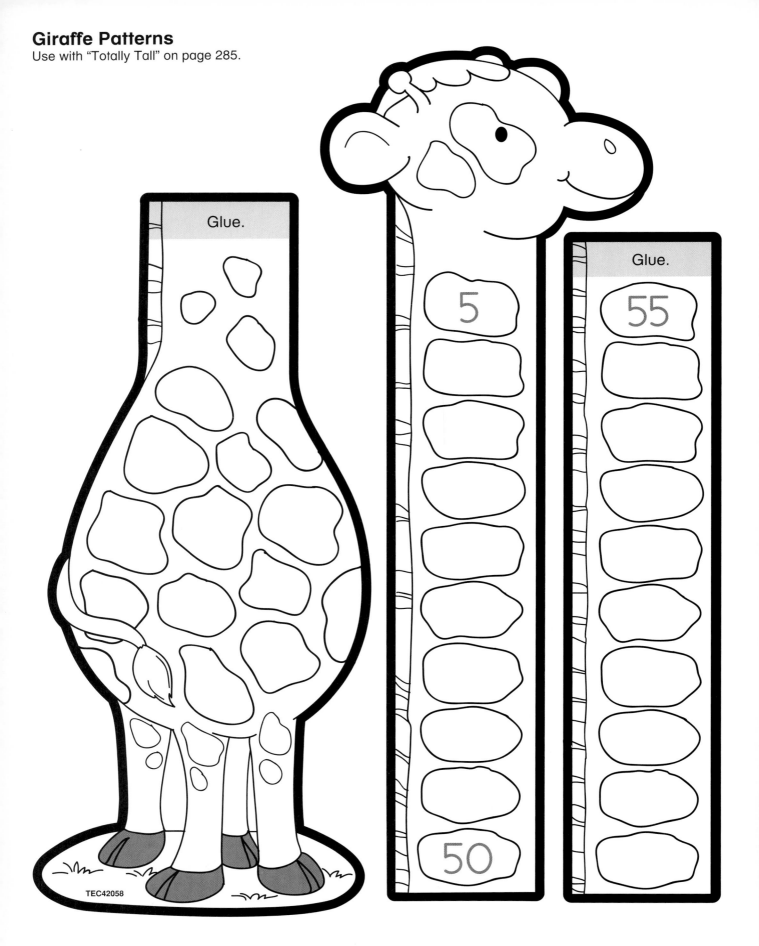

Glue.

5

50

Glue.

55

TEC42058

Presenting
Healthy Smiles

Youngsters are sure to show off their pearly whites with this collection of dental health ideas.

Something to Smile About

This collage project is the perfect addition to your dental health activities. Set out a length of bulletin board paper, a supply of recycled magazines, scissors, and glue. Throughout the day, give each child the opportunity to go to the area, cut out a smile from the magazine and glue it to the top portion of the paper. After each child has added a smile, post the paper. Then ask volunteers to name good dental health habits and write each students' response below the pictured smiles.

Jennifer Frankle, M. C. Riley Early Childhood Center, Bluffton, SC

Crocodile Cavities

To prepare for this small-group game, color and laminate a copy of the gameboard on page 288 for each child. Then cut apart a copy of the game cards on page 288. To begin, stack the cards facedown and give each player a gameboard and a dry-erase marker. In turn, each child turns over a card. If the card shows a frown, the child names an unhealthy dental habit and draws on his crocodile's teeth the number of cavities indicated on the card. If the card shows a smile, the child names a healthy habit and compliments his crocodile on not having any new cavities. After all the cards have been turned over, each child counts the number of cavities on his crocodile. The child whose crocodile has the fewest cavities wins!

Jennifer Frankle

Smile!
No cavities!

Frown.
one new cavity

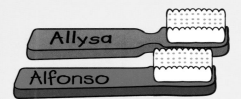

Allysa

Alfonso

Bring Your Brush

Toothbrushes are perfect for sorting. The day before the activity, send home with each child a personalized resealable plastic bag and a note. In the note, ask the parent to label the child's toothbrush, seal it in the bag, and send it to school the following day. Invite youngsters to study the toothbrushes, name different ways to sort the collection, and explain their reasoning.

Ada Goren, Winston-Salem, NC

Great Grin!

Teach this song to students to reinforce the importance of brushing teeth. For added fun, display a copy of the song and invite a youngster to use a toothbrush to point to the words.

(sung to the tune of "I've Been Working on the Railroad")

I've been brushing with my toothbrush,
Brushing every day.
I've been brushing with my toothbrush;
It's how I fight decay.
All my teeth are sure to sparkle.
The entire world will see—
Every time I show a smile,
My teeth will shine for me!

Linda Mixdorf, Edward White Elementary, Eldridge, IA

Gameboard and Game Cards

Use with "Crocodile Cavities" on page 287.

©The Mailbox® • TEC42059 • Feb./Mar. 2012

Smile! No cavities! TEC42059

Smile! No cavities! TEC42059

Smile! No cavities! TEC42059

Smile! No cavities! TEC42059

Smile! No cavities! TEC42059

Smile! No cavities! TEC42059

Frown. one new cavity TEC42059

Frown. one new cavity TEC42059

Frown. one new cavity TEC42059

Frown. two new cavities TEC42059

Frown. two new cavities TEC42059

Frown. two new cavities TEC42059

7 SUPER Seasonal Ideas

Pick and choose your favorite math, literacy, and science activities from this magnificent March collection.

ideas contributed by Jennifer Reidy, Halifax Elementary, Halifax, MA

1 MATH

Compare Golden Treasures

For this small-group activity, set out two brown paper rectangles (treasure chests), 24 plastic or paper gold coins, and a pair of dice. Have a student roll the dice and put the same number of coins on a treasure chest. Instruct each group member to write the number on a sheet of paper. Repeat this step for the other treasure chest. Then guide youngsters to circle the greater number. Continue until each child has had a turn to roll the dice. ***Comparing numbers***

2 SCIENCE

Form a March Weather Team

Your young scientists mimic meteorologists when they give this weather report. Display a chart similar to the one shown. Each day, designate each of three students to be the weather watcher, temperature taker, and season spy. To give a weather report, the weather watcher draws a small picture on the chart that shows the current weather conditions, the temperature taker

Date	Weather	Temperature	Season
March 26		48°	spring

records the day's temperature, and the season spy writes the name of the current season. Reassign roles on a daily or weekly basis to ensure each child gets a turn. ***Weather***

3 LITERACY

Use Shamrocks as Graphic Organizers

Give each child a large three-leaf clover cutout to plan her story. Have her draw on the left leaf the story's beginning, the middle of the story on the center leaf, and the end on the right leaf. Then have her write the story on a separate sheet of paper. Post each shamrock with its story. ***Planning and writing one's own story***

The bird is hungry. Its mom brings it some food. The bird is happy.

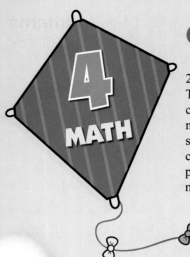

Create a Partner Game

Cut out a tagboard copy of the clock patterns on page 291. Use a brad to attach the clock hands to the clock face. Then write digital times on yellow paper circles (gold coins) and draw stars on several more coins. To play, partners put the coins facedown. A player takes a coin and shows the corresponding time on the clock. If he gets a star coin, he keeps the coin and picks another one. Alternate play continues for each remaining coin. The player with more gold coins wins. *Time*

Make Lamb and Lion Puppets

Have each child draw a lamb face on a small paper plate and glue cotton balls to the plate to represent wool. Then have her glue on ear cutouts. On the reverse, have her draw a lion face and glue paper strips around the edges to form a mane. Then staple the plate to a craft stick. As part of your morning routine, ask each student to hold up her puppet to show whether she thinks the weather is more like a lamb (calm) or a lion (not so calm). Next, encourage her to make a prediction about the rest of the day and flip her puppet as needed. *Weather, making predictions*

Use the Puppets Again!

Encourage youngsters to use lamb and lion puppets (see idea 5) to show the number of syllables in words. Name a one- or two-syllable word. If the word has one syllable like *lamb*, she shows the lamb side of her puppet; if the word has two syllables like *lion*, she shows the lion side. *Syllables*

Set Up a Center

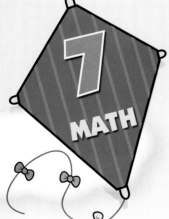

Set out copies of the recording sheet on page 291, one die, 12 cotton balls, and a large blue paper (sky). A child rolls the die, uses the matching number of cotton balls to form a cloud on the sky, and writes the number on his paper. Then he repeats the steps to create a second cloud. Next, he uses the props to help him solve the problem and then writes the sum. To continue, he simply removes the clouds, and he's ready to roll. *Addition with manipulatives*

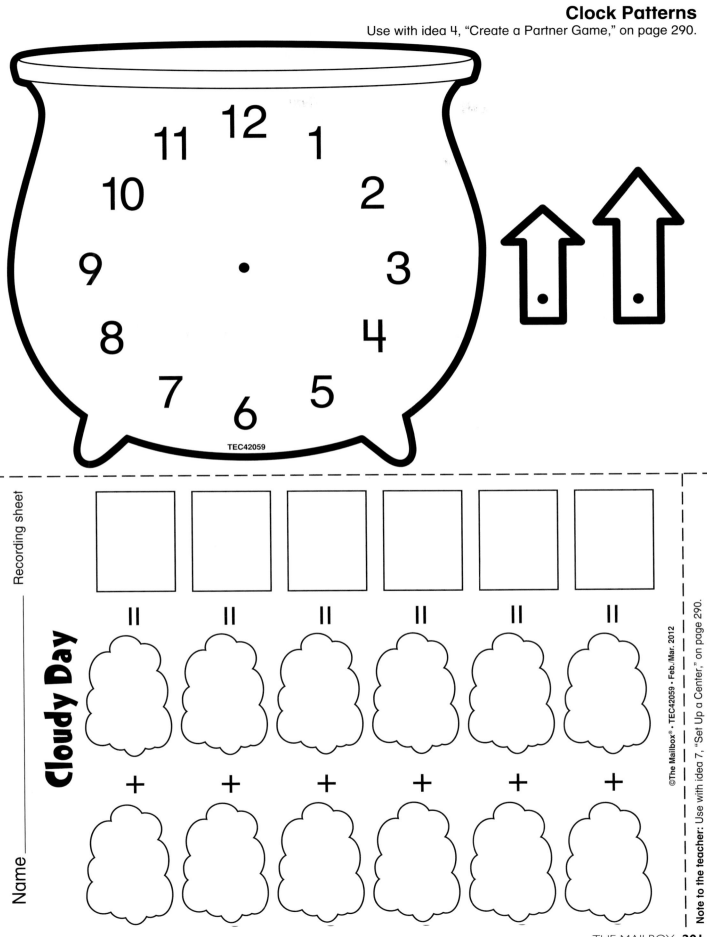

12 11 1 10 2 9 3 8 4 7 5 6

TEC42059

Recording sheet

Cloudy Day

Name _____

$=$ $=$ $=$ $=$ $=$ $=$

$+$ $+$ $+$ $+$ $+$ $+$

©The Mailbox® • TEC42059 • Feb./Mar. 2012

Note to the teacher: Use with idea 7, "Set Up a Center," on page 290.

Lucky Leprechaun

✏️ Write each time.

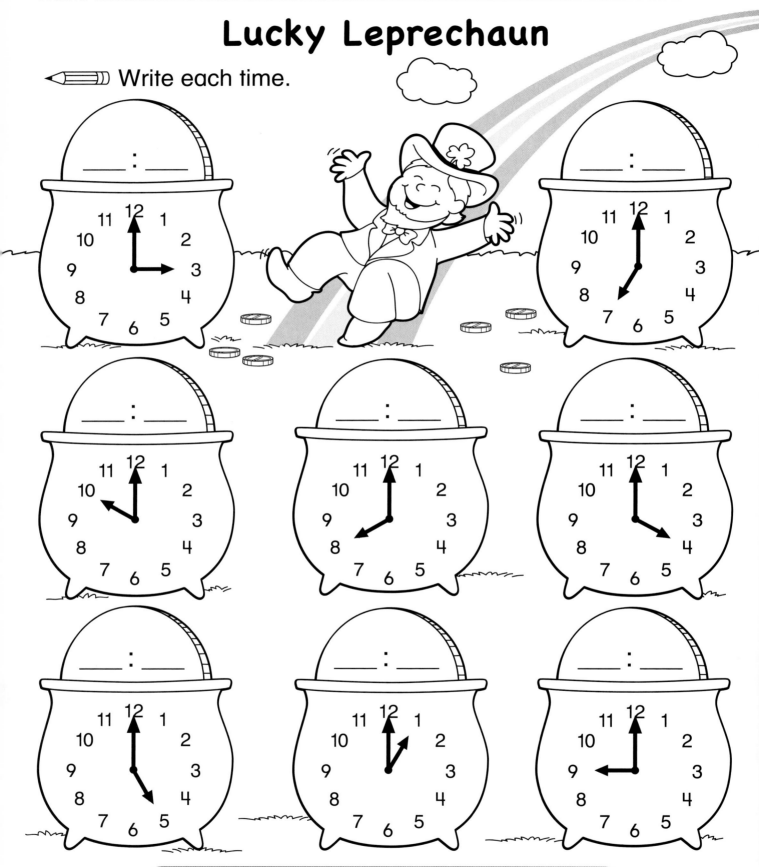

Bonus: Write the two numbers that clock hands point to at **6:00**.

©The Mailbox® • TEC42059 • Feb./Mar. 2012

This springtime collection of butterfly activities is perfect for incorporating reading, writing, addition, and more into your lesson plans!

SCIENCE
An Egg and Beyond!

Explore the life cycle of a butterfly with this hands-on idea. Have each child glue a pom-pom (egg) to a leaf cutout; glue three pom-poms (caterpillar) to a trimmed leaf, as if the critter munched the leaf; draw a chrysalis on a small paper bag; and glue a butterfly cutout (pattern on page 295) to a craft stick. Have her store the loose pieces in the bag. To demonstrate the life cycle, she removes the egg and caterpillar from the bag. She explains that when the egg hatches, out comes a caterpillar; it eats leaves and grows up. Next, she puts the caterpillar in the bag and tells about the pupa stage. Then she frees her butterfly from the bag, describing how a beautiful butterfly comes out of the chrysalis. Finally, she tells how the butterfly will lay eggs and how the cycle begins again. *Life cycle of a butterfly*

Jennifer Reidy, Halifax Elementary, Halifax, MA

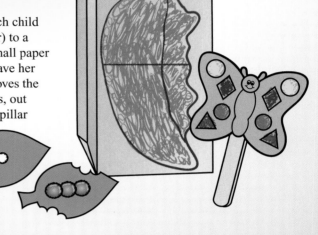

SCIENCE
Life Cycle Mystery

For this small-group activity, color and cut apart a copy of the butterfly life cycle cards on page 295. Display three of the four cards and ask what stage is missing from the life cycle. Guide youngsters to order the three cards and name the missing card. When named, show the card that completes the cycle. Continue with different mystery cards. *Life cycle of a butterfly, vocabulary*

Diane L. Flohr, Orchard Trails Elementary, Kent City, MI

LITERACY
Wonder Wings

When students assemble these butterflies, the result is a collection of compound words! For this center, cut out several copies of the wing patterns on page 295. To prepare each butterfly, write the first word in a compound word on a left wing, write the second word on a right wing, and draw a face on a paper oval (butterfly body). Draw a picture on each wing to match. When a child visits the center, she sorts the left and right wings. She reads the words to form compound words and puts the corresponding wings with a butterfly body. If desired, have her write each compound word and draw a picture to match. *Compound words*

Jennifer Reidy

MATH
Fluttering Around the Flowers

Uncooked bow-tie pasta and flower cutouts are perfect tools to review just about any math skill. Give each child 12 mini pasta pieces (butterflies) and a large flower cutout. Then lead youngsters to use the manipulatives to solve addition, subtraction, and story problems. The butterflies can also be used to compare sets, solve problems with missing addends, and discover equivalent sums. The opportunities are limitless! *Review*

Jennifer Reidy
Halifax Elementary
Halifax, MA

 tip → To colorize the butterflies, soak the uncooked pasta pieces in mixtures of food coloring and rubbing alcohol and then set them out to dry.

READING and MATH
Singing About Symmetry!

Guide students to paint or draw a symmetrical butterfly. After comparing the insects and their matching wings, have each child cut out and glue her butterfly to a craft stick to make a pointer. Then display the song shown. Invite youngsters to take turns using their butterflies to point to each word as you lead them in singing the song. When students are familiar with the tune, put the chart and butterflies at a center for youngsters to practice independently. *Symmetry, tracking print*

(sung to the tune of "The Itsy-Bitsy Spider")

The little butterfly is colorful and bright.
It has a pair of wings on the left and on the right.
Take a careful look—see the wings match perfectly.
Yes, on every butterfly, we can see some symmetry!

adapted from an idea by Jodi Darter, Cabool Elementary, Cabool, MO

WRITING
Pencil Pal

Students are sure to be inspired to write butterfly facts with this writing tool! Have each child color and cut out a copy of the butterfly pattern on page 295. If desired, post an example of how to color the wings symmetrically. When ready, cut slits large enough to fit a pencil at the top and bottom of his butterfly's body. Then help him slide the butterfly onto a pencil. Encourage him to look at his butterfly to help him write sentences about butterflies. **For a story-writing variation**, have him write a creative tale featuring his butterfly as the main character. *Writing sentences*

Jennifer Reidy

 See the word family skill sheet on page 296.

Butterfly Pattern
Use with "An Egg and Beyond!" on page 293 and "Pencil Pal" on page 294.

Butterfly Wing Patterns
Use with "Wonder Wings" on page 293.

TEC42060

TEC42060

Butterfly Life Cycle Cards
Use with "Life Cycle Mystery" on page 293.

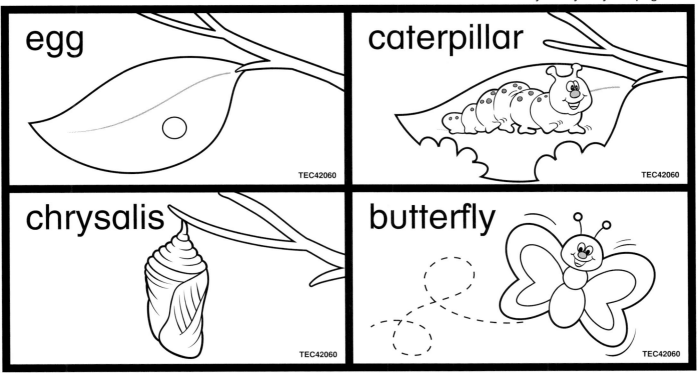

egg

TEC42060

caterpillar

TEC42060

chrysalis

TEC42060

butterfly

TEC42060

Name _____

High in the Sky

✏️ Write the word for each picture.

🖍️ Color the matching ⬭ .

snap

map

lap

clap

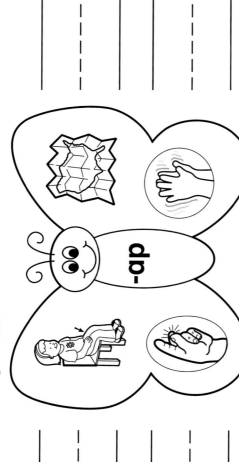

-ap

-op

Bonus: Pick a word family. Use each word in a sentence.

©The Mailbox® • TEC42060 • April/May 2012

hop

pop

mop

stop

Picnic

Serve several helpings of literacy and math practice with these picnic-themed activities.

ideas contributed by Jennifer Reidy, Halifax Elementary, Halifax, MA

LITERACY

A Seed Sort

This watermelon center can be used with just about any group of common words. Label a watermelon slice cutout for each category of words you would like to review, such as colors, numbers, and shapes. Then write several words in each category on separate seed cutouts. A child sorts the words to match the corresponding categories. **For an easier version,** draw seed outlines on each slice to show the total number of words per category. *Word categories*

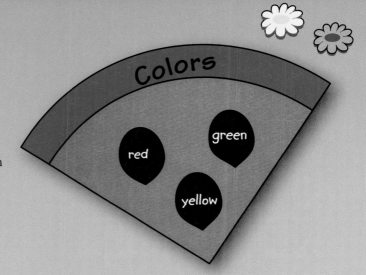

Colors

red   green   yellow

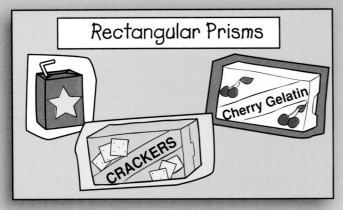

Rectangular Prisms

Cherry Gelatin

CRACKERS

tip → For added fun, label each of four sections of a checkered tablecloth instead of using the placemats.

MATH

An Assortment of Snacks

The materials for this group activity are all you need for a ready-to-use center! Label each of four sheets of paper with a different shape to serve as placemats. Then put food-related objects or photos of food that match the chosen shapes into a picnic basket. To begin, invite a child to remove an item from the basket and show it to the group. Lead youngsters to chant, "A tisket, a tasket, there's a [name of shape] in our basket." The child then places the item on the corresponding placemat. Continue with the remaining items in the basket. **For the center activity,** simply set out the picnic basket and placemats for youngsters to sort independently. *Recognizing shapes*

 See page 300 for a **practice page** on matching shapes.

A Walk in the Woods

What could be picnicking under a tree? Youngsters decide with this pocket chart activity! Display the poem shown in a pocket chart. To begin, encourage students to pretend they are walking in the woods and come across a group of picnicking animals. Next, lead the group in reading the poem. For each blank, invite a child to name the number of critters, the type of critter, and what they are eating. Record her responses on sentence strips and slide them into the pocket chart. Then invite her to point to each word as the class recites the completed poem. Continue with different volunteers as time permits. ***Tracking print, reading familiar text***

I walked into the woods today,

And what did I see?

Five furry cats

Picnicking under a tree.

They ate lots of cake.

It was such a fun day.

Then they all ran away

And went off to play!

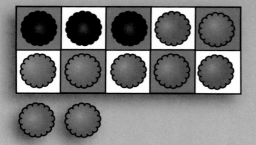

There are three black ants at the picnic. Then nine red ants joined them. How many ants are at the picnic in all?

Ants on the Move!

Several strategies can be used to solve problems associated with these picnic invaders. Cut a checkered tablecloth to make ten frames. Have students sit in pairs with a ten frame. Give one partner ten red pom-poms and give the other ten black pom-poms. Then tell picnic-related story problems involving ants. Have each duo move the pom-poms (ants) to help them solve the problem. Instruct each child to write the matching number sentence. Continue with different problems before encouraging each twosome to create their own word problem to solve and record. ***Solving word problems***

Serving a Story

These picnic pouches are perfect for storing students' work! Instruct each child to paint the back of a paper plate. When the plate is dry, cut it in half. Keeping the painted side out, help her staple the halves together to make a pouch. Then have her write the title of a desired storybook on a yellow paper strip (pouch handle) and staple the handle to the pouch. Following a read-aloud of the featured story, give each student a copy of page 299. Guide her to write or draw on each pattern to complete the page. Then have her cut out the patterns and store the cutouts in her pouch. Encourage her to use her work to retell the story to family members and friends. ***Identifying story elements and parts of a story***

The Teddy Bear's Picnic

Setting

End

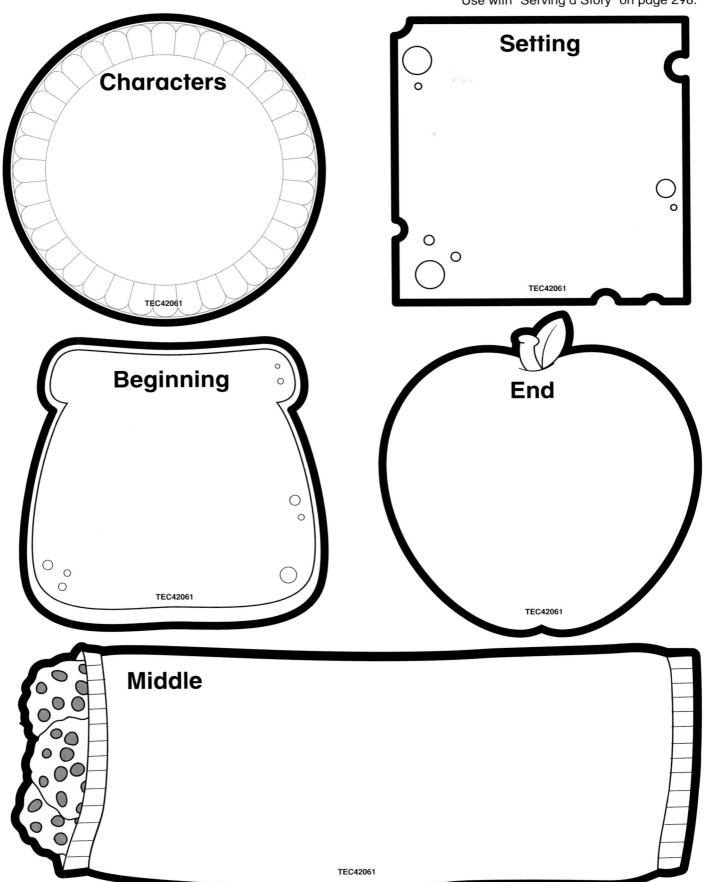

Characters

TEC42061

Setting

TEC42061

Beginning

TEC42061

End

TEC42061

Middle

TEC42061

Name _____

Yum, Yum, Yummy!

✂ Cut. Sort.

🍾 Glue.

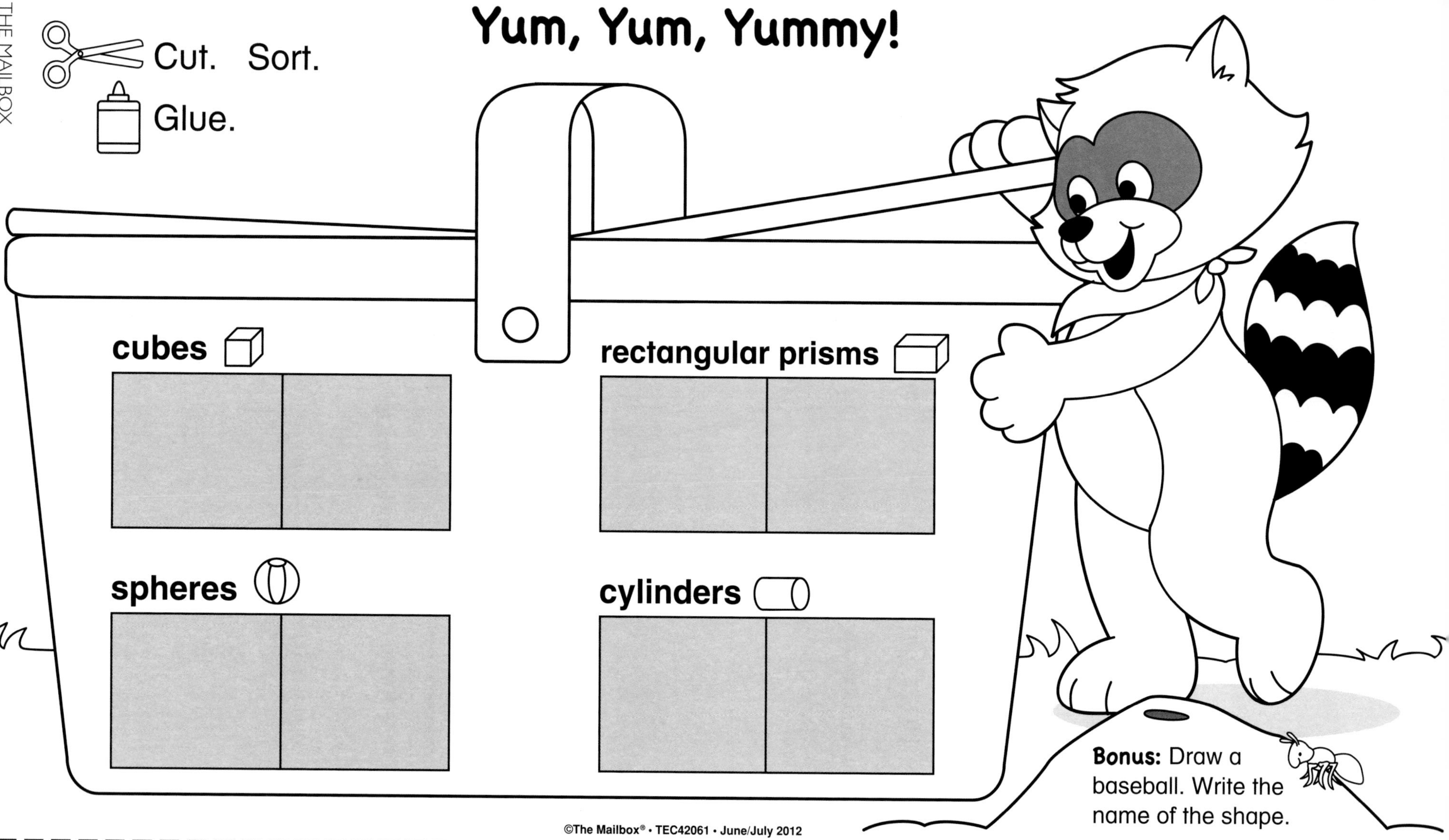

rectangular prisms

cubes

cylinders

spheres

Bonus: Draw a baseball. Write the name of the shape.

COOKIES

Celebrate Kindergarten!

Youngsters will give a cheer for these year-end ideas.

Memory Walk

This unique **floor display** helps youngsters recall their favorite kindergarten activities and events. Write the name of each month of the school year on a separate 12" x 18" sheet of construction paper (posters). Brainstorm different activities and events that took place throughout the year. For each memory, assign a student to trim an available photograph or draw a picture on a card, add a caption, and glue it to the corresponding month's poster. When the posters are complete, use clear Con-Tact covering to attach the posters, in order, to a long floor space, such as in the hallway by your classroom. Then invite youngsters to walk along the path of posters to remember the fun times they had in kindergarten.

Ellen McNeil
Naval Submarine Base Kings Bay Child Development Center
Kings Bay, GA

Squeaky-Clean Review

Here's a fun way to engage students in meaningful **skill practice** while enhancing the room's atmosphere at the same time! Squirt a generous dollop of nonmentholated shaving cream onto each child's desk. Have him use his hands to spread the shaving cream into an even layer on his desktop. Then call out high-frequency words, math facts, shapes, letter sounds, or other skills you would like students to review. As you name a word or call out a shape, have each child write or draw in the shaving cream to match the skill. After scanning for accuracy, direct students to smooth the shaving cream and wait for your next direction. At the end of the review, have each child simply wipe the shaving cream off his desk with a paper towel. Voilà! You have lots of skill review, clean desks, and a fresh-smelling room!

Susan Cortright, Pittsford Area Schools, Pittsford, MI

An Out-of-This-World Week

For the last five days of school, feature **favorite activities** for a different subject each day. If desired, incorporate a theme throughout the week as well. For example, to prepare a "Rocket Into Reading" (space theme) for the last Monday, invite students to share their favorite reading activities, such as partner reading, readers' theater, phonemic-awareness activities, and DEAR time. Then have students participate in nothing but their favorite reading activities on that day! At the end of the day, reading materials can be stored away for use the next year. For each remaining day, possible space themes include "Math on the Moon," "Stellar Spellers," "Astronaut Artists and Authors," and "Cosmic Center Stuff!"

Lorin Ervin, Greenwald Memorial Elementary, New Kensington, PA

Dear Mr. Hardy,
Thank you for helping me with my painting. I like your art class.

Destiny

Special Staff

Invite youngsters to express their gratitude to school staff members by writing **thank-you notes**. Have each child choose a staff member, such as the principal, custodian, or media specialist. Guide her to write a sentence or two thanking the recipient for something special they did that year. When she is finished writing, direct her to sign her name and add an illustration. When time permits, invite students to deliver their notes to the intended recipients.

Angie Kutzer, Garrett Elementary, Mebane, NC

Fabulous Frames

Make these colorful **keepsakes** for your students. To make one, glue a signed copy of the poem shown in the center of a four-inch tagboard square and attach magnetic strips to each of the corners. On the other side, glue a student's photo to the center of the square. Then glue a different-colored crayon along each edge to frame the photo. On the last day of school, present each youngster with his frame. It is sure to become a cherished kindergarten memory.

adapted from an idea by Susan Connolly
South Boston Catholic Academy
Boston, MA

Reading, writing, and drawing too—
Kindergarten work was fun to do!
Red, orange, yellow, or blue,
I will always remember you!

Ms. Connolly

TEACHER RESOURCE

Ready to Meet!

10 Tips for Terrific Parent-Teacher Conferences

1 Send Home a Reminder

Write on a strip of construction paper each child's name, her conference date and time, and a quick reminder message. Tape each strip around the corresponding child's wrist like a bracelet on the day before her parents' scheduled conference.

...rence Oct. 19 7:15pm

2 Share Skills

1st Quarter Conference

Prior to conferences, send each family a list of kindergarten skills and highlight the ones to be discussed. If desired, also let parents know at the end of the conference which skills you will be covering next so they know what to reinforce at home. *Tammy Lutz, George E. Greene Elementary, Bad Axe, MI*

3 Make Student-Made Welcome Cards

Parents will adore these heartfelt greetings! Prior to conferences, have each student write and illustrate a card for her parent, welcoming him to the classroom. Collect the cards. When each parent arrives, present him with the card from his child. When you wrap up the conference, give each parent a piece of paper on which to write his child a quick note. Have him tuck his greeting in his child's desk or place it in her cubby before he leaves.

4 Set Out Snacks

On the day of conferences, decorate a table with a tablecloth and a vase of fresh flowers. Then set out some refreshments for parents to enjoy as they arrive for their conferences.

5. Create a Slide Show

Use presentation software to make a slide show of class photos and other relevant classroom information. Play the show in a continuous loop for parents to watch as they wait for their scheduled conferences to begin. *adapted from an idea by Vicki Casso, Islands Elementary, Gilbert, AZ*

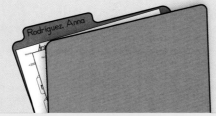

7. Prepare Conference Folders

Use these handy references to execute successful conferences. Personalize a folder for each child. Inside each folder, place a copy of the child's report card, work samples, and any other items you would like to share with a parent. When it is time for a conference, have the appropriate child's folder ready. The necessary items will be at your fingertips so you can easily answer parents' questions and address areas of growth and concern. *Jan Utesch, Remsen-Union Elementary, Remsen, IA*

9. Send Home Student Gifts

Make conference time special for students! Give each student's parent a small trinket such as a toy or a personalized certificate to reward her child for something done well. Ask the parent to present the gift with great fanfare to encourage continued success. *Marie E. Cecchini, West Dundee, IL*

6. Be Positive

Hannah is a good classroom helper!

Begin each conference with a positive comment about the child. This not only puts parents more at ease, but it also sets an upbeat tone for the conference. *Kiva English, Cato-Meridian Central School, Cato, NY*

8. Be Ready for the Unexpected

Set up a project table for students, siblings, or other visitors that show up unexpectedly for the conference. Attach a large sheet of white bulletin board paper to a tabletop and label it "Conference Masterpiece." Also set out a container of crayons. Then encourage visiting youngsters to color on the paper as you meet with their parents.

10. Write Thank-You Notes

Send a quick follow-up note to parents after the conference. In the note, thank each child's parent for attending, highlight a positive comment discussed during the conference, and encourage open communication to address further questions or concerns.

Keep Those Calendars!

9 Nifty Classroom Uses

Laminate the calendars for durability and so they are reusable!

1 Create a Number-Order Calendar

On each of several calendar grids, cover a few numbers with small white stickers. Place the grids, dry-erase markers, and paper towels at a center. A child reads the numbers on a grid and writes each missing number. After checking for accuracy, he wipes the grid clean and then continues with a different grid.

Janice Burch, Tri-Valley Elementary, Downs, IL

2 Prepare Bingo Gameboards!

Review a variety of literacy or math skills by transforming calendars into Bingo gameboards. To make a board, outline three full weeks on a calendar grid. Program each space in the outlined area to correspond with a skill, such as writing letters to review beginning consonants or writing numbers to review number identification. Make similar boards and a set of calling cards to match the programming; store the boards and cards in a resealable bag. To play, read a card and have each child cover the matching space, if possible, on her board. Play continues until a youngster marks seven spaces in a row.

Janice Burch

3 Use Photos as Writing Prompts

Use calendar photos as prompts for student writing. Give each child a photo and a sentence strip. Help him write a sentence that describes the picture. Next, put the pictures on display. Then have a child read his sentence. Ask remaining youngsters to identify the picture that matches the sentence. Continue until all the pictures and sentences are correctly paired.

Katie Zuehlke, Bendix Elementary, Annandale, MN

4 Reinforce Following Directions

Give each child a calendar grid. Then announce a direction such as "Use a blue crayon to circle each number three that you see" or "Use a purple crayon to color the box for the number fifteen." Continue giving directions as desired. Repeat the activity throughout the year, targeting different skills each time.

Litsa Jackson, Covington Integrated Arts Academy, Covington, TN

DECEMBER

S	M	T	W	T	F	S
	1	2	③	4	5	6
7	8	9	10	11	12	⑬
14	15	16	17	18	19	20
21	22	㉓	24	25	26	27
28	29	㉚	㉛			

5 Provide Practice With Adding Doubles

For this partner game, set out a pair of dice along with a calendar grid and 31 game markers per player. To play, each child takes a turn rolling the dice. If he rolls doubles, he adds them and places that number of counters on his grid. If he does not roll doubles, his turn is over. Play continues until a player covers his grid.

Janice Burch, Tri-Valley Elementary, Downs, IL

6 Make Puzzles

Riddles and puzzles go together in this entertaining small-group activity. Glue several calendar pictures on separate sheets of construction paper and laminate them for durability. For each picture, write a simple riddle on an index card. Puzzle-cut the picture and put the pieces and their riddle card in a resealable plastic bag. To use a bag, help a youngster read the riddle, predict the answer to the riddle, and then put the puzzle together to see the answer.

Janice Burch

Who am I?
1. I live in China
2. I have black and white fur.
3. I eat lots of bamboo.

7 Write Tales

For this shared writing activity, choose three or four calendar pictures that can be sequenced. Display the pictures and enlist students' help to put the pictures in order. Then lead little ones to write a story, encouraging each child to add to the tale.

Vada Boback
Alliance Christian School
Morgantown, WV

8 Reinforce the Concepts of More and Less

Give each child a calendar grid. Give a direction such as "Draw a purple X in the square that shows the number that is five more than three" or "Draw a blue X in the square that shows the number that is two less than twelve." Continue with different directions as time permits.

Yolanda Tatum
Jefferson Elementary
Carlsbad, CA

9 Establish Personalized Work Areas

Cut apart several calendars. Invite each child to choose a calendar page and write his name on it. Distribute the calendars (mats) when students need to work in a designated area or are working with messy materials, such as glue, paint, or clay. If a mat gets messy, simply wipe it with a damp cloth.

Bonnie Keller
Moore Elementary
Clarksville, TN

9 Neat Ideas for Lids and Caps!

Got lots of lids and caps? Try the following engaging and easy-to-prepare options!

1 Use for Sorts and Patterns

Have youngsters sort and re-sort lids and caps by a variety of attributes, such as color, size, and even product type. Then prompt students to use the lids to make a variety of patterns.

Randall A. Pellow, Shippensburg, PA

2 Make Graphs

Place an open two-column grid on a table and post a yes or no question. Then prompt students to use milk or bottle caps as markers to share their opinions and form a graph.

3 Build Towers!

Foster fine-motor development and provide math practice with a collection of bottle caps or milk caps! A child carefully stacks caps to make a tower. When the tower falls, he counts the total number of caps used. Then he tries to make a taller tower with a greater number of caps.

Cathy Bynum, Lafayette Elementary, Oxford, MS

4 Record Skip-Counting Patterns

Label sets of lids or caps to practice counting by twos, fives, and tens. Put each set in a separate resealable plastic bag. A child empties a bag, places the caps in order, and records the number pattern.

Jackie Wright, Summerhill Children's House, Enid, OK

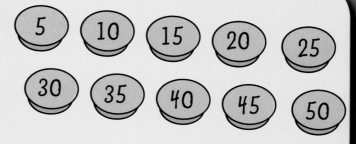

5 10 15 20 25
30 35 40 45 50

5 Create Shape Puzzles and Stencils

Draw a different shape on each of several plastic lids. Carefully cut along the lines to cut out each shape. Place the shapes and the corresponding lids at a center for students to match or use as stencils.

Rita Arnold, Alden Hebron Elementary, Woodstock, IL

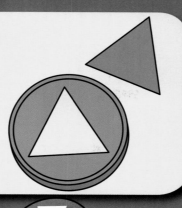

6 Count by Hundreds!

Got *lots* of caps? Then have students count to one thousand! Have small groups of students group caps into tens, count by tens to 100, and put each set of 100 caps into a resealable plastic bag. When ten bags have been prepared, lead the group to count by hundreds as you point to each bag.

Cathy Bynum, Lafayette Elementary, Oxford, MS

7 Segment Words

Give each child a set of three caps and have him arrange them in a row. Then say a CVC word and encourage him to touch or push each cap forward, from left to right, as he says each sound in the word.

Candy Channell, Fort Worth, TX

/c/, /a/, /t/.

8 Write Number Sentences

Set out a supply of caps, a die, and writing paper to set up a partner center. To begin, a child rolls the die and counts the corresponding number of caps. Her partner repeats the process, making a second set of caps. Then the students use their caps to each write an addition number sentence.

Randall E. Pellow, Shippensburg, PA

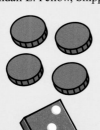

$$4 + 3 = 7$$

9 Practice Positional Words

Give each child a cap and a paper plate. Next, say directions to review positional words, such as "Put the cap under the plate" or "Put the cap next to the plate." Then have each child glue the objects to a sheet of paper and write a sentence to match the cap's placement in relation to the plate.

Randall E. Pellow

 Tip ▶ Ask students' families for help, and you'll quickly have a large collection of lids and caps!

6 Tips for Successful Field Trips

1 Make Reusable Nametags

Students' names are kept private when they wear these tags. Write the school name, school phone number, and your name on a class supply of colorful cards. If desired, include your cell phone number. Then laminate the cards for durability and reuse them trip after trip.

Barbara Mason Worobey
Deposit Elementary
Deposit, NY

> Deposit Elementary School
> 555-0198
> Teacher: Ms. Worobey
> 555-0123

2 Bring Bags for the Bus Ride

Give each pair or trio of seatmates a resealable plastic bag packed with small toys and trinkets. Invite youngsters to play with the objects until you have reached your destination. For longer trips, rotate the bags every 10 or 15 minutes.

Tammy Vincent, Northern Valley Schools, Almena, KS

3 Organize Lunches

Ms. Conroy
Jordan
Aidan
Melissa
Reilly
Shantay

Write the name of each chaperone and her assigned group on separate large paper bags. Before departure, ask each chaperone to name the students listed on her bag and have them put their lunches in her bag. With chaperones responsible for the food bags, there should be no more lost lunches!

Adrienne Hugo
Washington School
Mundelein, IL

4 Review Rules

Have students brainstorm ways to be safe on a bus. List the important bus-safety tips on a supersize bus cutout. Before each trip, reread the poster as a friendly reminder for students to follow the rules while riding on the bus.

Barbara Mason Worobey

Bus Safety Rules

5 Use Matching Cutouts

Have each chaperone and his group members wear matching labels such as shape cutouts or animal cutouts. To keep track of members in his group, the chaperone simply looks for the assigned cutouts.

Beth Parry, Zane North Elementary, Collingswood, NJ

6 Provide Numbers

Make a copy of field trip leaders' names and cell phone numbers for each adult. Encourage adults to use the numbers, as needed, to maintain communication while on the trip. Collect the lists upon return to dispose of them properly.

Have fun!

314

INDEX